# Our Trail Led Northwest

## True Tale of Romance and Adventure in British Columbia

### E. Madge Mandy

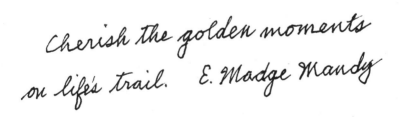

Cherish the golden moments on life's trail. *E. Madge Mandy*

### Photography — Dr. Joseph T. Mandy

**FRONT COVER**
The Mandys heading toward Squaw Creek, B.C., from Haines, Alaska, in 1934.

**PHOTO CREDITS**
B.C. Provincial Archives: 70, 131, 174; CPR: 8, top and bottom; Graham, Mildred: 224; Smithers News: 215; Tourism BC: 205; United Empire Mine: 159. All others by Dr. Joseph T. Mandy.

**CANADIAN CATALOGUING IN PUBLICATION DATA**

Mandy, E. Madge (Ella Madge), 1902 -
    Our trail led northwest

ISBN 0-919214-91-6

1. Mandy, E. Madge (Ella Madge), 1902 - 2. Mandy, Joseph T., d. 1968. 3. Frontier and Pioneer life — British Columbia. 4. Gold mines and mining — British Columbia — History. 5. British Columbia — Biography. 6. Gold miners — British Columbia — Biography. I. Title.
FC3826.1.M35A3 1992          971.1'03'0922          C92-091071-8
F1088.M35A3 1992

First Edition 1989          Reprinted 1992

**HERITAGE HOUSE PUBLISHING COMPANY LTD.**
**Box 1228, Station A, Surrey, B.C. V3S 2B3**

Printed in Canada.

# CONTENTS

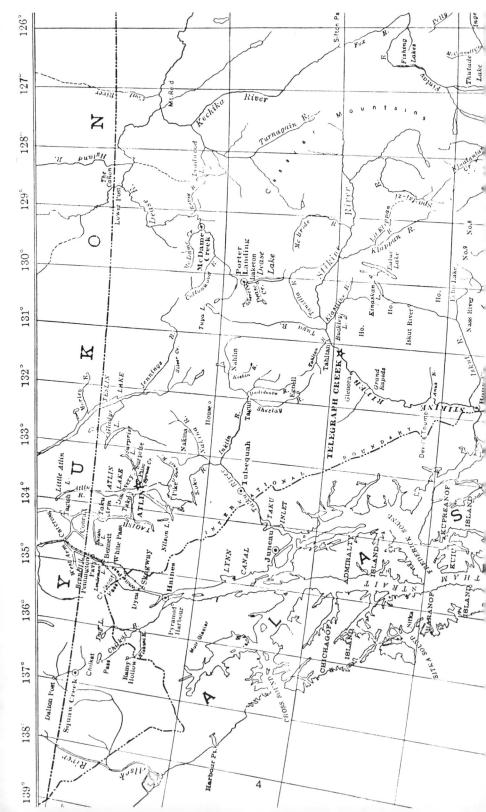

Map of British Columbia covering Northwestern Mineral District of the British Columbia Department of Mines for which Dr. Joseph T. Mandy was Resident Engineer headquartered at Prince Rupert.

# INTRODUCTION

Did you ever have a dream come true? I did because of a cruise from Vancouver, British Columbia, to Skagway, Alaska. With the fulfillment of the dream came a story book romance and marriage to a man met on the cruise ship whose profession in search for gold and other minerals took him and me into northwestern British Columbia. Access to that remote area of majestic, mountainous beauty was by coastal steamer along a world famous inside passage of the Pacific Ocean, through the Alaskan Panhandle and Yukon Territory and by dugout canoe, river boat, on foot or packhorse and in small freight planes flown by pilots relying on guidance by the "seat of the pants". What a challenge of "roughing it" we faced, travelling in a way that will not be done again and with few left to tell of such pioneering.

I share some highlights of the venturesome Mandys in OUR TRAIL LED NORTHWEST through dramatic and amusing incidents on the trail, in mining camps and isolated settlements or lone cabins and in acquaintance with optimistic prospectors, hardy pioneers and Indians of the wilds. The book is my contribution to Canadiana, a bit of history associated with mining exploration in the 1930's combined with the lasting love story of a tall, stalwart, mature mining engineer and a petite, naive, young college professor.

Appreciation is extended to all who encouraged or assisted me in any way to write my true tale which evolved in a part of British Columbia still little known and waiting for development of rich, natural resources. Come, take the trail with Joe and Madge Mandy and experience with us the joys, thrills, dangers and rewards of wilderness travel in the most westerly province of Canada.

E. Madge Mandy, B.L., M.A.

# PIONEER CITY OF PRINCE RUPERT

"NORTH. GO NORTH, NORTHWEST." These words rang in my ears and secretly directed my life when I was a small girl living in the city of Muncie in the American state of Indiana, far from the wilderness territory made so dramatically known to the world during the Klondike gold rush of 1898. Such advice to the shyest and most sensitive of the four children in my family was so surprising to me that I kept it to myself. My brother and sisters, had they known, would have teased me with, "What? Timid, little you going off to the wild west? Forget it, sis." I certainly did not intend to forget anything so foreign to my nature and offering such a challenge. It came to me through the shared experiences of a neighbour.

Mrs. Hettle was a chirpy, little, semi-literate old lady who lived across the street from my home. She looked, with her Victorian dress and heirloom brooch, like some of my ancestors in the family album. I was fascinated by her long ear trumpet, but my treble voice shouted down it could not be heard by her, for I was told in the prevalent phrase of the day that she was "deaf as a post". She came frequently to our house because she could enjoy vibrations from the piano practice of brother Dohn and I and from sister Blanche's cornet playing. We were sorry sister Mabel's violin vibrated nothing to her. She lived alone and seldom went anywhere, so her announcement one day of taking a far away trip seemed unbelievable.

"Folks," said Mrs. Hettle to the assembled Jones's, "I'm agoin' to Alaska. Ain't that somethin'? My son's up there. I ain't seen him for a coon's age. Glory be, he's up and sent me money to come. He's got hisself a wife. Now they's two to visit. I means to have me a great trip, I does."

At that time, in the early nineteen hundreds, such a journey by train and steamer was long, tiring and perhaps dangerous for the elderly, very deaf widow, but go she did. How I admired her adventuresome spirit! I wondered, too, if I should ever have as much courage to travel alone to an unknown, distant place. She came back to stir my imagination with snapshots of prospectors, trappers, pioneer settlers and their one-room log cabins, Indians, Eskimos, mining and logging camps, mountains higher than I ever visioned land could rise, glaciers, rivers, lakes and waterfalls. There were also impressive pictures of deer, moose, caribou, bear, wolf, wolverine, mountain goat, mountain sheep and powerful huskies.

Did those big dogs pull you on a sled? I asked Mrs. Hettle.

"Sure they did," she answered. "Skeered me, too. Why they's 'normous and fierce. My son says, 'Don't touch a husky.' I didn't not do that. Stayed as fur away from them critters as I could. My, my, it was kinda fun havin' them dogs harnessed up to act like horses."

Mrs. Hettle's tales of life in far off Alaska sparked my desire to live in the Northwest. To do this I knew I must overcome my timidity. Wise parents, aware of my shyness, assisted by giving me elocution lessons and they led to some measure of self confidence through my presenting readings to dissimilar audiences and to an interest in all phases of speech. My father furthered this interest by taking me to

In the dining room of the steamer *Princess Louise* Madge met mining engineer Dr. Joseph T. Mandy. The meeting led to marriage and years of adventure in the wilderness of Northwestern B.C.

Madge at Alert Bay during her 1931 coastal cruise.

hear well known lecturers, among whom was one of the most famous orators of the time, William Jennings Bryan.

It was logical when leaving high school that my major subject in university should be speech, and I decided to teach the subject for which I had shown an aptitude. Luckily for me, Departments of Speech were being introduced in a number of schools across the United States at that time and there was a scarcity of speech teachers. Upon graduation I had no difficulty in securing a position. I deliberately started a career away from my home state, first in an Illinois high school, then in a Texas technical school and finally in a Kansas college. I felt that I must try to achieve as a stranger in localities where it was up to me to sink or swim, unaided by relatives or friends. In this way I hoped to overcome my innate timidity and acquire the courage to confront and conquer any problems or difficulties that I might encounter in the future.

All the while, during those brief teaching years, I was building a fund to take me Northwest where I should discover whether my dream of living in that area might come true. I wanted to shout, "Glory be," like Mrs. Hettle when the journey became possible. In August of 1931, with rosy expectations, I travelled to Vancouver, British Columbia, where I embarked on the Canadian Pacific Railway Company's coastal steamer, Princess Louise, bound through the famous inside passage of the north Pacific for Skagway, Alaska. The ship sailed late in the evening with a light passenger list, undoubtedly due to curtailed spending of the Depression. This was disastrous for the steamship service but beneficial to me, as it meant I did not have to share a cabin with a stranger.

I was so happy to have my secret desire become a reality that I wanted to share my joy with someone and hurried to breakfast in the morning. A fatherly steward escorted me to a table for four, telling me he had just seated there an English couple now residing in Victoria, B.C. He probably thought they would provide companionship for a young woman travelling alone, and I hoped so too. I sat down with a smile and a cheerily voiced, Good morning. They answered with a courteous but frigid, "Good morning" and lapsed into silence for the rest of the meal. I could only presume they were the reserved old country type I had met only in novels, but their lack of friendly response discouraged me from trying to converse with others when I went up on deck.

I quietly followed fellow tourists and walked along the one street of Alert Bay, an Indian village where the steamer stopped briefly. I found the symbolic totem poles in the cemetery there were colourful and fascinating. Passing the school for Indian children maintained by the Anglican Church, I met a pretty, little native girl and stopped to ask, Will you please tell me your name? I expected to hear a name which would be unfamiliar and perhaps difficult for me to pronounce, but her answer was, "Jones." She confirmed what I had heard all my life, "Your family name will be found wherever you go." Well, the incident gave me something important to tell my students at the Kansas college. It brought to mind Abraham Lincoln's often quoted assertion, "God must have loved the common people because he made so many of them." Surely one could equally declare, "God must have loved the Jones's because he made so many of us," and this would account for the wide spread popularity of my name."

At lunch my tablemates said, "Good afternoon," and continued their meal without further speech. Afterwards, I sat alone in a sheltered and secluded spot on deck enjoying silent thoughts. I breathed deeply of invigorating sea air while feasting my eyes on the colourful Pacific shore and the loveliness of mountains glimpsed in passing. The scene was as captivating as Mrs. Hettle's pictures had shown and assured me this beautiful part of the world was where I wanted to spend the rest of my life.

My first view of Prince Rupert was breath taking. What a beautiful, magnificent setting! How very different, I said to myself, from the flat land which has always surrounded me. I'd like to live here. The city towered above the Pacific Ocean, its houses on hilly streets silhouetted against a lovely backdrop of mountains. Residents faced the ocean and mountainclad islands in the near distance. There was no beach, the city rising high above the water and requiring a climb of steep steps to reach the business district and houses. Walking to the main street, I saw a pioneer aspect of the city in a few board walks, type of building construction and friendly faces. The shops had Indian and Eskimo handicraft to sell which I could not afford to buy. Cheaper souvenirs were hurriedly selected for I remembered the warning, "Return to the ship when the whistle blows. We'll sail without you if you're not on time."

Back on the steamer I watched preparations for departure, ending with the drawing up of the gangplank. Seconds later, a taxi speeded onto the dock and drove to the edge of the wharf. Out jumped quite a big man who waved an arm and shouted, "Captain, take me on. Must go North." The Captain evidently knew him and ordered the gangplank lowered. The late passenger boarded, his face blurred by a brimmed khaki hat, his loose jacket with many pockets, baggy pants and high leather boots clearly not the attire of a tourist. He was encumbered by a bulging packsack on his back, a sleeping bag under his arm and a small kit bag dangled from his wrist. I was impressed and so were other watching passengers. We all thought he must be an important personage to receive such royal treatment. I hoped to find out who he was and what all those bags meant.

Only the words, "Good evening," were spoken to me by the Victoria couple when I joined them at dinner. My dining partners seemingly had no conversation in them — they didn't even talk to each other. I ordered a favourite dish, so often served by my mother, stewed chicken and dumplings. Imagine my disappointment when I couldn't cut into that fowl! A second try slid it across the plate and the third attempt almost sent it flying above the table into the faces of my quiet dinner companions. Had I been an experienced traveller, I would have sent that uncooperative chicken to the kitchen with a demand for edible replacement. Instead, the habit of trying to complete anything attempted kept me trying to accomplish the impossible. I was so intent on successfully carving the chicken that I was unaware of someone being seated beside me until I heard a musical, masculine voice. Certainly embarrassed, I turned to look into the tanned face of a handsome man with graying hair, expressive eyes and a sympathetic smile.

"You have a difficult problem," he said. "May I help you?"

Relief must have been in my voice when answering, "Would you? I really do need help. I - I can't get to first base with this chicken."

Placing my plate in front of him, the man identified himself as the tardy passenger boarding at Prince Rupert. He soon had that tough bird in pieces, though even he found it hard to dissever. His remark while carving, "Every problem can be solved," indicated a persistent, practical person and his face radiated kindness. I ate every bit of that chicken in appreciation for his assistance, in spite of this being an ordeal. The helpful stranger had dressed for dinner in a becoming beige suit and I thought him one of the handsomest men I had ever met.

Our introduction was unusual and comical enough to have us laughing together. Laughter removed the restraint normal between strangers and led to conversation which didn't stop until tired stewards told us, through deliberate clattering of china and cutlery, that all other diners had left. The two days following were the two happiest I had ever known as an adult. My rescuer and I walked the decks, played shuffleboard and strolled through the Alaska ports of call — Ketchikan, Wrangell and Juneau. We were in a world of our own, seeing and conversing with nobody else, a bond evolving based on mutual interests, common ideals and outlook on life, an identical sense of humour and a physical attraction.

The affable man asked the steward to reserve a dining table for two in a secluded corner where we could converse in partial privacy over meals together. I hardly slept at night, fearing I might not waken in time for our breakfast appointment. Somehow I was punctual for our start to the day and so was Dr. Mandy. I had never before met a man with whom I felt so at ease or one with such interesting and entertaining conversation. I intuitively knew he was a person I had heard about, "a gentleman of the old school." Such a charming and outstanding personality had not been in my dream of the Northwest, but oh how glad I was that he had appeared. He seemed to belong in my life from the moment of meeting, yet I dared not think of romance. My father's words of wisdom were with me, "Always proceed slowly and cautiously when your emotions are aroused and think with both your mind and heart." His advice restrained, at least outwardly, any display of my feeling.

I was enchanted by Dr. Mandy's background — born to English parents in South Africa where he spent his earliest years, secondary schooling in England, degrees in mining engineering and geology from German universities, service in Siberia with the Canadian army during the World War and mining employment in eastern and western Canada. Currently, he was Resident Mining Engineer for the Northwestern District of the British Columbia Department Of Mines, headquartered in Prince Rupert. Part of his job required following trails in isolated wilderness areas to give technical direction and advice to prospectors and exploration companies. Expeditions like his sounded exciting and challenging and made my profession seem prosaic.

Dr. Mandy was interested in my background. I didn't have an exten-

Miss E. Madge Jones in 1931.

Dr. Joseph T. Mandy in 1931.

sive and impressive past. Even my surname was not uncommon like his. I was one of numerous Jones girls, born and reared in the state of Indiana, graduating with a major in Speech from Northwestern University in Evanston, Illinois, and adding an M.A. in Speech from the University of Michigan in Ann Arbor, Michigan. After teaching briefly in Illinois and Texas, I was at the moment an assistant professor of Speech at Kansas State Teachers College in Pittsburg, Kansas. Dr. Mandy knew little about American universities except that they had social activities which were not in the schools he attended in England and Germany, and asked me to tell him about them.

Usually reserved about personal matters at that period of my life, I astonished myself by confiding what my university days were like to this interested man. They did not include much social activity. My parents had been concerned about my future and wanted me to have the university education which would prepare me for the teaching career I had decided to follow. I had no money and my father could afford only tuition, books and a little pocket money. It was up to me to earn my board and room. I did this by working for a very wealthy widow who lived near the campus. Instead of keeping a cook and maid after her banker husband died, she helped girls like myself by providing room and meals in return for household duties. I became her companion, housekeeper, cook, maid, cleaning service, etc. I must admit her introductory remarks intimidated me. They made me doubtful of living up to what she expected.

Said the dominating, white-haired Mrs. Trelease, "You look very young, Still, you look very healthy. I'm used to giving orders to be followed exactly and demand a quality service. This is what I expect. You must have a school schedule suited to my convenience. You'll dust the living room every morning, clean the whole place thoroughly on Saturdays and prepare and serve 3 meals a day. At lunch and dinner you'll engage me in interesting conversation. You may attend church on Sunday morning and join the university student's group at the church on Sunday evening — the Methodist church to which I belong and of which, I understand, you are a member. Occasionally, you may go to a movie or concert with a friend on Friday or Saturday night. Breakfast will be brought to me but you must never say I have breakfast in bed. Rather, you'll say I have breakfast in my room. You will not be paid any salary. Board and room are sufficient payment."

"She was an arrogant, selfish and miserly woman," commented Dr. Mandy.

Yes, she was, I said. Learning to co-ordinate Mrs. Trelease's requirements with those of the university was a full time job of long hours. My day started at six in the morning and generally ended at 1 or 2 the next morning. However, the greatest difficulty I faced was adjusting to a dictatorial 70 year old woman. Mrs. Trelease was one of those people who thought herself always right about everything, her schooling was quite limited, her sense of humour almost non-existent and she had no conception of how much study was necessary for my classes.

As a Speech major I had to practice speeches and platform readings orally. Part of this was possible in a room at the School of

Speech reserved for the purpose. Further practice in my temporary home was in a subdued voice or whisper while vacuuming, dusting, washing dishes, scrubbing the kitchen floor or when taking a bath. Many a poem and story I memorized from a copy propped in front of me while preparing meals. I guess grim determination and stick-to-it-iveness saw me through quite a trying period. Incredibly, I even became rather fond of that lonely, old lady, who had money but not real happiness, and to whose every whim I catered. She meant well and her behaviour was probably due to an inferiority complex. I can truly think of her with gratitude. She made my attendance at universi-ty possible and the result had been a successful career. Looking back, I'm sure those years with Mrs. Trelease were a valuable education for practical living. They taught me good housekeeping, organization, patience and tolerance. Then, too, the experience proved that one tends to achieve more if there are difficulties to overcome.

"That's true," said my sympathetic, listening companion. "Dif-ficulties are an incentive to accomplishment and also develop character. Working as you did, and studying, was not an easy thing to do. Your achievement is most commendable, Miss Jones. I say, as the headmaster at my boy's school in England would have said, 'Good show.' Do you know, I've never before met a girl who worked her way through university. Wasn't it unusual?"

You're right, I replied. Few did in the 1920's. There are more now though, and their numbers will grow in years to come.

We called each other, in spite of complete compatibility, Dr. Mandy and Miss Jones. We were following wise parental guidance which required friendship to advance slowly. I wished our association could continue and become less formal, and Dr. Mandy's conversa-tion subtly indicated he had the same wish. Too soon for us the steamer docked at its northern destination of Skagway, Alaska, the historic town founded in days of the Klondike gold rush. From this port I would return south to resume teaching and the mining man would leave for a wilderness journey. Our goodbys were said with a lingering handclasp in the Blanchard garden of Skagway, famed for a variety of bright flowers which grew extremely large during a short summer of constant daylight.

My sentimental companion bought me a pansy nosegay in the garden and accompanied the gift with a guiding and heartwarming question for the future. "You know pansies are for thoughts. I hope they will speed from Prince Rupert, British Columbia, to Pittsburg, Kansas, and be crossed by those hurrying from Pittsburg to Prince Rupert. Will you write to me?"

My quick response was, Oh yes, I will. We have so much to say to each other. Your friendship will give me moral support in a challeng-ing year. Professor Pelsma, Head of the Speech Department in my college, will be away on sabbatical and has chosen me to be Acting Head during his absence. I appreciate the honour, but the respon-sibilities of the position weigh heavily on my mind. I'll be extremely busy but I'll find time to talk to you by pen or typewriter.

Dr. Mandy soon became Joe to me and I became Madge to him. His messages were those of courtship, telling me that fate had decreed he meet and marry the girl he met on the Princess Louise for whom he had felt an instant and abiding affection. Letters permitted us to express our thoughts and feelings fully and melted my restraint. I finally confided my love which had been almost as immediate as Joe's had been for me. Our romance now demanded a reunion and on holiday leave Joe spent Christmas week with the Jones family in Richmond, Indiana, where my folks now lived. Our joyful reunion and suitability as life partners was so apparent that when Joe traditionally asked my father's permission to marry his daughter, it was given with dad's blessing. The consent of my father, and approval of my mother, was what Joe had hoped for. However, he felt it necessary for me to have a little more time to consider marriage.

"Your parents," he said, "are willing to have you spend the rest of your life with me. That's what I wanted the night of our meeting. I had boarded the Princess Louise thinking only of a hazardous field trip ahead. Truly I had no thought of romance, having resigned myself to being a lonely bachelor. While being escorted to your table, a voice spoke to me. I'd never had this happen to me before. I heard, 'You will sit beside the girl you will marry.' I must say you attracted me and as we conversed, your personality, matching mind, identical sense of humour and the same spiritual views were equally attractive. I was determined to make the prediction of the voice come true!

"We were kindred souls and my reaction to you was an instant falling in love. Recent letters have told me your love for me was also instantaneous. Oh my dear Madge, we were fated to meet and marry but I want you to be absolutely certain of it. We've only had 9 days together, 2 on the Princess Louise and 7 here in your Indiana home. You may find some of my idiosyncracies distasteful to you and you may also hesitate to give up your profession. Although I'd like to marry you now and take you back to Canada with me, I suggest you return to Kansas and think of all factors involved in marrying me. This seems to me the fair thing to do. When your decision is final, send me a telegram, perhaps in a week."

I weighed all the arguments for a successful professional career against those of an entirely different life in another country. I knew that any advancement in my field meant attaining a Ph.D. which would qualify me to teach in university. That choice could take years. After meeting Joe, I realized how wonderful it would be to share my days with a congenial husband. Certainly I loved developing public speakers, platform readers, story tellers and the dramatic ability of those chosen to act in plays and I dearly loved my responsive students. Both my mind and heart told me, though, that I loved Joe Mandy very much more. He offered not only a loving, understanding companion but the fulfillment of my secret dream to live in the Northwest. I would have a home in Prince Rupert, that scenically situated city above the sea about which I had said as a tourist, I'd like to live here. At the end of the week, Joe had his telegram saying, "Yes, I shall join you in British Columbia."

Joe wanted our marriage to be in early April so I could accompany him on his spring field trips. I had to complete my college's winter term and resign before the spring semester started. Breaking my teaching contract was disturbing but justified by knowing someone would be needing a position like mine. My love story had been a carefully guarded secret which had to be revealed to the head of my department, John R. Pelsma, and college president, Dr. Brandenburg. Both were surprised, impressed and concerned for my future and voiced the same opinion.

"Your romance sounds like a fairy tale. You've met your Prince Charming and he wants to carry you off to distant parts. Just a word of fatherly advice. You've known this man briefly, mostly through correspondence. Are you sure you are following the right course in linking your life with his? Your face and eyes say yes. They radiate love and one cannot deny that love is the greatest thing in the world. It is with regret your resignation is accepted. You and your teaching will be greatly missed. Should you again want a teaching position and there is a vacancy in the Speech Department here, it is yours. The best wishes of faculty and students will go with you when you leave the college. After marriage may you and your Prince live together happily ever afterward as in all fairy tales."

There was seldom a faculty marriage in the Kansas college, for most of the professors were married men and the few lone women professors were devoted to their careers. The men and women on the campus agreed that the romance of "little Miss Jones" was a fairy tale consistent with the dramatic subjects I taught. News of my approaching marriage and distant new residence travelled to all departments and was related to me by a young co-ed. She rushed to my office to get the whole story.

"Miss Jones, they say you're getting married and going to live in another country. Is that right? How did you keep this a secret? I'd have told everybody. The editor of our college paper titles your story 'Love at Long Range.' Isn't that cute? They say you'll live in Africa or South America or — was it in the South Sea Islands? Any of those places are far from Kansas and sound exotic. They say, too, you're marrying a Prince. Is that true?"

I had to laugh at these inaccuracies and correct them. Do tell all those who distort and embroider the truth, I told her, that I shall be married in April. My new home will be on an island in Canada's most westerly province, British Columbia, where there's a city named Prince Rupert. Study a map and you'll see exactly where I'll be. I'm delighted to hear I'm marrying a Prince. That is true. Dr. Mandy is a Prince of a Man.

At the end of my last class at the college, one of the girls rose to say, "I speak for your Speech students here and those who aren't here. Your life is going to be so different from that of a professor. Just imagine our little Miss Jones way up there in Alaska, no — Canada — with a big, handsome husband on wilderness trails! Your romance is simply enchanting. It's special. Of course we're glad for you but we'll miss you dreadfully. We'll be thinking about you and wishing you the best forever and forever."

I was almost speechless with emotion and could only reply briefly, I've been very happy here and loved my teaching and you whom I've taught. For you I wish the best too. Now, please go before I start to cry.

It was with mixed feelings that I attended dinners and parties,

17

featuring presents for the bride, hosted by faculty and students. The Pittsburg Business and Professional Women's Club, of which I was a member, draped a chair for me in pink and black at a parting dinner. Such a combination of colours for the occasion puzzled me until the President explained while presenting a gift, "The pink is for happiness wished you in marriage and the black for sorrow at your leaving us." Everything seemed in accord for departure. Then the morning before leaving, I met history professor Dr. Elizabeth Cochran when crossing the campus. She stopped me and anxiously asked, "What are you going to do? I've just heard the news."

What news and how does it affect me?

"President Roosevelt has declared a Bank Holiday to straighten out banking problems. It begins tomorrow, the 6th of March, and continues for a week or more. Nobody can draw money out of a bank or conduct any business with a bank. How can you travel without money? Thank goodness I have a small amount hidden at home. I'll loan you some."

I laughed and explained why I could be so cheerful. Don't worry about me, Elizabeth. A woman's intuition compelled me to draw all the money out of my bank account yesterday. Thanks for your offer.

I had decided to spend a month with my parents in Indiana before heading for the Northwest, travelling by train to Kansas City with a change at Mattoon, Illinois. There I boarded another train en route to Richmond. I had not gone far eastward before noticing a well groomed, prepossessing, middle aged man in the coach staring at me from across the aisle. Finally he spoke.

"May I sit beside you and chat for a few minutes?"

I was tired and wanted to doze but he was perplexed about something. That aroused my curiosity and I answered, You may.

"I am an official of the railway company and travel all around the United States. Having observed many people, I pride myself on cataloguing them quickly as to age and occupation. I've been studying you and you baffle me. There's a portable typewriter at your feet but you're not a stenographer or secretary. Your hands indicate no manual labour. Your face shows the scholastic but it includes a sensitive mouth and expressive eyes, so you're not a cold intellectual. You look like a college student. Yet, if so, should be in school. How old are you and what do you do?"

Really, I replied, you're old enough to know a woman's age is her most cherished secret. The heroine of a famous play, "She Stoops to Conquer," gives the reason in a conversation — "I must not tell my age. They say women and music should never be dated." As for employment, I teach.

"You don't resemble any teacher I know. Kindergarten?"

No. I was a professor at a college in Kansas.

"You're too young to have a position like that."

I was a very young professor. However, I look younger than I am and have had laughable experiences being mistaken for a student on the campus.

"Why are you here? Shouldn't you be on the job?"

I resigned and I'm on my way to spend a month with my folks in Indiana.

"These are Depression days. It's hard to find work. Why did you resign? I'm talking to you like a father because I have a grown daughter. My dear girl, why did you do such a foolish thing?"

Because I'm getting married in April to a man in the Canadian Northwest. We'll live in the province of British Columbia.

"So you fell in love. Are you sure you're marrying the right man and that you should go to another country?"

My Joe and I are completely compatible and I look forward to living in Canada, a country with a developing future.

The man smiled and shook my hand. "You've stars in your eyes and I know how you feel. I was once in love with a lovely lady from your state. We married and were very happy. She died young. I have a second wife who is also dear. God bless you and I'll tell my wife and daughter how you brightened my day radiating romance."

My parents had moved from the city of Muncie where I grew up and I did not know people in Richmond where they now lived. Actually, this was beneficial for allowing us to devote all our time to each other. How satisfying the days were as we revived precious memories of our closely knit family. I found myself appreciative in a mature way of my parent's loving, wise guidance and the sacrifices they'd made to give me opportunities. I knew now that mother, who had been an outstanding teacher of seven grades in one of the single room schoolhouses which dotted the rural Indiana of her youth, had given me invaluable coaching in home study and set a pattern for my teaching career. Father, born in a log cabin, had achieved without aid the status of a successful business man. What an example he had been of ambition and hard work, his fortitude shown in cheerfully bearing the constant pain of a leg impaired by typhoid fever. I also had a joyous reunion with brother Dohn, my close childhood companion, and his wife Kathleen.

A highlight of that March month was shopping for a trousseau with mother and Kathleen. Many firms had closed their doors or were operating with a skeleton staff during the Bank Holiday because people were afraid to buy on credit and few had ready cash. I was one of the few and very welcome at a shop where I was the sole customer.

My traveller's cheques were displayed before I said I wanted to choose a trousseau. Mother emotionally informed that I was marrying a mining engineer met on a ship in Alaska, that the wedding would be in Vancouver, British Columbia, and that Dr. Mandy and I would be living in northwestern Canada. I introduced mother and Kathleen and they were seated on comfortable chairs while waiting to advise me about what to buy. A smiling manager and four smiling clerks immediately bustled around me with decided interest. Never before or since have I been the recipient of such prolonged and efficient service. A woman press reporter wandered in to be greeted by the clerks with:

"There's a grand story here today."

"Meet Miss Jones. She's a Hoosier who's been living in Kansas. Her folks live here in Richmond."

"What do you think she's going to do? Go off to some place in Canada to get married."

"Her love story is so romantic! She's buying her trousseau from us."

The reporter insisted on interviewing me and the next day I read an account of my shopping in the local newspaper from which I quote excerpts:

"Trousseau! Such a magic word. The purchase of enchanting frocks and lingeries in almost wholesale quantities. Soft fabrics, laces. Smart new dresses. Hats for every ensemble. Hose and handkerchiefs to last a year. Novel accessories. Suits and coats and blouses and negligees and lounging pajamas. Small wonder that brides go haywire when they assemble their trousseaus, buying without discrimination as to suitability and serviceability. (Some city clothes were required, but the thought of negligees, enchanting frocks and lounging pajamas in the wilds where Joe said we would spend much time made me smile.)

"When I left, Madge had made a number of selections. I can't tell you about the wedding gown except that it is lovely and also practical and white, for I do love white brides. The foundation of her trousseau was a stunning navy blue suit with leg o' mutton sleeves and an impudent row of buttons down the front. To wear over the suit in chilly weather or over her other frocks is a navy blue coat with an Ascot tie of gray. There is a gray crepe afternoon dress, a jacket frock cut down the back to reveal a pink blouse, very lovely and very simple. And there is another dress in an ashes of roses colour with puffy sleeves of taffeta. I can't begin to describe all her dresses. But you can understand why even a bystander would get a thrill watching her buy, buy and buy! (That last line, impossible with my limited funds, made me feel rich and with cash in my pocket during the Bank Holiday I was.)

"Watching with admiration and a thrill of vicarious pleasure while Madge Jones selected the major part of her trousseau in a local shop, I was astonished to see her calm, sane approach to the problem — if such a delightful procedure can be called a problem. While she selected the army of bewitching frocks, she kept in mind all the time their suitability for travelling, for as the wife of a mining engineer and geological explorer Madge will tour with her husband over the resort regions of Canada." (I laughed for a long time over that summary. "Roughing it" as the Mandys must do would not resemble a resort tour and would be confined to the province of British Columbia.)

At home there was talk, talk, talk and much lingering around the table over mother's delicious meals of my favourite dishes. We all regretted that cost and time prevented Joe from coming to Indiana for our wedding and that the same reasons would keep my relatives from the ceremony in Vancouver. The month had to come to an end and then I had to say goodby to my family. My farewell to sisters Mabel and Blanche, respectively in Illinois and New York, was by letter. Mother, father, Dohn and Kathleen were as tearful as I when parting, for we did not know when we might meet again. Feeling very alone, I started a westward journey by rail to Chicago, changing there to head into Canada. The border was crossed at two in the morning and then the train stopped and a man's voice wakened me in the sleeper asking a question.

"Will you please put your head outside your berth?"

Somewhat frightened I countered, Why?

"Regulations," he answered. "I'm a customs officer."

I complied with his request and was surprised to hear what he said. "You're the American girl going to Dr. Mandy to be married in Vancouver."

This made me feel like a package to be delivered. Then came the offical question.

"Any wedding presents to declare?"

No. They've been mailed to my new address.

"Good. That was a sensible thing to do. You're wondering how I know about you and your plans. I'm real glad to tell you. That man of yours must be mighty thoughtful to write the customs office here to ask that every courtesy be given his bride. Seems like a good start to a happy marriage. I'd bet on you having a very fine husband."

Joe had also alerted the Canadian National Railway of my journey and our impending marriage. This news spread throughout the train and soon proved the popular saying, "All the world loves a lover," to be true. Both passengers and crew trooped through my coach to meet the bride, wish me well and help me assemble jigsaw puzzles friends had provided for recreation along the way. All remarked, "You'll have to have web feet to live in Prince Rupert. It rains every day of the year there." Such gloomy prediction did not dampen my spirits for I was happily going to the man I loved and a home with him in the pioneer city which had captivated me with the beauty of surrounding sea and mountain setting on seeing it from the coastal steamer Princess Louise.

When the train stopped in Vancouver at eight in the morning, I think my heart stopped too. I was terrified to find myself in a strange country where I knew nobody but my prospective bridegroom. My feet lingered and I was the last person leaving the train. Joe had considerately prepared for this reaction by having friends with him, a Mr. and Mrs. Welsh. They had been born and reared in Scotland and even after thirty years in Canada their speech was the same as in the old country. They welcomed me with a hug and a kiss, but their friendly voices spoke words I couldn't understand. Perceptive Joe sensed my dilemma and translated "Scottish," which I'd never heard before, to the merriment of the Welsh's. I laughed with them and gradually picked out meaning from their unfamiliar speech and I was cheered when they asked me to call them Uncle Jimmy and Aunt Jessie. They assured me that I now had relatives to attend my wedding and that my folks in Indiana would be with me in spirit.

After collecting my luggage, Joe and I were served a big breakfast in the Welsh's apartment. I had eaten earlier on the train and wanted no more food on this special morning, but politeness required at least some nibbling. Joe had planned and organized everything for the day. The wedding, timed for high noon, required hurrying to get ready. Can't we have the ceremony a little later? I gasped. I must have a shampoo and hairset first. Joe's response was, "That can be done right away." He consulted the telephone book for the number of the nearest beauty shop, called there and spoke to the manager. She promised to send one of her staff to the apartment in half an hour. I had a hasty bath before the arrival of the hairdresser while Aunt Jessie pressed my wedding gown. Meanwhile, Uncle Jimmy took the bridegroom, who was walking nervously in circles around the living room, for a soothing stroll.

We arrived at the church on time and how bridal it looked with a florist's arrangement of daffodils and tulips decorating the pulpit as directed by Joe. My wish for a quiet church wedding was carried out. Only Joe, Aunt Jessie and Uncle Jimmy, the organist, a tenor who sang a sentimental song, "God Gave Me A Rose," the minister and myself were present. The organ began playing the wedding march and the four of us walked slowly down the aisle. Joe led with Aunt Jessie on his arm and Uncle Jimmy followed with me, very proud of his role to give the bride away. Proceeding slowly and sensitively aware of Joe's height, a single thought stirred in my mind. I was sure that I looked quite tall in my floor length white gown carrying Joe's long bouquet of twelve Easter lilies held together artistically by a very wide, white satin ribbon falling from a bow to below my knees. The wedding was of short duration and very impressive with the vows promising fidelity until death do us part. The minister, Rev. Andrew Roddan, added words of wisdom and both Joe and I were so happy that tears of joy came to our eyes.

After signing the register, Joe rushed Uncle, Aunt and me to a photographer's studio for pictures and then we returned to the Welsh's apartment for a hearty lunch. Half an hour later, Aunt Jessie helped me change from wedding attire into a dark blue suit before a taxi drove us to the Georgia Hotel. Joe had reserved the bridal suite there and shortly after settling in a second luncheon was served in the spacious sitting room of the suite. I was certainly not hungry and ate lightly of an assortment of salads, cold meats, rolls and rich dessert. Aunt Jessie patted my hand and said to my husband, "Joe, 'tis a shame the wee lassie canna eat." I cut the wedding cake with Joe's assistance and grim determination tolerated a small slice of it, although my stomach was now in revolt against food.

We then went window shopping to acquaint me with Vancouver's leading stores. Although it was April 4th and the sun was shining, there was still a chill in the air and this soon sent us back to the hotel suite where Uncle Jimmy and Aunt Jessie ordered tea with sandwiches, crumpets and petit fours. Later, dinner in the elegant dining room of the hotel was an endurance test that almost sent me falling to the floor. I weakly inquired of Joe, after the Welsh's said goodnight, Do all Canadians eat as much as our wedding party did today? He emerged from a bridegroom's daze, suddenly conscious of what I had endured.

"My dear, little wife, I guess we overdid the eating." he admitted. "We were trying to keep you so occupied you'd have no time to think of your folks and friends left across the border. Don't worry about the quantity of food you'll prepare for me or Canadian guests. I'm sure food consumption here is the same as for Americans."

We sailed north after a romantic honeymoon in Victoria, the capital city of British Columbia, where flower gardens were everywhere, hanging baskets of flowers adorned lamp posts and afternoon tea at the stately Empress Hotel was an event with English atmosphere prevailing. Then I stood hand in hand with Joe on the deck of the Canadian National Company's steamer Prince George when it dropped anchor in the Prince Rupert harbour and fondly remembered

Pioneer city of Prince Rupert on Kaien Island.

my first glimpse of him as the tardy passenger on the Princess Louise. He pointed out Mount Hays, which dominated the entrance to the south, a backdrop of Mount Oldfield and rocky Mount Morse across the harbour. Dear Joe, I exclaimed, I love the city's setting. The green clad mountains are beautiful and the houses set on scenic hills, with an added seascape, resemble a pretty picture postcard. Thank you for bringing me here.

We were driven to a residential district in the same taxi which had brought Joe to our ship of destiny. It was separated from the rest of the city by a long viaduct over a deep ravine from which a turn to the right brought us to a street overlooking the ocean. There were no buildings in front to mar a lovely panorama of sky and ships, fishing boats and various small craft passing frequently on the sparkling sea with a background of islands. "Here's our home," exclaimed Joe when the taxi stopped in front of a brown, shingle-covered house trimmed in white. It nestled confortably on a lot, flat in front but sloping into a hill behind. Across the fronting street of Graham Avenue, a cliff dropped to Canadian National Railway tracks beside the shoreline.

I had expected to find a primitive residence in a pioneer city, but to my surprise the houses were really modern. Ours was maintained by the British Columbia Department Of Mines for the Northwestern District Resident Mining Engineer. It was well planned, spacious and included a coal and wood burning furnace, electric range and the luxury of an electric fireplace. Poems of Robert Service had acquainted me with the outstanding friendliness of people in the Northwest and this spirit of the north was soon verified by our first caller. Neighbour Harry Pullen, owner and editor of The Prince Rupert Daily News, came to extend a welcome from himself, his vacationing family and the community. Mr. Pullen was a booster for his city and anxious for me to learn its history and potential. I listened to him with great interest and tried to absorb the information he poured out.

"I'll probably sound like an editorial in my paper but there's some facts you should know about Prince Rupert, Mrs. Mandy. This is a young city, just twenty-three years old and it's still very much a pioneer settlement. The founders were strong, optimistic people. They blasted a dwelling place out of rock and built on sour muskeg. Walk around here and you'll see boulders and your feet will sink on spongy ground. There's been, I must say, great progress since incorporation in 1910. We can boast of having the largest city north of Vancouver on the Pacific coast. Our population is over six thousand. We're also proud of having the Canadian Fish and Cold Storage Plant, the largest of its kind on the continent. Do take a tour of it, you'll find something worth seeing.

"Dr. Mandy, you'll agree on the importance of Prince Rupert as the centre of a huge mineralized and forested area. I'm sure you'll want to show Mrs. Mandy the reduction plant where fish oil and fertilizer are produced, the grain elevator, dry dock and ship building plant. Have you told her how the city came into existence? No? Well, I will. Prince Rupert was the dream of Charles M. Hays, General Manager of the Grand Trunk and Pacific Railway. He planned to extend the railroad to a northern British Columbia port which could compete with Vancouver in shipping. This site on Kaien Island was chosen because it has one of the finest natural harbours in the world. It is fourteen miles long, landlocked, ice free all year and five hundred miles nearer the Orient than Vancouver and Seattle. Unfortunately, construction of both the city and the railway was delayed because Hays died in the tragic sinking of the Titanic. What cheers there must have been when the first train from Winnipeg arrived in April, 1914.

"By the way, Mrs. Mandy, I suspect many people living here don't know the city was named for Prince Rupert. He was a first cousin of Charles II who was the first governor of the Hudson's Bay Company. I believe the dream of Hays for expansion into a major port will be realized in time. We're in the throes of a Depression now, waiting for something to turn up and it will. Prince Rupert is destined to prosper. I'm your neighbour and if there's anything I, or my wife, can do for you, let us know."

I had reason to be grateful that a considerate man was the first caller in the newly established Mandy home because of what happened during the course of the evening. Former communities in which I had lived housed coffee drinking people, so I was unprepared when my husband asked, "Harry, would you like a cup of tea and some biscuits?" His reply, "Indeed I would," sent me to the kitchen. I had never brewed a cup of tea but remembered reading that the English preferred it strong. Pullen was English. Tea bags were not in vogue then so I opened a package of tea and dumped eight heaping teaspoons into a small teapot filled with hot water. Several minutes elapsed before I nervously wheeled the results, on a new but slightly creaking teawagon, into the living room.

Harry Pullen and my husband were truly gentlemen. They not only drank three cups each of that bitter brew but, at my insistence, told me how to make good tea and assured me they wouldn't tell anyone about my humiliating moment. I'm sure had a woman guest been involved, the related error would have amused at numerous tea, dinner and bridge parties as too good a story to keep secret. Then, as stories change with repetition, the number of heaping teaspoons might have increased from eight to fifteen or more with a resultant branding of Dr. Mandy's bride as most inept in the kitchen. However, the information gained that night was beneficial — how to prepare the community's popular beverage and also to graciously accept hospitality without visible aversion. The latter was quite necessary when, in future days of wilderness exploration, I was offered the prospector's and pioneer settler's much stronger tea and coffee than I had brewed.

The thought did not occur to me that, as the bride of a well known local man, I would be an object of local interest and speculation. Prince Rupert was still a pioneer city where contact with people from the outside world was limited to visiting relatives or friends, travelling men and passing tourists, all transported by coastal steamer, small boats, railway and occasionally by plane. Joe said the whole city buzzed with excitement and curiosity when a newcomer planned to locate there and the romance linked with my decision had the appeal of a novel. Shortly after arrival, a long-time resident asked if she could introduce me to a group of Prince Rupert women at an afternoon tea. This was a gracious gesture and I became her guest of honour from two to five one April day, dressed by request in my wedding gown.

Of course I felt very self conscious being observed and appraised by over eighty strangers in the claustrophobic dimensions of a small apartment. I also found it difficult to juggle a cup of tea and dainty delicacy while shaking hands sandwiched between crowded guests. The clatter of continual small talk in women's high pitched voices kept me from hearing correctly most of their murmured names when introduced, but the friendliness of acceptance was heartening. One matron manoeuvered me into a corner for a gossipy monologue.

"My dear girl," she gushed, "you've been the talk of Prince Rupert since we heard Dr. Mandy, our most eligible bachelor, was getting married. Were we ever surprised about that! He chose a bride from a long way off, didn't he? Indiana is where you came from, isn't it? Looked it up on the map of the U.S. to see just where that place is. I'll bet you feel dreadful so far from your kinfolk. Confidentially, some hopefuls here tried to nab your man. Don't let them losers bother you! Didn't stand a chance they didn't. We've all been dying to meet you and see what you're like. You look so young and Dr. Mandy is such a mature man and much older than you I'd say. Oh well, you'll make a real nice picture together and you'll keep him young. I'm sure we all hope you will be happy here."

It was easy to be happy in Prince Rupert. I was not only in love with my husband but with the exceptional beauty of the locality and the kindness of residents gave me an "at home" feeling. What did people in this pioneer city do for recreation? There were several clubs and lodges to provide social gatherings and projects and a theatre entertained with moving pictures, although not the most recently produced. The sports minded could choose tennis, badminton, fishing, hiking, boating or skiing. Community activities included teas, dinners, dances and bridge playing. Bazaars kept many constructively busy in financially assisting seven churches — United, Catholic, Presbyterian, Baptist, Salvation Army, Lutheran and Pentecostal.

Afternoon teas of fifty to one hundred guests were a major event for women in the Prince Rupert of the 1930's. They were an outlet for chatting and culinary talent which encouraged friendly competition in the variety and originality of dainty sandwiches, crunchy cookies, shortbread, cakes covered with delicious icing, petit fours, scones, candies, etc., offered to please both the eye and palate. What a drastic change from my afternoons with students! The teas were popular but the overwhelming obsession of both men and women was bridge. The game absorbed them at afternoon and evening parties and the desire to win transformed the game of bridge into a warring contest. Four prominent ladies of the city who excelled at bridge were called "The Big Four" and devoted many mornings to the game. The most fanatical of the four accosted me, a bride of a few weeks, when I attended an afternoon tea.

The plump matron was wearing a high, wide hat with an ostrich feather descending from it to tickle my face as her head moved vigorously near me. Her shrill voice stopped the chatter of assembled guests who listened wide-eyed.

"You're Mrs. Mandy, aren't you? I hear you and Dr. Mandy are not going to play bridge. I must tell you this. You can't live in Prince Rupert, isolated as it is, without a hobby. That means you have to play bridge."

My answer was simply, I don't have one hobby but several. I expect them and field trips with my husband, my home and participating in community projects will take all my time. Joe's reply when I told him of the incident was reassuring.

"Madge, I don't think it advisable for you to play bridge here. I've spent the odd evening at Prince Rupert bridge parties and always came away exhausted from fiercely fought battles. Now, with you, I can enjoy leisure pursuits which are really pleasurable instead of excessively competitive. What do you say?"

I agreed. Neither of us thought of a repercussion from our decision but it came from the member of "The Big Four" who told me I couldn't live in Prince Rupert unless I played bridge. Because of this, she refused to speak to me when we met while shopping, at a tea or any social gathering. I was distressed about such pettiness until I spoke to Joe about it and he responded emphatically.

"Such behaviour is childish and not worth a thought. That woman lives only for bridge and such limited living is pathetic. Be glad you live fully and feel sorry for her that she does not."

I had arrived in Prince Rupert on a sunny day prepared for rain and it soon came and stayed awhile. The Welsh's had warned in Vancouver, as had travellers on the train, that I should expect rain every day in the year there. Time proved the city had a goodly amount of rain but certainly not that much. I soon wrote to my mother to tell her Prince Rupert rain was dry, an observation she never understood — neither did local residents. This conclusion came from having lived in Texas and Kansas where cloudbursts kept me indoors. In Prince Rupert I could walk through a more gentle downpour and keep dry dressed in raincoat, rain hat and boots while clinging to an umbrella and listen to the soothing song of raindrops.

Some benefits of the fairly damp clime were greener lawns and flowers that grew bigger and brighter than in the drier, sunnier south. Many floral gardens flourished and interest in them developed a Horticultural Society in the mid-thirties with Harry Pullen as president and myself as vice president. Our club held meetings and shows where flowers were displayed which thrived on the Rupert rain and tender, loving care. A professor from the Agriculture Department of the University of British Columbia attended the shows to judge and award prizes for best flowers and best arrangements of flowers. He also selected, from a tour of the city, two gardens for medal recognition. Residents were especially proud of their huge, colourful dahlias and begonias. Joe and I were pleased to produce sweet peas along the side of our house that grew to a height of twelve feet. They were in clusters of large blossoms with very long, strong stems and bouquets of them had to be picked from a tall ladder. Our Society discovered that the rose adapted well to the local climate and chose it as the city flower. Gardeners co-operated and hundreds of rose bushes were imported and planted. I encouraged this floral beautification by writing an article which was published in the Vancouver Province newspaper titled, "ROSES REIGN IN PRINCE RUPERT." Surely roses were compensation for sometimes excessive moisture and reigned as an asset for the city.

Every community has characters and one couldn't reside in Prince Rupert without being aware of a conspicuous two who were totally different. Foremost was patriarchal furrier William Goldbloom whose shop was on the main street. On fine days he eased his portly frame into a wide chair on the sidewalk outside the store, usually with his little dachshund beside him. He was always dressed in a beige suit with a gold nugget chain holding his stretched vest in place, his head topped by a Stetson. He had observant eyes set in a broad face with a prominent nose above a gray Vandyke beard and enjoyed smiling at and talking to passersby. Joe liked and respected Goldbloom, whom he knew well. One story he told me of their association was that of an experience they shared when both chanced to be travelling on a coastal steamer.

"It was evening," Joe said, "when our ship stopped at a small village. Some Indians came aboard to tell Goldbloom they had trapped some black marten and wanted to sell the skins. The merchant went ashore to inspect the catch but made no deal. He confided to me, 'These Indians ask too much. I'm not to be taken over. You go to them and they'll sell for what the marten is worth. Take this money for the furs, the market price today. Good luck.' I was successful and turned the purchase over to him. Next morning at breakfast Goldbloom looked across the table at me and chuckled as he said, 'Dr. Mandy, you followed instructions but I was skunked. Sure those skins were black marten. Smoke made them black. The colour came off on my hands. I know tricks of the trade and should never have looked at them in the darkness of night.' He laughed at his stupidity, refusing to condemn the cheaters because 'Cash is so hard to come by these days.' Quite a man!"

An equally interesting character was "Holy Joe," infrequently seen in the city centre, alone and silent. He was about five feet ten, had a long, black beard, wore a brownish jacket over baggy, black pants and perched a peaked hat on his head. He was barefoot all year around, paying penance for a brother who was acquitted of a crime for which he was charged. His home was a little shack and the garden behind it provided vegetables for his meals. His income came from the sale of potatoes that he produced and wood he cut and delivered. "Holy Joe" helped the Catholic Church in every way he could and though eccentric was considered a good man. I often wished someone could ease his self-imposed penance and loneliness.

How pleasant it was to live where only petty violations of the law attracted police attention. Absence of serious crime was possible because of the type of citizens in Prince Rupert and the island's isolation which made a get-away difficult. The only violent incident during my time of residence occurred on July 4th, 1938. On that American holiday an American navy vessel was in port and a cruise steamer was entering the harbour. An official on the wharf cleared passage through the crowd gathered to welcome the ships and the group held back responded good naturedly. Then a taxi drew close to the docking area and the officer called loudly, "You'll have to park farther back. You're blocking the way."

The driver of the car jumped out, angrily shouted something unintelligible and hopped into the taxi. He raced home to pick up a gun and speedily drove to the Court House. There he rushed into the building and then into the headquarters of the provincial police. It was just after the noon hour and Inspector William Service and Corporal Robert Gibson were at their desks attending to correspondence. When Service got up to speak to the caller, the agitated man pulled out his gun and fired. The Inspector had no chance to defend himself and fell to the floor dead. The surprised Corporal was also quickly shot and died shortly after in hospital.

The gunman ran out of the Court House and drove to a hotel beer parlour on the main street. Swinging through the door he fired wildly. Frightened sailors from the visiting American navy ship and other patrons shrieked and dived under tables. Three pursuing constables, exchanging gunshots with the killer, fatally wounded him and he died instantly. News of the tragedy spread and put all of us who heard it in a state of shock. We were saddened that such senseless murder of two fine men could happen in our city. Doubtless the American sailors from the naval vessel were fearfully surprised by the melodramatic pursuit and shooting of the killer. They would tell their folks and friends back home, "Why, being in Prince Rupert on that July 4th proved shoot-outs do happen in the Northwest. It was scary there, just like the shooting in western movies we saw when we were kids. You know, we could have been bumped off, too. Prince Rupert? We'll never forget that place!"

With the coming of May in the first year of our marriage, which was 1933, Joe outlined what our living course would be. "My field work begins this month and continues into the fall. I have a large district to cover. It extends north from the Queen Charlotte Islands to the Alaskan and Yukon borders and east to the Babine mountains. Of course you'll go with me. The map of British Columbia will show you where we'll be going. Only a part of the district can be covered each year. We'll be in isolated places often and travelling will usually be rough and tough. Madge, my dear, you'll stand up to it like a trooper."

I was glad Joe had confidence in me — but could I be a trooper I asked myself. My life had been one of study — school, elocution and piano lessons in the shelter of my parent's home, childhood summers spent on my Jarrett grandparent's farm, courses in university and further instruction for self and students when I became a teacher. I had never participated in sports, except hiking. I had never ridden a horse, climbed a mountain, rowed a boat or even been on a camping trip. Still, being in love made all things possible and a thoughtful, caring husband wise in the ways of the wild would surely give me courage and help for our rugged ventures. Actually, it was good I didn't know the dangers of wilderness trail travel. They would have appeared impossible to confront and conquer and I should have missed unusual, thrilling and happily memorable adventure which became mine through accompanying my husband on his field trips.

We Mandys were away from home most of spring, summer and early fall. During winter residence, Joe wrote reports of his field work for an annual publication by the British Columbia Department Of Mines. It was then I became fully occupied in conducting a weekly story hour for children, giving speeches to various organizations and sharing trail experiences in a travelogue illustrated by Joe's pictures. I also presented evenings of entertainment in the reading of poems, stories and one act plays for the benefit of city churches. My husband and I assisted each other in all activities so that I became conversant in mining and he in speech. True love dominated our lives and drew us ever closer and, though we retained distinct personalities, people never thought of one without the other.

After six adventure filled years with Joe, I gave up trail travel to happily stay at home with a baby boy. It was such a joy to us to have a child and so sad that World War II started that year of his birth and changed our city drastically. Prince Rupert became the most important port in the Pacific Northwest due to it's strategic location nearer the Orient than any other north Pacific port and the fact that it adjoined potentially threatened Alaska. Almost overnight it changed into a bustling, over-crowded community with Canadian Navy, Army and Airforce stationed there, as well as an American contingent. Supplies for newly established protection posts of the Northwest, comprising British Columbia, Alaska and Yukon Territory, were rushed through this all important centre by rail from the east, ships from the south and planes from numerous points. The road to link Kaien Island, on which the city stood, with the mainland had long been under construction, advancing only a few miles because of muskeg, rock and exorbitant costs. Joe had calculated that the time required for completion at the continued slow rate would be ninety-nine years. With the advent of war it became an almost instant accomplishment and proved invaluable then and for the future. The reputation of a "wild city" developed because of problems associated with war and hundreds of service men passing through or remaining in the port and was temporarily descriptive.

I loved and shall always love the Prince Rupert of the 1930's where

Joe and I established our first home. My happy years of residence in that scenic city were enhanced by it being a peaceful haven for return from hazardous, wilderness trails. There, as throughout Joe's entire mining district, I was encircled by a lovely setting and the neighbourly spirit of the Northwest which drew every resident into a special bond of kinship. What a privilege for Joe and I to live in pre-war Prince Rupert and pioneering from it become a part of Beautiful British Columbia's history.

Prince Rupert in the 1930s. To Madge and Joe the city was a peaceful haven following weeks of wilderness travel. After returning from a field trip, opposite, they pick their sweet peas. The plants were over six feet tall.

# THE QUEEN CHARLOTTE ISLANDS

"We go to the Queen Charlotte Islands next week," said Joe on our first May day in a Prince Rupert home.

You have so many regal names in British Columbia, I remarked. Were the islands named for Queen Charlotte?

"No," answered Joe. "Captain George Dixon sailed to them in 1787 and gave the islands the name of his ship, Queen Charlotte. The archipelago is the home of the Haida Indians, highly intelligent and powerful people who used to travel to Victoria in dugout canoes. They are world famous for their carving of argillite totem poles which are rapidly becoming a collector's fancy."

Where are the islands located? I asked.

Joe knew his assigned territory and replied without hesitation, "140 miles northwest of Vancouver and 60 miles west of Prince Rupert. The two largest, which we shall visit, are Graham and Moresby and form the most westerly extremity of our province. Population is confined to Graham Island where you'll find the Indian villages of Masset and Skidegate. The Queen Charlottes are in the southern part of my district, what I call the Near North. Travel there will not be as difficult or dangerous as in the Far North where we'll be in summer and fall. You might call this minor expedition a gentle introduction to my type of field trips."

What I knew about his field trips was limited to romantic imagination about episodes he had told me. I lacked the experience to really comprehend what they involved. However, I could sincerely say, I'm so glad my first roving with you will be on the Queen Charlotte Islands. They hold a special place in my heart.

"Why is that?" he wanted to know.

Because of a letter you wrote me. You not only described their charm and included sketches of prospectors and settlers but let me have a clear insight into your character. That letter solved a question in my mind. Do you truly love the author? It made you irresistible and deep affection admissable.

Joe's response was, "The Queen Charlottes will be special to me from now on."

Let me refresh your memory and mine by a section of the letter, I reminisced. Turning to a personal file I read aloud what had so enchanted me.

"As I hike along the miles and miles of golden sand beaches fringed with the foaming surf rolling in, I wish you, too, could enjoy the unsullied beauty of the mighty ocean far from the sordid surroundings of men.

"The east coast of Graham Island (the north island of the Queen Charlottes) is remarkably interesting and characterized by a fascinating and lengthy stretch of sand beach that spreads out in the sea from wooded cliffs and dunes. I hiked about 75 miles of this stretch with short incursions into the fringing plateau behind. Two island settlers and four or five prospectors populate the area. On such a trip I generally carry enough grub to see me through and what other paraphernalia I need in the way of instruments, etc., but as this constitutes a pack of 40 to 50 pounds, which begins to feel like 100 at the end of the day and about 15 miles of hiking, I did not bother with my sleeping bag and its extra weight. Graham Island is drier and balmier than the mainland, and with plenty of matches and lots of dry driftwood for fire one can generally fix up a comfortable nest for the night should one not be able to reach a prospector's or settler's camp. However, on this trip I was fortunate to be able to reach a camp each night.

"On the fifth day at about 9 p.m. I came to the sumptuous and hospitable confines of Madame Rajout's resort hotel, 'The Dunes,' on the Tlell River — tired, dog-hungry and dirty. And then a bounteous repast of wild rabbit, gallons of fresh milk and cream, soft music on the radio, a shave, a refreshing hot bath and the most comfortable bed I have ever slept in, with the dull roar of distant rolling surf for a lullaby. Madame Rajout is an interesting Belgian woman who found her way to Canada after her home in Liege and all her possessions were destroyed in the German invasion. She is a wonderful worker and is a splendid example of an indomitable spirit in the face of adversity. With her daughter and son-in-law she is building a beautiful and somewhat unique resort at Tlell — peaceful and restful, far from the madding crowd.

"The old prospectors and settlers one meets on these trips are great characters and full of interest. With what little and rough habitations they have to offer, they are hospitality personified. Calloused and sometimes dirty in habits — they love to chew tobacco and spit, but generally into an old coffee can and with unerring and nerve-trying marksmanship — they are mostly diamonds in the rough. Sometimes through years of living alone, they harbour 'notions' and have become soured of the world. Usually they have developed a philosophy of life logically sound, to suit their individual conditions. The only urge I can figure out for a settler to seek isolation is the desire to get away from people and the frustrations of the world. Yet they appear overwhelmed with joy to meet somebody from the outside, if only to have someone to talk to for awhile.

"Near the Oeanda River I spent a night in the one-room shack of an old fellow, Jimmy White. His cabin was filled with rusty odds and ends, sacks of flour, beans, mouse traps, knicknacks and junk picked up from the flotsam and jetsam of the ocean. A goodly layer of sand carpeted the floor. The shack was built of jetsam lumber found on the beach. Nearby was an enormous barn with nothing in it, a construction of huge timbers thrown on the beach, each of which would represent a good day's work to carry up. This had taken the old man seven years to erect and it is not yet fully completed. His homestead covered 100 acres of swamp land which he had drained by enormous ditches, any one of which would represent Herculean labour for an individual and one of which caused the whole Oeanda River to change its course and come surging through the land in a new channel about 1½ miles from its original course.

"And here old Jimmy White has been living for 30 years, his sole companion a horse named Nellie and a lone Dutchman settler a short distance away. Over 60 years of age, with not a gray hair in his thick, tousled mat like a buffalo's mane, the old chap talked incessantly like the purr of a cat, reminiscing of days spent all the way from Quebec to Idaho, the Klondike and back again. He did not seem to want conversation for which, being tired, I was grateful. And when I woke after inadvertently falling asleep, the old boy was still prattling along of days gone by. He never noticed my napping.

"At midnight I turned in on a makeshift bunk of boards — much against the will of hospitable Jimmy White who needed much persuasion to prevent him from giving up his bed to me. Possibly still desirous of a sympathetic listener, Jimmy went outside the cabin and called long and loudly into the night for Nellie. 'Come on. Come on Nellie.' His plea was like a drawn-out wail of anguish. 'Come on Nellie and get some sugar.' But Nellie never came from her hiding place in the swamp and only the howl of the south-easter as it swept over the homestead answered the old man's call into the night.

"The following night I spent in the cabin of a Frenchman 15 miles further on. He had come out from the Klondike in 1924 for the first time since he went in with the gold rush in 1898. His cabin was neat, spic and span, and he spent his time washing gold from the 'black sands' of the beach nearby.

"Such a trip is teeming with interest in people and the geological story of the perpetual conflict between land and sea unfolded by the pebbles on the beach, the cliffs, sand and rock. The struggles of nature and the struggles of men are inspiring in the extreme. I think you would love it and I hope some day you may take it, but with a kindred spirit by your side. And if you do hike along the sands of the Queen Charlottes at some time, you will not be stranger to the symphony of nature there for your personality and charm have already blended with the beauty and inspiration of the song of the ocean as you walked the strand hand in hand with me. And into the salty sea breeze and away into the southeast horizon of Pittsburg has been whispered the refrain — 'Madge, dearest pal of mine'."

Shall I meet Jimmy White and his beloved Nellie? I inquired.

"Not this time, but you'll meet other islanders and you'll admire the self-reliant men who eke out a living from mining the sands on the beaches."

My next question was a woman's. What do I wear?

"Not what you wore in the classroom, my dear. You'll need woolen longjohns, woolen socks, woolen shirts, woolen sweaters, woolen jacket and high leather boots. Then you'll add those golf knickers you wore for hiking in the States, a raincoat and a khaki hat like mine. Wearing these duds won't qualify you for a place in a fashion show but they will give protection for changing weather. That's important."

It was fun shopping, accompanied by Joe, in a men's clothing shop for my "bush" wardrobe. Bill Stone, one of the owners of the shop said, "I've never outfitted a lady for lengthy trail travel. Dr. Mandy, you'll know what your wife ought to have. Just tell me and I'll put it together. Size? Let's go over to the boy's section." I told the women at an afternoon tea about my new garb which I would wear to the Queen Charlotte Islands the next day and listened to questions and comments.

"Don't you think those wooly longjohns will make you scratch?"

"I've never been to the Islands. Hear they're lovely. Lucky you!"

"They say the crossing to get there is simply terrible, worse than the English Channel. You'll be dreadfully seasick."

"Do you know that the Queen Charlottes are simply out of the world? Why, they're cut off from everything."

"Watch out for bears. Somebody told me there are ever so many over there and they rob gardens. Don't know what they do to people."

We embarked on the Prince John of the Canadian National Railway Steamship Services at ten in the evening. My husband prepared me for the sailing by saying, "The Prince John is small but seaworthy and has weathered many a stormy passage. I should warn you that this crossing to the Charlottes is usually very, and I mean very, rough." His prediction and that of the pessimistic tea guest was wrong on this trip. The water on which we sailed was calm and the moon spread a silvery path across its passive surface. It remained quiet during the night and so continued until Graham Island was sighted next morning, the island rising like a mirage out of the ocean, an exciting happening to landlubber me. At that moment an elderly, dignified lady approached me and when she spoke revealed a cultured English woman. She introduced herself as a resident of Graham Island and, having acquired some information about the Mandys, gave me a bit of local history.

"You're a newcomer to British Columbia, aren't you? That means you know little about the Queen Charlotte Islands. Many of the white settlers here were lured from England by a slick promoter. He promised a thriving community where we would prosper and grow rich. Instead, we found ourselves pioneers who had to learn a new way of life, building homes in isolated wilderness. We didn't have money for passage back to the old country, so we had to stay. In spite of a distressing entry, we've learned to love the islands, so peaceful and beautiful. Then, too, the Haida Indians here are good neighbours and their traditions merit respect. We're coming to two settlements soon, the Indian village called Old Masset and the white village of New Masset. They're close together.

"Captain Vancouver was here in 1793. Long time ago, wasn't it? He didn't know that the Sitka spruce, which grows profusely on the Charlottes, is superior to spruce in other places. It was used in construction of fighter planes during the World War. We've had some mining on the islands, but logging has been the major industry. Now mills are closed and there's only a few logging camps left. Lumber companies were beneficial in providing employment locally and much needed cash for our scattered communities. However, I criticize them for disfiguring the land with bare spaces and for abandoning their donkeys. Look! You can see some donkeys from this deck where we're sitting."

I looked shoreward and couldn't see any forsaken animals, even with Joe's field glasses. I told my husband such cruelty shouldn't be tolerated. His answer was, "Shed no tears for cruelty, my dear. Those donkeys are engines used in logging operations. They've been left because it is more economical to leave than to remove them from such an isolated location."

I was told the entrance to Masset was difficult to navigate as it was filled with hidden reefs. Such menace held no fear for the Captain of the Prince John. He brought us safely into port where we were greeted by a crowd of Indians and whites elbowing harmoniously. All were there to watch merchandise unloaded and passengers land. This contact with the outside world was an eagerly anticipated event and smiling faces welcomed. The group soon parted to allow a very tall man in uniform to stride forward and speak to Joe and me. His words were brief and to the point.

"I'm Constable Gerald Sharpe, recently assigned to Masset. You must be Dr. and Mrs. Mandy. I was informed of your coming by radio. Your presence is timely, Dr. Mandy. Prospectors here need your help. Nice you could come, too, Mrs. Mandy."

I looked up, from my five feet, into the face of that very tall officer and couldn't stop myself from asking, How tall are you? He probably had been asked the question hundreds of times but politely answered, "Only 6 feet 6 and ½." His height and big, sturdy frame must have been an asset in policing. He had kindly told the proprietor of the only and small Masset hotel that we would be his guests and a young chap from the lodging was on hand to carry our luggage there. Genial Mr. Frost, who also owned the adjoining general store, was at the door to shake our hands and launch into an informative monologue.

"Glad to see you folks. So far, you're my only guests this week. Once the hotel was always full up. Quite profitable it was. The Depression has hit us hard, but all in all Masset's a good place to live. We aren't just common folks in this out of the way place either. We have Dr. Dunn. He's well educated, a good doctor and he has travelled a lot. There's a Sandhurst graduate and more who are really somebody, and I haven't always been a poor inn and storekeeper. A foolish lad I was to run away to sea. That's why I haven't had much schooling. The rest of my family in England have all been teachers. There's little money floating around Masset these days. Everyone manages though. Getting something to eat is easy. We dig clams, catch fish, pick wild berries, raise vegetable gardens and shoot deer and rabbits. Wood to build a house or cabin is ours for the taking. I've got a nice house, wonderful wife and a fine boy. What more could a chap want?"

We met several villagers that day as we mingled among them learning where Joe's assistance was needed. I discovered they were an example of genuine neighbourliness. When lacking cash, the islanders bartered. The doctor took care of the sick in exchange for whatever his patients could offer and all residents shared their skills and possessions. Entertainment was primarily community get-togethers such as picnics and evenings passed pleasantly with conversation and radio listening while tea and biscuits were served. We were immersed in an atmosphere of good will and contentment where everything was leisurely. This insular fragment of British Columbia bestowed inspiration in scenic beauty, gave a liberal supply of food from land and sea and provided sincere fellowship with peace of mind. No wonder people liked living on the Queen Charlotte Islands. I, too, could have loved residing there.

The next morning Joe said at an early breakfast in the hotel's little dining room, "My schedule won't permit me to spend much time here and I mean to make every minute count. Today you'll hike with me on the beach I wrote you about. This is a working day for me, an instructional one for you. While walking by the water take time to look at the colourful seascape painted by nature and listen to the song of the ocean. Oh, here comes the man I've hired to take us to the ruby sands. Let's go out and get into that rattling, old Ford truck of his."

The truck barely fitted on the road which was constructed of planks laid on wooden ties. This pioneer type of roadway trailed across swampy land which could mire cars slipping into it. Our driver was so used to this constant menace that the occasional shifting of the truck to the plank's edge did not disturb him as it did me, accustomed to the broad, smooth highways on solid ground in the States. We soon reached a forked turn and from there walked to the beach.

Why is this beach called Ruby? I asked. "Look at it closely lying on your stomach and you'll know," was Joe's answer. I saw red particles when my eyes were close to sand and concluded islanders thought they were

Typical plank road on Graham Island in the Queen Charlottes.

rubies, which must be valuable, and consequently named the strand Ruby. Unfortunately, Joe's examination proved the red specks were garnets too tiny for commercial value. "Oh well," said the islanders when informed of this fact, "it doesn't matter. We had fun dreaming of what we'd buy with money made from mining the ruby sands."

We walked for miles on this stretch of sand. I did listen to the singing surf and stopped frequently to view the expanse of pictorial water and sky, sensing its attraction for the venturesome to explore a mysterious beyond. While Joe took samples of sand to assay for gold inclusion, I filled my pockets with agates and pebbles of various sizes, shapes and colours found lying on the beach. Joe said some could be cut, polished and made into unusual pendants, brooches and bracelets. The hours passed so quickly and pleasantly that I was surprised when Joe called a halt for lunch in mid-afternoon. The tasty meal of tinned meat, cheese and crackers was welcome. I had been used to walking all my life, even during professional days when my salary did not permit the expense of a car. However, this demanding tramp on squishy sand, combined with the effects of the sun and sea breeze, wore me out! I almost fell asleep during supper and don't remember undressing and going to bed. I awoke in the morning with stiff, aching legs but was cheered by Joe's application of soothing lotion to my sun and wind burned face.

For that day Joe had planned examination of black sand where a few prospectors were mining fine, flour gold and a little platinum. Our truck driver of yesterday arrived to take us through an open field to a trail near the sea. Then we walked into dense undergrowth and obstructing trees where I had to push away brush, boughs and twigs. What a wet trail it was, untouched by the sun and enjoyed by slow, slimy slugs. We sloshed on to reach a campsite of several small and mostly deserted cabins and an abandoned sawmill.

A young man, in clean but much patched clothing, came out of the largest cabin to exclaim, "Constable Sharpe told me you'd be here. Ain't never mined before. He said you'd tell me the best way to do it, Dr. Mandy. This your wife? Want to come with us and see what I'm tryin' to do? This way. There's my claim."

Joe had referred to placer mining on the Charlottes before we came here. Ignorant of what placer meant, I had turned to his copy of "A Glossary Of The Mining And Mineral Industry." Placer was defined as a place where gold or other valuable minerals of an alluvial or glacier deposit were obtained by washing. Now I was to see a placer operation. An essential piece of equipment for this mining was a sluice box. The box I saw was made of wood and was about two feet wide and twelve feet long. It slanted down to the beach, allowing water from a small stream above to flow over the contents and carry the light gravel to a tailings (refuse) pile. The bottom of the box was covered by blanket cloth and fitted with wooden bars called riffles which were fastened at regular intervals to help retain shovelled gravel. Black sand of the gravel, with holding riffles removed, stuck to the blanket beneath and the residue was then washed into a round, shallow pan designated the gold pan. Further washing, with skilled manipulation of the sand, left only gold which was heavier. It was exciting to see the prospector's demonstration of gold extraction known as the clean-up.

I watched dots of yellow slowly visible in the black sand and called out, The gold appears like stars beginning to shine in a dark sky.

The prospector thought of the mineral less poetically and drawled, "Reckon that's likely, Ma'am. Me, when I looks at it I think of bacon, beans, bread, coffee and dry socks."

When the inspection of this claim was finished and advice given, another young chap came along. Said he, "I was sleepin' in this mornin'. They's no time schedules on the Charlottes. Well, the grapevine just told me you was here, Dr. Mandy, and your wife. So, I hustled over to meet you. Over there's my cabin. You two come there after I've grabbed some grub and we'll talk minin'."

As the leisurely man disappeared, a hurrying man strode into the scene saying, "Dr. Mandy, I don't know nothing about mining. What I do know is there's gold on this beach and it'll keep me off government relief. I don't want no handouts. I want to support myself. Let me show you my outfit."

This man was anxious to learn and Joe was equally desirous of helping him. So much time passed in conversation between the two that I thought Joe had forgotten my presence. About three o'clock my husband glanced at his watch and then at me. "I'm sorry," he apologized, "I was so intent on assisting that self reliant chap that I didn't think of the many minutes ticking away. You must be hungry and the man who went off for brunch will be wondering why we haven't showed up. Let's go to his cabin. We can lunch there and dry out a bit during discussion."

Rain had been persistently pouring on our waterproofs, dripping on our faces and sneaking into our boottops. The warmth from the cabin's stove was welcome and so was the hot, strong coffee offered to top sardines, crackers and cheese we carried. A middle aged visitor was chatting with our host and waiting to consult Dr. Mandy. He had operated a cannery in the island's prosperous years and at present was cheerfully trying to make a living from mining the black sands. I hated to leave that cozy cabin but I had chosen to join my husband wherever his trail led and that meant, at this moment, trudging with him and the prospectors to their claims. I spent the rest of the afternoon observing consultations, much talking, taking of samples, notes jotted down and pictures snapped. Merely from standing by to watch and listen, I liked what I learned about placer mining and what it involved. The miners were battling discouraging odds to reap a small reward of gold but more important to achieve and maintain self respect, patience and optimism. What an example of mental courage and physical stamina they were!

The following day was Sunday, a day which the prospectors devoted to weekly washing of their grimy clothes and visiting. Dr. Dunn sent word to our hotel that we were to be guests in his home for the noon meal and that he would call and drive us there. Hotel proprietor Mr. Frost informed us, "You'll be part of a group. The Dunns are fine people. Great on sharing. Usually have fifteen or more guests for Sunday lunch." The doctor's large, log house was a few miles from Masset near the mouth of the Sangan River, set back from the road and nearby were four sturdy log cabins which he told us he had built with a holiday resort in mind.

"You built these, Doctor?" exclaimed Joe. "Have you had any construction experience?"

"None. Neither did Robinson Crusoe. I believe as he did, where there's a will there's a way. My venture is a gamble but should pay more than mining the black sands. You've heard how my family and I came with others from England in 1922. We were lured to the Queen Charlottes by brochures promising 'a land of milk and honey!' The reality was wilderness and unprepared pioneers. We've learned to love the islands and probably wouldn't be happy any other place. Though we're poor in cash, we're wealthy in friendships and beautiful surroundings. It's a good life here."

The next morning Joe and I set out in a little boat for an island near Port Clements. The boarding was scary for me, descending from the dock by a swaying, narrow, rope ladder to lower myself onto a small deck from which I poked my head briefly into a tiny cabin partially filled by a smelly engine. The crew consisted of an English owner and an Indian skipper and we and a fishing bound man and his young grandson were the passengers. I went ashore with Joe when we reached the isle where an absent prospector had staked a claim and by letter had asked Joe to examine it and write a report on the showing. A long afternoon passed before Joe's work was finished and then we hurriedly fought our way to shore through tangled brush because the sky had turned very dark. We were barely back on the boat before a northeaster struck with furious force and a wind driven rain beat against us.

Joe guided me to the shelter of the only cabin and, manlike, remained on deck to test his strength against that of the storm. I sat down on a bunk to read a magazine spread there and soon became so sleepy I had to lie down, my eyes closing before I could feel the cushion under my head. Joe sought refuge with me awhile later. His question, "Some storm, isn't it?" brought no reply even with repetition. Fortunately, boatwise as I was not, he realized when calling my name loudly and shaking me brought no response that my slumber was too sound. Quickly seizing a blanket, he wrapped me in it and carried me to the deck where he let cold rain pour down on my face. How long I was unconscious, I don't know and Joe never told me. When aroused, I couldn't understand why my husband was letting me get so wet and whispered weakly, What am I doing here?

Joe huskily answered, "Thank God you're alive. My dear wife, you almost died from carbon monoxide fumes. I swear I won't let this happen to you again."

When the rain stopped, my mind cleared enough for me to think of what Joe had said before we set out for the Queen Charlotte Islands. I remembered his words, "Travel there will not be as difficult or dangerous as in the Far North. You might call this mining expedition a gentle introduction to my type of field trips." My thoughts formed a silent monologue. Gentle that man of mine said. There must be the risk of a more violent death ahead. Why, it's a good omen for the future, since I've survived this near fatality, if I think positively. I shall keep the fact in mind that the Mandy's trail will be dangerous, stimulating, exciting and pleasurable to recall and to relate to others. Then I prayed I might be given strength to carry on as fearlessly as possible.

Being near death was a shock to my entire system and I felt quite sick. Joe knew this and yet had to continue his field work. I assured him there was no cause to worry as my usual good health would shortly return. We landed at Port Clements to find that the once bustling, prosperous logging community had a hotel which had become an empty building. No accommodation was available, so Joe hired local taxi owner, Bob Dyson, to drive us to Madame Rajout's resort at Tlell. He and his wife insisted on serving us sandwiches, tea and biscuits in their extensive, typically English garden where hundreds of flowers beautified the grounds. I was suffering from nausea and had to refuse food, feasting my eyes instead on a border of purple violas a foot wide on either side of a broad walk leading to the Dyson home.

It was now evening and we were driven over a two plank road, a third plank added in some places. Joe thought I should lie down on the back seat and Mr. Dyson, quite disturbed by what had happened on the boat, tucked a blanket over me. By eleven o'clock we reached "The Dunes" resort hotel. The family operating the inn had gone to bed and Mr. Dyson had to knock loudly to arouse them. The Belgian owner, Madame Rajout, came to the door and pleased to see a former guest greeted him with, "Dr. Mandy, again are you here. Bride, too.

Of you, I hear, Mrs. Mandy. Welcome are you." She led us into a homelike sitting room where daughter Camille with her husband Jim had hastily come.

Madame Rajout was a short, stout, gray haired woman with a round, genial face and hospitable manner. She asked Jim to escort us to our room while she prepared refreshments for us. I felt very tired and so weak that Joe carried me to the lounge downstairs. He explained my condition as the after effect of a brush with death. Madame Rajout and her daughter immediately propped me up on a sofa with pillows while serving cinnamon toast, cake and coffee. My stomach rebelled against eating and the coffee tasted so bitter I could only sip a little.

Madame Rajout sympathetically patted my shoulder assuring, "Better feel you when a good night's rest is gone. Hot water for one bath I have. Comes morning, hot water for bath two."

My considerate husband responded, "The ready bath is for my wife. Ladies should always be first. A hot bath for me in the morning will be a perfect start for the day."

When I awoke after a restless night, the wind was howling and rain played loud tunes on the window. Madame Rajout declared such weather was unusual on the Queen Charlottes in May and would disappoint many people on this holiday of May 24th, a national holiday honouring Queen Victoria's birthday. She felt sorry picnics and fishing parties would have to be postponed. Neither holidays or storms kept my husband from his consulting work and he was off for the day right after breakfast. I had looked forward to observing mining activity on this part of Graham Island but had to be content to recline in the lounge, still a victim of nausea, dizziness and chill. Madame Rajout provided warmth with hot water bottles and entertainment with a small radio. I was grateful for both, physically and mentally.

The hard working proprietress took time from her numerous chores to tell me about her dream of making "The Dunes" a family vacation home. I could picture, as she talked, children climbing up and sliding down adjacent sand dunes and collecting shells and pebbles on the beach. I agreed the kiddies might like to help bring in eggs laid by her many chickens, watch the resort's cow milked and munch on tender new peas and young carrots just as they were, fresh from the garden. She was positive hunting and fishing would attract fathers and they and tired mothers would enjoy sitting on the wide balconies both upstairs and down to sun, read or drowsily listen to the music of distant, rolling surf. I suggested she emphasize in advertising what had appealed to my husband when writing about "The Dunes", a beautiful and somewhat unique resort at Tlell, peaceful and restful, far from the madding crowd."

After two days at Tlell Joe hired Jim to drive us to the small settlement of Skidegate. There he planned to examine the closed Southeaster Mine for determination as to whether it could profitably re-open. We shared our journey with shy deer, curious bears, beautiful pheasant and scurrying rabbits. The adjoining Indian village of Skidegate resembled Old Masset, both almost deserted at this season because the Haida families were away fishing. Joe had made arrangements to stay in the home of Mrs. Gordon, whose late husband had been involved in mining. She retained an interest in his properties and looked forward to Joe's report on them. Seeing us coming, the little widow tripped out to meet us with a smile and eyes as eagerly inquiring as a child's. No wonder she looked at me with surprise, for my walking was a stagger even with Joe's support. When Joe told her why I was unsteady, her answer was positive and practical.

"Dr. Mandy, you go out and tend to mining. I'll tend to your wife. I've heard she goes everywhere with you. Not this time she doesn't. Don't worry about her. I was a nurse before I got married and still know what to do when anyone's sick."

Mrs. Gordon kept me lying on a chesterfield with hot water bottles fore and aft and a covering of heavy blankets for added heat, a combination expected to extract poisons from the system by perspiration. The food for invalids she prepared for me wouldn't stay down and she wouldn't stop trying to find something that would. Her persistance won when I was able to retain jelly and a little weak tea. Of course this led to more substantial nutrition and a happy nurse. I wanted to read but couldn't concentrate and had to be content with drowsing. In this semi-conscious state I heard her softly spoken words more than once:

"Poor little bride, so far from her folks. And — she almost died. How terrible to think about. My, my, what might have been!"

Mrs. Gordon's sympathy almost made me feel sorry for myself, an emotion in which I believed nobody should indulge. Under her ministrations I improved but not enough to join Joe to meet prospectors and watch mining activity in the Skidegate area. By the time we embarked on the steamer Prince John sailing back to Prince Rupert, the only remaining effects of inhaling toxic gas was a bitter taste in food and beverage which lasted for over two months.

A request for examination of two lode (ore deposit) claims on Moresby Island of the Queen Charlotte group, took the Mandys back to Skidegate the following year. Mrs. Gordon housed us for a night and served me huge helpings at dinner "to make up for what you couldn't eat when you were my patient." In early evening we called on her Haida neighbours, Mr. and Mrs. Ed Stevens. They were to give us information about transportation to the west coast of Moresby and then to the Haida Gold Mine. As we neared their house, a large, black bear ambled out of the bush and blocked entrance. We stopped and stood motionless and I held onto Joe's arm tightly. The teen-aged son of the family saw the defiant animal from the window and rushed out with a gun. His shot missed and the intruder fled with the boy and his dog in pursuit. Such a menacing visitor at the door must have been a common occurrence, for no mention was made of the bear during the ensuing consultation.

Stevens proudly told us, "My son-in-law, Bert Ingraham, superintendent is of Haida Gold Mine. Me, what you call proprietary vendor. Me, own most shares in Mine Company. Becomes Company May 15. Bert, he set up camp. Has log cookhouse, two tents for seven men. Comes winter and log cabins for crew. Part of mine is restaked Blue Mule old working. Bert, he stake claims for mine. Big property now. How get there? I have man drive you to Queen Charlotte City.

See Bert there. He gets Charlie Haan take you on freight boat longside west coast Moresby, Kootenay Inlet, then Kootenay Harbour. 'Bout fifty mile on water from Queen Charlotte City. Charlie get mine supply there once in week. Mine men carry freight he bring on back, maybe one mile, to camp on trail. Talk to Bert. He fix it all."

The hotel in Queen Charlotte City was an old, weatherbeaten but still sturdy frame building. The owners, Mr. and Mrs. Roy McKenzie, had known prosperity when logging boomed in the vicinity. On the day of our arrival, we were the only guests. The "grapevine" had spread the news of our coming and where we were bound. The McKenzies extended the typical friendliness of the islanders which included a leisurely chat over tea and biscuits. After this warm display of hospitality, we were directed to Ingraham's house. He was a recent arrival from England and Margaret was his Indian bride of a month. The competent mine superintendent had already arranged for Charlie Haan to transport us to Kootenay Harbour with him preceding us to ready progress reports for Joe to study. Ingraham warned me the sailing along the west coast of Moresby Island was so rough and dangerous that few chanced travelling there. I replied, Thank you for warning me, but if my husband chances it, so will I.

Margaret spoke coaxingly to her husband as Joe and I were leaving. "Bert, you take me to mine. You my husband four weeks and I not see Haida Gold Mine. Mrs. Mandy, she go. I come too."

"No," said Bert decisively. "I've told you a hundred times, a mine is not a place for a woman. You stay home."

I was still sleepy when Joe and I were called for a three o'clock breakfast. The McKenzies advised, "Stoke hearty if you must take that awful trip along Moresby's west coast. Are you sure you want to sail there, Mrs. Mandy? You could stay with us while Dr. Mandy's away. We'll give you a cut rate and show you lots of interesting things around here." I appreciated their interest in my welfare but could not accept their proposal. Accompanying my husband on his field trips, hazardous or not, was what I had decided to do and, besides, the journey ahead sounded too thrilling to miss.

Margaret was pacing up and down near Charlie's boat when we approached with our dunnage and called out, "I work on Bert. I tell him you don't like woman at Haida Gold Mine. Mrs. Mandy's a woman. You let her come. He has to say yes. I come with you."

Our skilled pilot, Charlie Haan, had known the islands and boats all his life and loved both. He said our early start was necessary to catch the full tide which would carry us safely over reefs and sand bars in the narrow Skidegate Channel. Emerging into a rolling sea, our boat was tossed and tilted by powerful waves. Luckily, I did not get seasick, instead I felt the certainty of being thrown overboard and sinking to the bottom of the sea from which there was no escape. I tried to centre my thoughts on the scene of surrounding grandeur and sombre beauty. Graham Island, visited the year before, was comparatively flat but along the west coast of Moresby Island rocky mountains rose abruptly from the sea with tree clad heights behind them. This was no sheltered passage, for the grim cliffs faced the pounding Pacific on its rushing way to the distant Orient. I whispered to the sea breeze, Ingraham was right. This is a rough, dangerous sailing. Though I'm really glad to experience the thrill of such a trip, I hope I'll never have to travel here again.

Margaret was talkative and Joe and I craved sleep instead of conversation. We left her chatting with Charlie and stretched ourselves out on bunks below. The porthole was closed so that soaring waves could not enter and flood the cabin. The oil burner at our feet, to warm against chilly morning air, soon drugged us into weird dreams. Joe decided the atmosphere was unhealthy and carried me to the deck where I slept fitfully. The brightness of the morning sun and a cold wind finally awakened me. Joe had been scanning the seascape and now turned to me with a question.

"You look quite alert and ready for what I'm going to ask. You'll make a lovely picture sitting in the bow looking out over this choppy water. Will you just walk over there and take that position while I ready the camera?"

His request caused the same disturbance to every nerve in my body as did stagefright suffered sometimes in my speech career. This seafright, my mind told me, was much worse — it might be fatal. Only Joe's belief I could pass this test of courage, which he knew it was for a landlubber, gave me the strength to do it. I clenched my teeth and hands, wobbled across the heaving deck and collapsed on a coiled rope in a paralytic state. Picture snapped, Joe beamed and guided me to the relative comfort of a folded sleeping bag that cushioned a seat of hard planks and a box of hardware provided a backrest.

I wanted to shout in relief when we entered Kootenay Inlet with stable earth on each side. Margaret prepared a delicious meal of blueback salmon, potatoes, pudding and coffee which we were enjoying when the anchor was dropped in Kootenay Harbour. Charlie blew the boat's shrill whistle and Ingraham, hearing it, came down to the boat. While Margaret served her husband lunch, Joe and I started hiking the trail to the camp of the Haida Gold Mine. It led through forested muskeg and the slugs there were the biggest and slimyest I had ever seen. I hoped future trails would not be like this one, constructed of felled logs connected at precarious angles with axed steps cut into them at very steep places. The logs were quite wet, as the sun never penetrated the dense growth above which darkened the slippery log trail and made it difficult to see clearly.

My husband trod ahead calling back, "Go slowly and carefully, Madge. Watch each step. Grab me if you start falling. Chin up, forge ahead and you'll make it."

The miners were on shift when we arrived at the mine's camp. Joe left a message with the camp cook for Ingraham, saying we were taking the trail to an upper level and would meet him there. On the way we came across an old deserted cabin which must have been built by a former owner of the Haida Gold property when it was staked as the Blue Mule. My imagination allowed me to see the hopeful prospector of yesteryear standing beside the remains of an old water wheel. While examining the cabin, now the home of mice and packrats, we heard the voices of Bert and Margaret and came outside to meet them.

Madge at Haida Gold Mine Camp on Moresby Island.

Ingraham said, "Dr. Mandy, I want to show you outcrops at a higher elevation. There's no trail to them and we have to slog through heavy brush. This rain that's falling will probably soon be worse and we'll get very wet so, Margaret you stay here and find a spot of shelter for Mrs. Mandy and yourself. Let's go, Dr."

Margaret was an expert in the survival lore of her Haida ancestry. In record time she built a fire in front of a three sided, wide lean-to below the decaying cabin. There we were dry and warm, though the downpour of rain continued to dampen everything but us. Ingraham and Joe returned pleased with their examination and then Margaret and I went with them into the old workings of the mine. Neither of us had ever been in a mine and we gingerly accompanied the men, attaching miner's lamps to our hats. Was I scared to go into the dark depths of the old mine? Of course I was, but I didn't let the men or Margaret know it. We entered a tunnel of blackness, the walls of the underground passage seen dimly by the feeble light from our small lamps. Joe chipped samples and jotted down notes in his field book before we descended to a lower level where two miners were drilling into solid rock. They looked at me in disbelief and stopped work briefly to question.

"How did you get here?" asked one of the men.

By boat and trail, I answered.

"You mean you come along that gosh-awful west coast of Moresby? By golly, you're a brave one. Don't mind sayin' I ain't so brave. If that's the only way out from this mine, I'll stay here forever."

Piped his partner, "That west coast of Moresby Island is one hell of a trip. Near scared me to death an' I don't scare easy. Do hear you can cross the island to the east coast. No trail part way, but solid land. Fightin' bush beats drownin'. I'll leave that way."

I was ravenously hungry when we got back to the cookhouse where the cook, who had gone to bed, had kindly left supper in a warmer for us. Bert and Margaret were to spend the night in a tent at the mine and Joe and I on Charlie's boat. It was dark by the time we started down that terrible log-felled trail which we could hardly see by the faint light of hand carried miner's lamps. Suddenly, something moved on the trail ahead, heard in the stillness of night and forest but not seen. It had to be an animal and perhaps one to be feared.

Joe whispered, "Don't move! Maybe the creature will be frightened by our lamps."

When we put our feeble lights together, there was a loud "Meow" and the cat from the mine came slinking toward us. She was used to men and obviously preferred them to women, ignoring me to become a problem for Joe. She stopped on steeply inclined logs to rub against his boot and wait to be petted, a difficult balancing feat for a big man on such a trail. Joe was kind to her, talking softly in what he hoped was acceptable cat chatter but gently urging her on with the tip of his boot. She led the way to the boat and then disappeared into the woods. Charlie had been watching for us and I told him how startled we had been by a gentle pussy. He laughed and said she was his frequent, welcome visitor.

"You know," continued Charlie, "that cat's a person. I anchor here when I bring supplies for the mine. I stay over night and it's lonesome except when the camp cook comes calling in the early evening. The cat's always with him, likes to visit. We three do nothing but sit and listen to radio. That tabby likes to hear news. Choosey when it comes to music. Purrs with the soft and hisses at the loud. Smart cat!"

Joe set out the next day to explore with Ingraham and I remained on the boat. Feeling cramped in close quarters, I asked Charlie to row me to the beach where I could walk. When tired, I sat down on a washed up log looking at and enjoying the music of a waterfall pouring into the inlet. Suddenly, I knew from intuition, I was not alone. I jumped up, looked nervously around and saw nobody. Then Charlie came to row me back to the boat for lunch, but I said nothing to him about the presence I had sensed. However, I looked back after climbing aboard and I was right. Standing where I had been was a black bear. Oh, Charlie, I gasped, he must have been near me. Charlie's response was simply, "Bears are curious. He was only checking up on you. If he'd come out close, he'd have been as afraid of you as you of him. One move from you and you can bet your boots he'd have run away." I'm glad I didn't have the chance to find out if that was true.

Joe came back to the boat with a raisin pie from the mining camp cook and he, Charlie and I downed it all at supper. Margaret and Bert sailed with us the next day to Mitchell Inlet. In spite of a violent storm, Charlie started off when the tide was right and roaring waves heaved us into the inlet's Gold Harbour, the site of an old mining operation, around midnight. A sudden flash of lightning showed me clearly, for a moment, Charlie's gangplank. It was a narrow board, without railing, stretching upward in a slope perfect for a climbing mountain goat and wrong for me.

My husband knew I mustn't have time to think about the flimsy, slanting gangplank and hurried me onto it. I started up with a small kitbag in my hands for balance, a pounding heart and a prayer that I would not slip and fall into the raging sea far below. I was supported somewhat by Joe close behind me with his hand on my shoulder and his flashlight dimly outlining the plank. Halfway up we sighted Billy Burke, watchman at the Early Bird Mine, swinging a lantern. To my dismay, he started down the gangplank to meet us, forcing we three to stop in the middle.

Bowing to me, Billy bellowed above the roar of storm and sea, "Shure pleased of your acquaintance. May I prove worthy, Ma'am, of the privilege of meeting you."

Such gallantry at such a place and time was so surprising that I might have lost balance and fallen off the dangerously inclined, narrow gangplank had not Joe's strong arm steadied me. Ashore, Billy guided us over logs, rain drenched board walks and moss covered stairs to a damp, roomy cabin housing two single beds, a chair, table, stove and coal oil lamp. He soon had a crackling fire in the stove and, satisfied we would be comfortable, said goodnight. Joe told me Billy had been cook for the last miners working at Gold Harbour and had stayed on when lack of funds closed the mine. He was watchman for the present owners, who wanted an examination and report on the Early Bird from Joe, and did a little prospecting for himself. Having visitors in this remote spot was a rare treat for Billy and in spite of the late hour he came back for a "visit". The cheerful, sentimental Irishman, whose deafness kept him from hearing us very well, wanted to talk and we listened.

"Been expecting you and been sprucing up for company. Don't have callers and a lady coming, well Ma'am, you do me honour. Charlie, he brings supplies, told me a week ago you was heading this way. Said you just got yourself married not long ago, Dr. Mandy. High time you did. Nice little bride you be, Mrs. Mandy. A good mate you are, standing up to a trip with your man longside this wild, west coast of Moresby Island. Now, Dr. Mandy, I've got a lot to show you inside and outside the mine. Never did the Early Bird get a fair deal. It's an old discovery. Too bad them as mined here was all for high grading. Didn't do no exploration. They was all for the gold brick. Nobody can develop a mine properly that way. Shure and somebody can do the job right."

Billy's chattering might have gone on for hours had Joe not interrupted with, "Billy, we have much to examine tomorrow and should get off to an early start. I suggest we turn in for a good night's rest."

Billy agreed, with an apology to me. "Right you are, sir. Your little lady is tired. Sorry Ma'am for keeping you up with my prattle. May you always have the luck of the Irish and your trail be bordered with flowers."

Billy was cut off from communication with others except for Charlie. He did have a row boat which allowed him to get away for necessary contacts. I was disturbed about his isolation as the boat could not help him when the weather was foul and the seas too rough for launching or rowing. Certainly if an accident occurred or illness happened, he might not be discovered in time to save his life. Apparently, Billy did not share my concern about him and lived happily with a dog and white Persian cat for companions. I suspected he entertained them with stories of the leprechaun and fairies in the old country and put them to sleep singing, "An Irish Lullaby".

At six in the morning a loud knock sounded at the cabin door and Billy shouted, "Breakfast is almost ready in the cookhouse. Come you over and eat breakfast with old Billy."

How nice it was to see the sun shining after last night's storm and to have Billy greet us at the morning meal with, "Ma'am and Dr. Mandy, the top of the morning to you. Nothing fancy on the table but food that'll stick to the ribs." Breakfast was the substantial one of mining camps — porridge, toast, bacon, eggs brought in by Charlie, flapjacks flipped high to turn in midair and then land safely on the griddle target, wild strawberry jam, marmalade and strong coffee. The Ingrahams arrived shortly after we finished eating and Joe, Bert and Billy set off at once to explore underground working and surface showings of the old mine which Billy believed had "never had a fair deal."

Margaret and I walked around the rough and rocky ground of the site, inspected a tailings dump and admired wild flowers bravely blooming in a tangle of weeds and bush. We had such different backgrounds that it was difficult at first to talk about anything but the weather and the Haida Gold Mine. Then I remembered Charlie telling me there was an interesting story connected with the old mine at Gold Harbour. I was sure Margaret would know it so I asked, Could you tell me about the mine here?

"Yes I can," answered Margaret. "Let's sit on those big boulders by the cookhouse where I tell you what is history, Mrs. Mandy. I am Haida and proud gold is found right here by Haida Indians in 1851. That's long way back. I tell you what many not know. Here is first what you call lode-gold discovery in British Columbia. My people trade in 1851 with Hudson's Bay Company in Victoria when they go there in dugout canoes. Sometimes they trade-pay in gold. Hudson's Bay Company finds out where gold is and brings thirty men for mining the gold. They come in Hudson's Bay Company boat UNA. Captain of boat is Mitchell and inlet to Gold Harbour is named for him. Soon Haida's say gold is on our land. Who is mine owner, them or Hudson's Bay Company? They have big fight with miners and Hudson's Bay Company gives up. Company gets more money in trade with Haidas than from mining gold. Years go and the man Mr. McClellan become now the mine owner because Haidas don't want it no more. He takes out some gold, finds to mine is too hard work and goes back to England. Comes now new owners and they wants to open old mine. That's why Dr. Mandy is here to see if that is good to do. Bert tells me."

1851, I exclaimed, when Margaret finished her tale handed down by Haida ancestors. The first recorded lode-gold discovery in British Columbia was in 1851! That's an important date and should be engraved on a permanent metal or stone memorial here and should also be featured in history books. I shall remember it and those who found the gold. When conversation lagged, I thought of something which could help us pass the time pleasantly. Margaret was conversant with the wild flowers growing profusely around us and I wanted to know their names and possibility for growth in Prince Rupert. She located a tool to dig up plants and a box in which to store them for travel. She also carefully packed them in damp moss for preservation until transplanted. After that, the banked fire in the camp's cookhouse warmed and cheered and crackers and cheese set out for a snack tasted unusually good.

Joe's examinations concluded, we sailed back to Queen Charlotte City and went on from there to Masset to board the Prince John for the return to Prince Rupert. Homecoming meant I could plant the flowers Margaret and I had collected. They would be a reminder of gallant Billy Burke and the historic mine over which he kept watch. Somehow, they confirmed my feeling that, having been at Gold Harbour, I was linked with the mineral treasure and happenings there. Memorable experiences had been mine on the Queen Charlottes accompanying my husband to learn about mining and what following a trail with him was like. Best of all remembrance was meeting the residents of those enchanting islands located in remote, natural beauty and splendour. I am told changes have not greatly altered the leisurely life, hospitality, neighbourliness and sincere friendliness which prevailed there in the 1930's and I am glad this is so. To me, the Queen Charlotte Islands will ever be gems of the North Pacific, isles of abundance, contentment and fine folks.

Madge on the log trail leading to Haida Gold Mine on Moresby Island in the Queen Charlottes.

# WILDERNESS TRAVEL INITIATION

With the coming of June that first year of my marriage came a telegram for Joe from mining promoter O. B. Frith. It read:
"A PLANE FOR SPENCERS PROSPECTING ON THE BORDER OF BRITISH COLUMBIA AND YUKON ABOUT JULY 6TH OR 7TH AND DR AND MRS MANDY WOULD BE WELCOME PASSENGERS ON FLIGHT TO SQUAW CREEK"
Where's Squaw Creek? I asked.
"It's way up in the northwestern corner of British Columbia, sandwiched between Alaska and Yukon Territory. You'll love going there. The trip will be your initiation into wilderness travel."
Do you mean it will be some sort of a test?
"In a way, yes. You'll start the trip with the comfortable amenities of civilization around you and have to adapt to the wilds where there are none. Dangers must be met along the trail different from anything you've ever known. Think how proud you and I will be when you face a fight, so to speak, with them and win. Picture, too, nature's unspoiled beauty and soothing solitude on the way to Squaw Creek which, with the mental and physical endurance required to get there, refreshes the mind and develops the body. How does this sound to you?"
Wonderful, I quickly responded. I can hardly wait to get started.
"Just be patient," advised Joe. "We won't go until you've had a complete physical examination. I want you to be sure you're in top condition."
Dr. Kergin's report of excellent health was what I expected, never having had any but minor childhood illnesses. He did warn, "Your husband tells me you've never ridden a horse. You'll have a painful experience when you do. There'll be stiffness and soreness for a few days and standing, sitting or lying down uncomfortable. Dr. Mandy will wisely counsel when this occurs. He is a knowledgeable, considerate man. You are an unusually healthy young lady and should enjoy trail riding. I think your days ahead promise unforgettable adventure."
I started packing for the northern trip after Joe announced, "We're leaving in two days and on the steamer, Princess Louise, where we were introduced by tough chicken, bound for Skagway, Alaska. We won't part there as we did on that August day in 1931 but go north together on the White Pass and Yukon Railway to Carcross in the Yukon. From there you'll have your first plane ride to Pringle Lake and ride on a packhorse to Squaw Creek. By that time you'll know the Far North attracts as few places do. You're familiar with the poetry of Robert Service. So am I and I can say the spell of the north about which he writes has captivated me as it will you when you follow northern trails."
Sailing along the sheltered inside passage of the north Pacific the second time was one hundred percent better than that wonderful first. Now, a fascinating, adoring husband shared information about the area which had not been relative to our getting acquainted during the previous voyage. After passing Wrangell and the old Russian town of Petersburg when we were asleep, the steamer entered Taku

Inlet for a view of a glacier at its end. The tide had not permitted entrance into the narrow channel two years ago, so this was our first sight of something truly sublime. We stood on deck with other passengers in silent awe looking at an immense formation of ice, indented by numerous crevasses and blending a lovely blue with its dazzling whiteness. The director of social activities voiced statistics:

"The Taku glacier you see is a mile wide, 100 to 200 feet high and extends back 15 miles from the ocean. When the ship's whistle blows, vibrations sometimes cause bergs to break and fall into the water. Listen and watch."

The hoped for result of the whistle did not happen and I was glad no weighty chunk fell. I recalled vividly the true horror story in my childhood days of the Titanic's collision with an iceberg and subsequent sinking with such a heavy toll of lives. My mind pictured a sizeable berg induced to fall here, injuring the Princess Louise and those she carried. I did not dwell on this thought and certainly had no inkling of my association with a menacing icefield in the future. Sailing on we came to Juneau, capital of Alaska. My husband was attracted by the buildings of a mine seen high on Mount Roberts overlooking the city. When he told me why he was interested in the Alaska Gold Mining Company's operation penetrating the mountain, I was too.

"This Juneau mine is perhaps the largest low-grade gold mine in the world and provides a big payroll for people living here. I wish we could go through at least a part of it."

Limited time in port did not permit a visit to the famous mine but did allow us to see the Territorial Museum which boasted having the best collection of Eskimo artifacts to be found anywhere, as well as Indian handcraft and numerous exhibits which portrayed the history of Alaska.

"The curator of the Museum is history himself," informed Joe when we entered the building. "Father Kashavaroff was a Russian missionary and one of the few survivors of the Russian occupation. He is largely responsible for the remarkable memorabilia assembled here."

A slight, sprightly priest came forward and recognizing Joe impulsively seized both his hands saying, "Last year you come. You like Museum. Ah, little lady, wife? Good. Blessings! Come."

Father Kashavaroff guided us to a group of tourists and we listened to his lecture while he was directing our attention to the treasures of the Museum. Among them was the highly prized bill of sale by which the United States had acquired Alaskan Territory. History books called the purchase, at the time it was made, "Seward's Folly," Seward having been the Secretary of State who negotiated the agreement. In spite of the price, $7,200,000, the U.S. must now consider "Seward's Folly" a bargain as mining and fishing have already contributed much more than that to the economy and there is promise of other resources to develop. When the tour of the Museum ended, Father Kashavaroff took us into his office to show us a small, very finely woven Indian basket with colourful native designs around the sides, which had been brought in that morning. He cradled it reverently in his hands and appreciation of the art it represented was in his voice.

"Two baskets in whole world like this now. Worth? $1,000.00. Beautiful — most beautiful. How much in more years? Do I not know."

Back on the Princess Louise my husband said, "The ship will soon be entering Lynn Canal where there's a wonderful panorama of mountains and glaciers on either side. You'll be a part of such scenery on the trail. Exciting prospect, isn't it?"

The steamer docked at Skagway which rested on Yukon River flats where chilling wind from surrounding snow topped mountains swept across the town to prove its apt name of Indian origin meaning north wind. We hired a local boy to help us carry a suitcase of "outside world" clothes and "bush" dunnage of suitable wilderness togs, sleeping bags and packsacks to the station of the White Pass and Yukon Railway. The train was due in four hours and we decided to spend that time walking around the historic town, stopping when we heard a shout.

"Hello there! Wait up Dr."

The call came from a man named, Joe whispered to me, Martin Itjen. He stood beside an old Ford truck which had been converted into a bus with the words SKAGWAY STREET CAR painted on each side. The ingenious chap had a stuffed black bear at the entrance to the bus and demonstrated its assistance as co-conductor by manipulation of an extended paw, an opened mouth and the lighting of glass eyes when a gong sounded to warn almost non-existent traffic to beware of a collision. Martin resembled the pictures of old-timers that Mrs. Hettle had shown me with his wrinkled face, alert eyes, determined expression, ready smile, handlebar moustache and a gold nugget watchchain draped across a colourful vest. He struck a dramatic pose, hand on a huge, gold nugget (actually a gilded boulder Joe laughingly told me later) that was attached to the car's radiator, and barked a sales pitch inviting us to tour Skagway with him and a group of tourists.

"Dr., you meet old prospector Martin last year. Remember me? I remember you. Who's this cute chick with you? A wife you say? Some bargain you got. Take the little lady for a ride in Skagway town where thousands come in them good old gold rush days of '98 and goes on to make a famous trail to the Klondike. Swing her aboard, Doc, and take off with the crowd."

Martin had a salty sense of humour and entertained us with stories of the past, some lurid and melodramatic. He told the true tale of a notorious gambler whose real name, Jefferson Smith, became "Soapy Smith." In Colorado the wily man drew crowds on a busy street corner with a medicine-man type of selling. After a hypnotic spiel on making money, he held up a cake of soap over which he placed a $5.00 bill and wrapped them together. Then came the question, "Who will give me $1.00 for this bar of soap and a fiver and get $4.00 free?" A confederate rushed forward, handed up a dollar, took the soap and tearing off the wrapper held the $5.00 bill high for everyone to see before quietly walking away. All others who paid $1.00 for soap had just soap. Escaping angry customers and the law, Soapy left for the Northwest where he and his followers terrorized Skagway.

Martin shrewdly remarked, "Anyone thinks he get $4.00 for $1.00 is wrong in the head. Soapy brung them gambling ways here and one day Sheriff Reid shoots it out with him, right on the dock. Both gets killed. I show you Soapy's saloon where he and his gang held out. They fleeced suckers for quite a spell."

The reconstructed saloon had wax figures of the gambler and some of his gang, their dress representative of the era and complete with guns in position ready to draw. The evil stamped on their faces must have frightened the bravest of those who opposed them. It was good to leave the desperados to see many lovely flower gardens, including the Blanchard's, where Joe and I had sadly parted in 1931 and to which he always referred as "our enchanted garden." Martin then drove us from floral beauty to a sombre survey in the cemetery where Sheriff Reid's and Soapy Smith's graves were side by side. Reid's stone memorial was given only a passing glance by most viewers and some deplored the heavy mesh wire protecting Soapy's monument, necessary because of souvenir hunters who often had chipped pieces from it. The climax of the tour was a stop beside a small stream in the outskirts to demonstrate the art of panning gold. Martin winked at Joe, knowing he was knowledgeable in mining trickery, while he slyly "salted" gravel to insure having real gold nuggets to please his tourist audience.

The train puffed in on schedule on tracks laid down on Broadway, the main street of Skagway. Along with its arrival came several local residents to enjoy the "event" and among them was Martin Itjen. He insisted on seeing us into the observation car remarking, "Costs $2.00 more and more you gets to see from big windows. Let little wife pay, Doc. See you next year, mebbe?" Martin represented the spirit of the north, displaying that true friendliness which enfolded me as Joe had predicted. Many passengers from the Princess Louise crowded into the railway coaches for a half day's journey before turning homeward.

Soon the train, pulled by three engines, began an ascent, threatened in places by overhanging ledges of granite, climbing around gorges, hovering on the edge of canyons, passing through one tunnel cut through solid rock and offering spiritual beauty in mountains, waterfalls and glaciers along the way. At Inspiration Point the train stopped long enough for the passengers to take photos of a monument erected by The Ladies of the Golden North and Alaska Yukon Pioneers. This memorial for the packhorses of Dead Horse Gulch, overlooking remnants of the famous trail of '98 which claimed their lives, bore a tribute:

"The Dead are speaking. In Memory of us three thousand pack animals that laid our bones on these awful hills during the Gold Rush of 1897-1898. We now thank those listening souls that heard our groans across the stretch of years. We waited but not in vain."

Learning the fate of those horses brought tears to my eyes and I said, It is so sad they died in the search for gold. Joe comforted me by telling of the good that resulted from the sacrifice of their lives.

"Those horses and the stampeders, many of whom also died on the trail of '98, opened up the north. Without them Whitehorse, Dawson and other settlements might not now exist and neither would the

White Pass and Yukon Railway. Their part in pioneering will live on to encourage further development of northern wilderness."

The train crossed the International Boundary twenty miles from Skagway on White Pass summit where the Union Jack and Stars and Stripes flew side by side. A red-coated Mounted Policeman boarded the train there to routinely question passengers before the train moved on into the Canadian province of British Columbia. Look, Joe, I exclaimed, according to a brochure, we're on a thirteen mile plateau where we see many small lakes filled with trout and grayling. This section would surely be a paradise for fishermen. A lunch stop was scheduled for Bennett station at the head of large Lake Bennett where there was a population of 10,000 in the rush of Klondike days, the gold seekers building rafts and boats here for continuing on a waterway of lakes and rivers to Dawson. At present it was a lonely place, important only for a restaurant maintained by the railway for tourists.

Everyone got off the train, many women of all ages lingering beside it to have their pictures taken standing beside the Mountie who had questioned them. Joe and I watched for a few minutes and listened to such gushing by female tourists as:

"Isn't he just too handsome? I could go for a man like that."

"What a pretty red jacket he's wearing. I'd like a blazer in that colour."

"I've always wanted to meet a Mountie since I saw that movie about Rose Marie."

"Wait till Ah gets home and Ah shows me with a Mountie. Ah heah they allus gets theah man. Ah wish Ah did."

Eventually we joined the crowd in the dining room where long tables were crowded with hearty food, including three kinds of meat, canned salmon, fresh fish, bowls heaped with vegetables, jam, honey, bread and heavy-crusted pies. We wanted a light lunch and Joe asked the friendly cashier who also served as waitress, "Could we have a sandwich and a cup of coffee?"

The girl was astonished at the request and answered seriously, "I have to tell you folks you can only get one lunch here, all on the table. Costs $1.00 no matter how much you eat. Most people take seconds. Sorry, no sandwiches and coffee only with the dollar lunch."

We went back to an empty observation coach to munch apples bought at Skagway. The young Mountie we'd sympathetically watched posing with feminine admirers soon hurried in, asking "May I sit down and talk to you two for a few minutes?" When we said we'd welcome his company, he poured out his suppressed feelings.

"I'm so glad you're a Canadian couple who don't feel compelled to have a picture taken with me."

He was so very serious I had to laughingly ask, How do you like being so popular with the ladies?

"Might I say, I'm not a lady's man and becoming conditioned to what you've witnessed takes some getting used to. I've only recently been posted here and sentimental women capturing me, so to speak, is embarassing. Of course I realize a Mountie has become a symbol of Canada and being gallant to women tourists is a part of my duties. By the end of the season I may be adjusted to the emotional admiration they show me. Just hope I'm never asked to sing 'The Indian Love Call.' I'm not musical, can't even carry a tune."

Leaving Bennett, the railway hugged the shore of very clear Lake Bennett for twenty-six miles to Carcross at its northern end in the Yukon Territory. Joe spoke of the mountains skirting it, "You'll soon see, while trail riding, how many flowers grow on them. They're proof the north is not perpetually frozen. That fallacious belief is held by the general public." Carcross was originally called Caribou Crossing because of the large herds of caribou that used to ford a narrow neck of water there between Lake Bennett and Nares Lake. Joe and I stepped down from the train at Carcross station to see a few scattered houses, a trading post and a sizeable building. We were the only people getting off and a waiting big, husky, outdoor type of man recognized us instantly.

"You're the Mandys? I'm Frith and you'll fly to Squaw Creek with me?"

Joe nodded and answered as brusquely as the questioner. "Yes, we're the Mandys. Your telegram said take off July 6th or 7th. Today is the 5th. When do we go?"

"Don't know. I'm waiting for the company plane from the south. You folks can stay at the Caribou Hotel. I'll let you know when we'll fly."

Frith strode away and we registered at the only accommodation available. The turn of the century hotel represented history in a weather-beaten appearance with worn and shabby furniture throughout, sagging beds and yellowed, tattered curtains at the bedroom windows. The long, wide and cosy lounge had walls symbolizing the north with mounted heads of moose, caribou and bear and smoked animal skins. Indian artifacts were displayed on small tables and shelves. The room's hostess was named Polly, a vivacious, brightly feathered, talkative parrot, presumably brought to the Yukon during the Klondike gold rush. She was looked upon as a fascinating "person" with a reputation for an extensive vocabulary of profanity and drinking of "hard" liquor and had the reaction of falling to the floor of her cage drunk, to stay there in a stupor for some time. Polly was considered an outstanding personality in the community whose fame travelled far. I learned years later that she became a teetotaler and died peacefully at the age of 125. Her death became an appealing news story of an unusual celebrity with a wide circle of friends.

We were told by a friendly waitress in the hotel that Indian Patsy Henderson gave a daily lecture for visitors in Carcross during the summer. "Don't miss him," she advised. "Why he was in on the Klondike gold discovery." Pleased at this prospect while waiting to go on to Squaw Creek, Joe and I went to the community hall the next morning. There we met Patsy Henderson in the centre of a tourist group stopping briefly en route to Whitehorse. He was impressively costumed in a tunic of fringed and beaded, smoked mooseskin, matching trousers with beaded bands at the knee and his beaded mooseskin moccasins were sewn to the pant legs at the ankle. His lively personality and expressive, laconic use of English held our complete attention.

"Patsy Henderson I am. I make a talk. No talk English pretty good. No school. I show. I tell. Cost twenty-five cents. You lissen. You see. Show bear trap, beaver trap, mink trap, marten trap, fox trap, gopher trap, lynx trap. Indian know how trap."

He proceeded to show us Indian handwork and to demonstrate the different methods of trapping animals. When he came to the lynx trapping he said contemptuously, "Lynx easy for trap. No smart. No know how make home. Go everwhere. Now I show 'bout canoe. Take moose skin when go hunt for make canoe. Water no hurt. No go in skin. Make new skin canoe all time. See medicine man's rattle? He shake. Noise come inside. He dance. Sick in man go way. No need pill like white man. Now I tell 'bout gold. First white man Caribou Crossing George Carmacks. He go down wiver. Stay three year. No come back. We go find. Me go. Charlie go. Skookum Jim go. Carmacks north with Indians fishing. He say see white man Bob Henderson. Henderson tell Carmacks he see gold in wiver. He go way. Carmacks look, mebbe three, four mile from camp. He tell Skookum Jim, Charlie, me, he find gold in wiver. He excite. Skookum Jim drink creek water. He see gold. Me no see gold in creek. No care 'bout gold. No savvy, see? Carmacks make big money. Lots people come, go Dawson, find gold. Hard work get gold. Fish, hunt more good. Trap and fish in wiver. Call animal for kill. Indian know long time how live. Lissen!"

Joe said that the sounds Patsy produced were true reproductions of animal calls in the wild which would certainly get a response. For a grand finale of his talk Patsy announced, "Me sing now. Indian love song." This was rhythmic and very loud, accompanied by enthusiastic beating of a drum. We could understand how it could set the blood tingling, promoting an ardent courtship and marriage. Patsy Henderson and his illustrated talk were a delightful introduction to the Yukon.

A message at the hotel asked the Mandys to call on the Forresters that evening. They lived in a little log cabin on the lakeshore which was brightened by flowered cretonne drapes at the window and cushions covered by the same material. Mr. Forrester, a pilot, was trying to establish an air service at Carcross and encouraged my entry into the north with, "The wife and I came here from eastern Canada. We were certainly chechakos. That's what the Northwest calls greenhorns. I understand, Mrs. Mandy, that you are a chechako too. It won't take you long to fall in love with this wonderful northland as we have done."

Mrs. Forrester added, "At first we felt cut off from what is called civilization. Now we're glad we are. Actually, the radio gives us all the important news and entertainment. Besides, it's better not to know all the disturbing things happening around the world. Life is peaceful in Carcross and I don't think genuine northern friendliness can be duplicated in many places."

Frith appeared in the morning to say, "Get ready Mandys. Can't wait any longer for the company plane. Will pick up what supplies I can in Carcross. Forrester will fly us to Pringle Lake after lunch. See you then."

Joe bought groceries to stow in his packsack and when I looked surprised at the amount he was buying said, "I can't be sure how long we'll be in the bush. There aren't any shops where we're going. My work requires all my attention, so there'll be no time for fishing and I never carry a gun which could supply meat. One is apt to get into more trouble packing firearms than not doing so. I couldn't kill any of the animals we may meet but we will eat their meat if a prospector, trapper or Indian has killed them for necessary food and offers us a share of it. Your initiation into wilderness travel starts as soon as we get into Forrester's plane. There are thrills ahead for you, little pal."

Weather was not favourable for flying but by two in the afternoon had cleared somewhat and Forrester was confident that "It's safe to go up now." The plane for my first sky ride was small, barely large enough for the pilot, Joe, Frith, me, dunnage and freight — all squeezed in tightly. Claustrophobia gripped me and I closed my eyes during a run on the lake before take-off. When I opened them we were airborne, flying over mountainous country carpeted with a variety of trees displaying varied tints of yellow, blue and gray in their green foliage. Valleys were deep and wide, cut through by creeks and winding, rushing rivers. The naturally painted, inspirational panorama of beauty quelled my fear of flying. Like all bush pilots of his day, Forrester flew by innate skill and "the seat of the pants." I trusted him to land us on little Pringle Lake, just one of numerous small lakes beneath us and all looking the same size to me. Guided by Frith, who may have jokingly estimated a two hundred and fifty mile flight, the pilot landed smoothly on the right body of water after about an hour and a half. We passengers discharged ourselves and Forrester helped unload dunnage and freight, anxious to fly away because of a threatening storm.

Frith expected to be met by a man with horses, but he had not come. Angrily Frith growled, "Drat that man! Why isn't Harry here? Guess I'll have to hike with you Mandys to Dalton Post. Freight can be picked up later. Five miles to go, Mrs. Mandy. Trail is plenty rough. Take yourself. I'll pack your stuff. Let's shove off."

I thought I should carry something and the men reluctantly placed a small packsack on my back, as they knew even a little load would feel like a ton to a chechako like me before reaching the Post. When the sun came out, we became so warm that we shed our sweaters. The northern summer was colourful with acres and acres of wild flowers. How surprised my family in Indiana and friends in Kansas will be to learn this, I murmured. We hadn't gone far before I heard bells ringing. Where are they? I asked Frith.

"They surprise you?" and he laughed. "Not church bells, little lady. Up here we hang cowbells on packhorses. That's so we can find the critters if they skedaddle off. The bells you hear now mean Harry's coming."

We soon met Harry Fromme, a tall, blond, handsome young Canadian. On hearing his name, I recalled what Joe had told me about him. Harry had been unable to find work in his prairie home town and decided to go west and prospect for gold in British Columbia. He and three other youths came to the province by hitching a ride on freight trains. They read my husband's report on Squaw Creek in the annual publication of the British Columbia Department Of Mines and considered it a favourable mining locale. Joe interviewed them in his Prince Rupert office and advised against trying to make a living from a placer operation at Squaw Creek, since they were totally ignorant of wilderness living and lacked funds to buy necessary mining equipment and provisions. The lure of gold was stronger than his counsel and the four young men worked their way to Squaw Creek and staked claims there. They didn't find enough nuggets to pay their expenses and three were so disillusioned that they left the north. Harry stayed on to freight for Frith from Dalton Post to his camp at the mouth of Squaw Creek in the Yukon.

Frith was irritable, anxious to get to our destination and snapped directions. "Get going Mandys. Straight ahead is a creek with a log bridge over it. A short cut to Dalton Post is on the other side. Me and Harry will pack the horses with us and the freight left at Pringle Lake. We'll catch up with you."

One of the northern log bridges Madge and Joe crossed.

He relieved Joe and me of our packs and I was grateful, having resigned myself to never straightening up again. The single log across a wide creek looked to me like an enlarged pencil in width and a city block in length. Joe had predicted thrills and this crossing was to be one of them. At this point it was the only way to get to the other side. Unpertubed, Joe calmly cut walking sticks for us and handing me one spoke encouragingly.

"What a solid log! Going over a typical bush bridge will give you something to be proud of and prepare you for others. Hold this stick in one hand for support and give me your other hand. I'll lead. Ready?"

If left to myself I should never have been ready but stalwart Joe gave me the courage to proceed and I managed a weak, Lead on.

Joe began to walk slowly and steadily across the damp, ridged surface of the bridge and my shorter legs attuned to his pace. We had almost reached the log's end when Joe slipped on loose bark, losing his balance. "Jump," he shouted, letting go of my hand as he fell into the creek with a great splash. I jumped and landed unhurt on a mossy bank. My dripping-wet husband pulled himself up and declared, "Just an example of roughing it, my dear. Now, let's look for a blaze. That's an axe slash on a tree trunk to mark a trail."

On our way we saw an Indian camping ground with many racks for drying fish. Scattered clothing and empty tin cans indicated recent habitation. The trail led down to the historic Post on the bank of the Tatshenshini River. Almost there I saw little log cabins with moss covered roofs perched on stilts. Joe, I cried out, Look at those tiny shacks! Do people live in them?

"Oh no. Each is a cache high above the ground to keep prowling bears and other animals from breaking in to eat meat, dried fish and other food stored in them. Close up you'll see tin nailed along the supports to prevent mice from running up for a meal."

We passed open drying sheds for fish and meat, their pole roofs covered with twigs, before entering the once prosperous community of Dalton Post. Only ten sturdy, one room log cabins remained. Frith had told me the cabins were often occupied by Indians during trapping and fishing seasons and all passersby could stay in them at any time. He also said there was one family living permanently at the lonely village. Their large log house was built by owner Jack Pringle, an adventuring white man, for himself, Indian wife Susie and their fourteen year old adopted daughter Hazel. Jack was away at the moment cooking for Frith's camp. Frith arrived at the same time we did and introduced us to the Pringles.

Susie came shyly to meet us, apprehensive because white women did not visit Dalton Post. She was the Indian woman of paintings and story books with wise eyes, skin burned dark by sun and wind and a face indented with many wrinkles. It was impossible to guess her age and, judging from Indians met on the Queen Charlotte Islands, she would probably look the same for years. Susie was wearing a short-sleeved cotton print dress, undoubtedly purchased from a mail order catalogue, the "shop" of most people in remote northern locations. Her brightly coloured garters, well below the knee, held up black stockings and the mocassins she wore were beautifully beaded in several colours. Frith had prepared us for the fact that she knew only a few words in English, although she had been married to a white man for thirty years. There was no need to know her husband's language as her associations were mostly with her own people.

Hazel was Susie's niece, her ancestry a white father and a mother who was Susie's sister. She spoke English well, having spent the early years of her life in Haines, Alaska, where she attended school. Hazel was a pretty girl, the type glorified in songs like "The Indian Love Call." Her hair was the black of Indian forbears and bobby-pinned to form a severe frame for her intelligent face and large, dark eyes. I took a womanly interest in her attire — a red jersey, a knee length fully gathered, beige coloured cotton skirt and white bobby socks encased in criss-crossed leather "store" sandals, all topped by a coat sweater of purple trimmed in bright red and orange. A native love for vivid colours was shown in her dress and also in a heavily applied spot of rouge on high cheek bones. She was reservedly friendly and spoke softly.

"Frith and Harry tell me you come. I am glad to see a woman. Good you both come to Dalton Post."

Frith offered a cabin, in which he usually stayed when at Dalton Post, for our temporary residence. Said he, "You'd freeze in your tent. Darned chilly along the river at night. Cabin stove here heats up fast. And, Mrs. Mandy, you can write home and tell your folks you stayed in the home of an Indian princess, Alice. She's Susie's sister. Claims the place. Away mostly, sponging off relatives. You'll likely meet her. Princess Alice is quite a gal!"

The occasional home of Princess Alice was a one-room log cabin and the inside walls captured and held my attention. They were decorated with pages from mail order catalogues representing various phases of human interest and small spaces between them showed patches of chinked logs. A large, hand hewn bed with a lumpy mattress filled one corner of the room. Suspended above it was a net mosquito tent, gray from age. Joe said we'd have to drop the tent over our sleeping bags for the night, otherwise mosquitoes would keep us painfully awake. There was no curtain at a tiny window and its glass pane was so grimy nobody could see in or out of it clearly. Furnishings included two straight chairs, an incongruous deck chair, a small wood-burning stove, a few dishes, a couple of granite cooking pots, a teakettle and a tin wash basin. The cabin offered the bare essentials for living and shelter, sufficient to serve the transient who stopped there briefly.

Frith advised us to make a deal with Susie to cook our meals and to pay her with bacon, tinned meat, oranges and coffee from our provisions. Harry acted as interpreter for this arrangement and Susie's response was, "Cook. House. Hazel tell." Translated, her words meant she was agreeable and her daughter would let us know when to come for supper. At six o'clock Hazel came to walk us to the evening meal in her home with me exclaiming, I'm so hungry I could eat anything.

The Pringle's log house of two large rooms dominated the small cabins lined up with it in a row on the bank of the Tatshenshini River. The parlour-bedroom was crowded with a battered bed, an old sewing machine, a sagging couch and a large chest on which were thrown smoked mooseskin jackets and beaded mocassins. A kitchen-living-dining room was filled by guns and hunting knives on the wall, dishes, pots, pans and cutlery on shelves, a big stove for heating and cooking, two straight chairs and a roughly constructed wooden table covered with a worn oilcloth. Seats for dining were wooden boxes in which merchandise had come with names of firms standing out distinctly on the sides. Light entered through two small windows and an open door which faced the river.

Hazel pointed to where we were to sit at the table and Susie placed a plate of food in front of me muttering something that Hazel translated into "moose mulligan." On top of the stew of meat, potatoes and vegetables rested two fried eggs, gifts from Frith's camp provisions. Fork in hand, I looked down at the mixture and suspended it in mid air. Two big mosquitoes were imbedded right in the centre of the eggs. Good heavens, I silently said to myself, do people up here eat mosquitoes? If this is part of my wilderness initiation, I'll have to flunk it. I just can't eat mosquitoes. Of course I didn't want to embarrass Susie and slyly cut the offending insects out and hid them under a mound of mulligan which was left untouched. I should have known my action would not escape the keen observation of my husband.

"How did you like your supper?" he asked later.

I stammered, It - was good. Very filling. I hadn't tasted moose before.

"Nor mosquitoes? For a minute I thought you were going to eat them just to be polite. They wouldn't have hurt you but the thought of them might have made you sick. I saw your cover-up. Susie and Hazel didn't. Don't worry about mosquitoes being a part of northern diet. You saw how easily they can be. If you'd been the cook, they would probably have flown into eggs you fried. The difference between you and Susie is that you would have cut them out before serving. She's so used to these nuisances she didn't even notice they were there."

That evening there were more arrivals at Dalton Post. Indian Johnny Fraser had heard through bush telegraph that Dr. and Mrs. Mandy were at the Post and required packing and transportation. He came to provide both and make money while so doing. He was accompanied by his son, three other teenaged Indian boys and several horses. Johnny and his companions cooked their supper over a campfire on the river bank and then came to the Pringle house to watch the Mandys finish supper. The meal over, the boys pulled out a portable phonograph hiding in a corner under a mooseskin cover. It was an old machine with cylinder records sending sound through an attached horn, just like one I'd enjoyed as a child at my Jones grandparent's home in Indiana. The Pringles had only two records and one was so cracked it scratched out an ear piercing tune which the youths liked. They discarded it after a third playing for the undamaged recording which blasted through the horn in a man's loud, nasal voice, "The Strawberry Roan." They played it over and over and after I went to bed the song was a serenade outside my window. I appreciated their entertaining attention but the fate of the "bronco bustin' " cowboy in the musical tale sent shivers down my spine and prevented peaceful sleep. All through the night I had frightening dreams of a "strawberry roan" throwing me off his back when leaving the safety of Dalton Post to cross the adjacent wide, flooded Tatshenshini River.

Joe and I were persuaded by Susie to stay for awhile after supper, that first night in her home. She led the way into the windowless "parlour-bedroom" which was dimly lighted by a coal oil lamp and pantomimed circle seating. Then she, Johnny and the teenagers sat silent and motionless appraising us, their faces disclosing no sign of their thoughts. Hazel spoke one sentence about the weather before lapsing into silence and I, not knowing what to say, said nothing. Joe, adept at adapting to circumstances, launched into a monologue about Squaw Creek gold and amused with his trick of tearing a cigarette paper into four parts and, after much manipulation, restoring it to one piece. The boys asked him to repeat the performance twice, surprised as much by the third success as by the first. "You like medicine man," they chorused.

By this time Hazel decided appreciation of Joe's entertainment could be expressed by showing some of Susie's handwork. I especially liked mocassins made of white caribou skin lined with gopher fur, trimmed around the top with baby mountain goat fur and embroidered with a fusion of coloured porcupine quills to resemble a flower. She also showed us a pair of lightly smoked mooseskin gloves beaded in a design of red, green and white. Shy Susie was a shrewd woman and, noting my interest, wasted no time in selling the mocassins and gloves to Joe as a gift for me. They've been carefully preserved through the years, a priceless memento of meeting the Indians at Dalton Post.

Suddenly, we heard the fierce barking of big huskies chained beside the house. The Indians all rushed outside. Joe and I followed to see a tall, broad, sedate Indian riding into the Post, three horses ambling behind him. His high cowboy hat, fringed and beaded mooseskin jacket with matching pants, mocassins and leggings were distinctive and his manner regal. The boys evidently knew the man well and welcomed him with a shout of, "Jimmy Kane", but did not approach him until he dismounted. His face was impassive listening to the news of the plane bringing Frith and a white man with his bride.

Doesn't that powerful looking Indian have anyone with him? I asked Joe. I had learned on the Queen Charlotte Islands that Indians travelled with their families.

"Your question will be answered soon," replied my husband.

Jimmy Kane's wife and teenaged daughter walked into the Post half an hour later, bent forward from bearing a weighty pack on their backs. Trotting behind them was a heavily packed big husky. Hazel told us, after talking to the wife, that she and the girl had hiked thirty miles that day. Again I questioned Joe. Why have the women walked and carried those cumbersome loads when three strong horses were following Kane? They could have been riding and the animals packing.

"I've been told," answered Joe, "it's the custom up here for the men to ride and women are taught to fear the horses and consequently prefer to walk."

Kane remained at the far end of the village talking to the teenagers, who listened attentively, until his family plodded their way to him. He ordered them to put up a tent, build a fire and cook his supper immediately. Those women must have been very tired but they obeyed his command, throwing off packs to follow directions. Leaving them at their assigned task, Jimmy Kane marched like a triumphant general to where Joe and I were standing in front of Princess Alice's cabin and spoke to my husband.

"I hear. You bring city girl. She not know up here. Mebbe get lost. Watch girl. You, tell Jimmy how get nuggets at Squaw Creek."

Joe was pleased at the concern expressed for my safety and taking my arm led me to the edge of the river where he tried to dispel my fears about crossing it. Dalton Post was situated on the junction of the Klukshu and Tatshenshini Rivers. Always a wide stream, at this point the Tatshenshini was now a swollen torrent carrying the melting snow of the mountains. Frith had warned of dangers it presented in rapids, log jams, whirlpools, boulders and holes. The broad expanse of swiftly moving, roaring water with those hidden dangers made my knees tremble and my stomach turn into a hard knot. Is crossing this wild Tatshenshini the only way to get to the other side? I asked.

"Yes, it is. This looks impossible to you but really isn't. The Indians constantly ford here. Johnny Fraser will guide us over when the time is right, which he says may not be for two or three days. We'll ride over on Johnny's pack horses. You've not been on a horse before so I'll put you on one and Hazel has agreed to lead you up and down the river bank to get you used to what riding is like. Another thrill is ahead for you, my dear."

In addition to these elementary riding lessons, I hiked many miles with Joe in the wilderness around us during the waiting period. We set out early in the morning with a lunch packed by Susie and wild berries picked along the way provided dessert. Joe studied the geology of the area while I collected flowers for pressing and framing. Susie was not at home when we returned to the Post on the third day. Harry was there to cook and serve our supper and afterwards drew my husband aside for a conference. I was surprised when this ended that Joe wanted me to have a walk before bedtime. I went along without comment, but after awhile the trailless bush caused my legs to buckle and it took all my willpower to keep myself upright. At long last, Joe gave a lift to my steps by turning back toward the Post.

"We'd better get to our cabin and go to bed," he said. "Johnny told Harry we can cross the river between two and four in the morning. The water will be at its lowest then. You're tired enough to sleep like a baby tonight and you'll be fit as a fiddle for plunging into the river tomorrow."

We heard a weird noise as we came to the door of our cabin and before Joe could restrain me, I turned and looked in the direction of the sound. I saw Susie, her hair streaming down her shoulders in matted disarray, swaying and shouting at the top of her voice. Hazel and Johnny's son were supporting her and vainly trying to guide her to the tent where she slept in summer. She refused to cooperate and kept running up and down screaming violently. Now I learned, after an explanation, why Joe had taken me for such a long walk. Harry had told him of Susie's sorry condition and considerate Joe had wanted to spare me the sight of kindly Susie crazed by alcohol. Her husband had taught her to drink with him, although liquor was prohibited for Indians at that time in both the Yukon and British Columbia. An unscrupulous white man had smuggled it in that day for Jack Pringle, and with him away Susie had imbibed without restriction. The result was sad indeed. In spite of this disturbing episode and my nervous anticipation of the next day's journey, I was almost asleep while fastening the zipper on my sleeping bag. I didn't even see Joe adjust the net tent over us as protection from the busy, singing, stinging mosquitoes.

Susie appeared in the early morning to cook our breakfast, sober but showing some effects of the drinking bout of yesterday. Johnny and his son readied the horses and Harry, who was to accompany as wrangler, helped to pack them. It was amazing to me how the packs were placed to achieve balance and then securely roped on. Sleeping bags were put behind our saddles to give comfort and back support. Johnny had trained his children to ride on a horse named Polly and thought I should be safe with her. Frith rode Spaghetti and the three Indian boys who had serenaded me with "The Strawberry Roan" came along just for the ride. They were experts in the saddle and rode up and down the river bank showing me tricks their horses could perform. I prayed Polly was not so talented. At last all was in order

Hazel and Susie Pringle and Madge at Dalton Post.

and we started off to test our mettle against the force and hazards of the river. Susie and Hazel waved goodby and Susie expressed fears in a quavering voice.

"Me — no cross wiver. No ride mountain up. I scare. Horse bad — throw. Bad! Bad!"

What a discouraging send-off! Harry led the packtrain, Frith and the Indians were next in line and Joe and myself last. My husband attached a long rope to Polly's neck and held the other end of the rope in his hand, speaking positively to counteract Susie's negative thinking.

"Remember I'm leading Polly. She and I will take care of you. Sit tight and hold fast to the reins. You'll enjoy a daring ride."

I heard a loud cry from Harry as the accompanying colt of the horse he was riding stepped into the water and disappeared. The colt had lost his footing and dropped into one of those holes Frith had warned us about. I sat frozen to the saddle and breathed again when the colt rose to the surface and began to swim. Harry shouted for Frith and the Indians to cross lower down. Finding the current there dangerously swift, they indicated by gestures that Joe and I should cross still lower where the ford might be safer. Just as Joe's horse entered the river Frith called, "You can get a good picture of a pack train, Doc."

Joe held up his camera to adjust it for a memorable action scene, but violently rushing water almost tumbled his horse and he realized all his attention was required for guidance. He quickly shoved the Kodak into the pocket which covered the back of his khaki jacket. The snap fastener for closure did not catch and he and his mount were moved on by the force of the river at a slanting angle. The camera shifted to his lowered side and slid out of the open pocket into the depths below and was carried downstream and out of sight in seconds.

My first impulse was to reach out and try to grab the falling camera which was an important part of Joe's field equipment. Fortunately, the law of self preservation instinctively prevailed with the realization that such an action would be futile and result in my falling and being carried away too. The fast and icy Tatshenshini River was not a river for swimming, so I held on like glue, my fingers gripping the reins as if permanently attached. I braced myself when Polly stepped into the water. Then the current struck her with such fury that she staggered and swayed until reaching midstream. There she stopped and stayed. My frantic, Go on, Polly, go on, fell on deaf ears. Joe had prepared me for being frightened but had said nothing about a horse's fright. I looked around and then down at the swirling water and, gazing in fascinated horror, my eyes became blurred and dizziness made me feel faint. With an effort I brought my head up and focused misted eyes on Joe and the rest of the pack train waiting on the other side.

I cried out frantically, Joe! Joe! My horse isn't moving. She isn't going anywhere. Polly doesn't want to cross. Joe couldn't hear my voice in the distance and above the noise of the thundering river. I felt very small, very alone and completely aware of nature's tremendous power. I made another appeal to Polly. Come on, Polly, I begged. We have to join the others. They're waiting for us. You can take me across. I know you can. Polly answered my plea, abandoned the attempt to walk and began swimming. Cold water rose above my boots and trickled into them and I didn't mind because we were on our way again. Progressing slowly, we reached the other side of the river and when Polly scrambled up on the bank I breathed a prayer of thanks for survival. Joe gave me a military salute and I was heartened with his commendation.

"Crossing the flooded Tatshenshini is the climax of your initiation to trail travel in the north. You've come through with flying colours, didn't panic when Polly balked in midstream. The men and boys have been watching with me and are as proud of you as I am. No time to rest though. We must push on up a mountain trail to Frith's camp. The pace will be slow and the ride exciting. Come Madge, let's follow the packtrain."

A scary, steep, brush covered rocky cliff rose before us. I saw immediately that the horses were sure-footed and trail-wise. Transport by them promised more safety than by recklessly driven cars in the city. The old Dalton Trail was almost obliterated in places, having been infrequently used by Indians in the past few years and they had not bothered to remove the obstacles of fallen trees or blocking boulders. Joe rode behind me to be sure all was well, whistling and singing to make me aware he was ever on guard. Hats protected our faces from overhanging branches and alert eyes allowed time for ducking if they drooped too low.

The trail led ever higher and we paused once in awhile to look down on the beauty of valleys or a sparkling lake. Occasionally, we came to a patch of snow and had to dismount and lead the horses around the swampy ground they refused to cross. When we approached the first of many little gullies, I saw the horses ahead of me hurdle the obstruction, the Indian boys shrieking loudly as they did so and then displaying galloping horsemanship as they rode on. I had a vision of myself sailing over Polly's head when she played "follow the leader," but I had not reckoned on the wisdom of my intelligent horse. Polly knew she had an inexperienced rider on her back and, disregarding the example of the other horses, stepped slowly over the gully and all the other gullies we encountered. At that moment, I learned the real meaning of "horse sense" and Polly demonstrated this each step of that trail.

It was late afternoon when we rode into the camp of B.C. Prospectors Company Limited. Although this operation was at the mouth of Squaw Creek in Yukon Territory, Joe deemed it advisable to examine the workings in correlation with the upper Squaw Creek in British Columbia. Drilling was being conducted under the supervision of O. D. Frith and H. McN. Fraser, with a crew of five men. The camp set-up was very compact with six sleeping tents and a cook tent. Supper was almost ready and Frith invited us to share it.

"Gosh, Mandys, what a day we've had! Even I feel tuckered out and you must be as ready for grub as me. Come on and eat with me and the miners. They'll sure like seeing new faces and — here we are. Fellows, meet callers, Dr. and Mrs. Mandy."

Jack Pringle was the camp cook, a friendly man with weathered face and graying hair. I wondered if he had regrets about leaving the outside world to spend the last thirty years with Indians in isolation. He inquired about his adopted daughter Hazel of whom he appeared to be quite fond. Pringle also apologized for the meal served as needed supplies had not come in until now with Frith and a variety of food was lacking. Whatever he cooked would have been tasty to me after my long, tiring and danger fraught initiation day.

Hearing through "bush telegraph" that Dr. Mandy of the British Columbia Department Of Mines had come to the B.C. Prospectors Company camp, two of four men prospecting nearby came to request a favour of Joe. They asked if he would go with them to their claims and give them some advice about mining. This request was unofficial they said, since their workings were in the Yukon. Joe, always willing to help others when possible, agreed to accompany them. He was tired and knew I must be exhausted after the river crossing and gruelling mountain trail. He walked me to our night's lodging in Mr. Fraser's tent. Fraser had given us his quarters to save us the chore of erecting our tent, saying he could bunk with one of the drillers. He added, "It's a little something I can do for you folks. Sure is a treat to have visitors. Your inspection of what we're doing here is important, Dr. Mandy, and having a lady in camp is - well - special."

Joe laid our sleeping bags on the ground floor of Fraser's tent and placed a packsack behind mine. He looked at me with compassion while saying, "Sorry to leave you but the prospectors do need assistance. I'll only be gone a short time. It doesn't get dark in northern summer nights. Quite light now and will be when I come back. I hope you can sleep after your first ride on a horse. If you need anything, just shout and the fellows here will rush to help you. You're safe in these mining camps. The men in them respect a lady."

I was tired and yet the hour was too early for bed so I stretched out on top of a sleeping bag, using a lumpy packsack for a pillow, and read. A Magazine Digest kept me company and when words in the publication began to blur and run together I knew I was ready to sleep. I stood up with my back to the tent entrance, which was closed by a flap, and had unbuttoned my shirt collar and taken off my tie when I sensed a presence. I had heard nothing but knew I was not alone. Turning slowly, I was surprised and rather frightened to see our supplier of packhorse transportation, Johnny Fraser, standing just inside the tent. I was sure he meant me no harm and I was positive Joe would expect me to handle this situation without rousing the camp. We stood silently staring at each other for several minutes before I could stammer, Hello - hello - Johnny. There was no response and I nervously picked up a wild flower from a collection acquired along the trail and asked, Don't you think this pretty?

"You know him?" questioned Johnny.

No, no. I don't know him.

"He wild carrot."

After several more minutes of silence I asked, holding up another flower, What's this, Johnny?

"Fire weed."

And this purple one?

"Onion. Onion wild."

Here's some pretty blue flowers. What do you call them?

"No forget me."

My floral assemblage was limited and Johnny was not inclined to introduce another topic of conversation. He sat down, folded his arms and looked at me intently. I sat down also and puzzled what to do when a native of an unknown territory called unceremoniously. There was another period of silence in the tent. Outside all was quiet, too, where birds slept and animals were resting or stealthily prowling. I fingered the Magazine Digest, opened it and tried to read without success, although turning pages as if getting meaning from them. An hour went by and I began to pray inwardly for my husband's return. Two hours later, when tension had stiffened my whole body, Johnny spoke.

"You got thread?"

Yes, I got thread.

"No need thread. You got needle? Big one?"

I have needle. Big one. I'll get it for you out of my kit.

My fingers relaxed enough to find what Johnny wanted. I handed it to him with a request. Please bring it back in the morning. Why do you want a needle?

"Fix saddle." Johnny clutched the needle tightly and slowly and contentedly left the tent.

I was in a daze for several minutes after the unexpected visitor left and tried to stay awake to tell my husband about him. Events of the day, however, and now the evening's incident had over-tired me and I fell asleep, not knowing when Joe came back. In the morning he listened while I gave a detailed account of what had happened and he wisely treated the episode lightly.

"How nice to have someone entertain you when I was away. You acquitted yourself well, waiting for Johnny to tell you the reason for his coming. His people are very informal and slipping into the tent as he did is a common practice among them. They have a leisurely way of living and take time to do everything. Had you been brought up with their traditions, you would think our conventional, scheduled life peculiar and unattractive."

Johnny completed his mending and brought back the needle without a word of appreciation, although thanks was indicated in its return. This time when he glided noiselessly into the tent, my husband was standing beside me to give him a nod of recognition and understanding. We heard Johnny say to his waiting son, "That good woman. Got needle."

When Joe and I came to breakfast, the cook and crew of the camp had finished their first meal of the day. They were all dressed in clean clothing, the previous day having been Sunday, which was their time for weekly laundry. Instead of going off to drill, they were lingering and eyeing me with sympathetic concern as each man spoke to me.

"Good morning, Mrs. Mandy. Sure's nice you're here."

"My gosh, but you had a tough initiation yesterday."

"Did you sleep all right last night?"

"Hard to walk today, ain't it?"

"Maybe you should stand up to eat."

Well, I was neither stiff or sore and demonstrated this by easily sitting down on the hard plank bench beside the table saying, Oh, I feel fine. The men responded with, "How can you feel fine? We can't believe it. Why it - it is impossible!" Neither my doctor or I could account for the fact that riding a horse merely made me tired and only that side effect continued throughout my trail riding days.

Northwestern B.C. was so sparsely populated that Telegraph Creek was the largest community for the 300 miles between Stewart and Atlin, then eastward over 500 miles to the Rocky Mountains.

The cook placed huge steaks of fibrous meat on our plates and Joe beamingly said, "This is a delightful surprise! Remember my telling you, Madge, that mountain sheep is choice game meat in the north? Jack has given you more than a sample. My, it's good, isn't it fellows? Don't hesitate to ask for a second helping. Pringle reports there's plenty."

The miners added their commendation. "Sure is some meat. Nothing better, Mrs. Mandy."

I couldn't understand the enthusiastic recommendation for the steak which my most forceful sawing wouldn't cut. Joe had to carve that tough mountain sheep for me, just as he did the leather-like chicken on the Princess Louise. It took me a long time to chew each bite sufficiently to swallow and then getting it down was difficult. This was strange in light of the praise given the meat of the mountain sheep by my husband and the miners. I thought their taste buds must differ radically from mine. The men watched me until Joe inquired, "How do you like mountain sheep?" I could only say, It's not exactly what I expected. It's - different. Smiling broadly, the men left for work and it was not until two months later that Joe confessed I had eaten bear that morning.

"I didn't know whether you'd want to eat bear. Many people don't. To think you were polite enough to eat it and only say it was different! Adapting to everything encountered is a test of the trail and you score high in adaptability. I conspired with the miners to imply you were eating mountain sheep. The joke turned on us instead of you. Let me tell you how that bear got to the table. It's a good story.

"I brought the meat back from the camp of the Yukon prospectors who asked me to advise them about their claims. They were asleep the night before I went there, all in one tent. John, the oldest, was wakened by a noise at four in the morning. He looked up to see the shadow of a bear standing with paws stretched toward the tent. Grabbing his gun, he crawled out and before the bear moved shot him through the heart. His startled companions were not only grateful to be saved from injury or death but thankful for meat which they'd been without for a week. Knowing Frith's camp was also meatless, they asked me to take a quarter of the bear to Frith. I've eaten bear meat that was tender and tasty, but that old one was the toughest meat I've ever eaten."

In addition to bear our breakfast had included eggs, mashed potatoes, rolls, bacon, toast, flapjacks, strawberry jam, apple sauce, prunes and coffee. It fortified me for the next part of the trail, three miles to the Squaw Creek Canyon. We didn't get started until after lunch as Joe spent the morning discussing mining problems while I napped. The day was sunny when we started and Johnny and the teenaged boys accompanied us. Half an hour before arriving at our destination, we were drenched by heavy rain and hail. The horses didn't mind the weather and carried us steadily forward until my husband reined up beside me with cheering words.

"Look! Look down, my dear. See Squaw Creek running through a canyon that's really grand? What an inspirational picture of natural beauty! Follow me and we'll soon meet those sturdy optimists who collect gold nuggets there."

# GOLD NUGGETS OF SQUAW CREEK

Joe had told me when we left Frith's camp, "It must be puzzling to you crossing from Alaska into British Columbia, then shortly into Yukon Territory and soon back into British Columbia."

It is, I agreed. I keep wondering exactly where I am.

"Study a map I have and it will help you locate yourself. Squaw Creek, and we're heading for that section of it in British Columbia, has been in existence for a long time but only recently named when gold was discovered in its gravel bed. The creek has a good supply of water but many big boulders which make mining difficult. I became acquainted with problems in the recovery of gold there when on field work last year. You'll meet mostly Indian miners at Squaw Creek and a remarkable woman, Mrs. Muncaster. Without her the camp wouldn't have developed as much as it has. She was the second staker of claims on Squaw Creek and holds a government mining position as recorder of claims. A real pioneer she is and a very charming lady."

We rode down from the elevated trail to ford Squaw Creek and drew up in front of the most picturesque and individualistic log cabin I was to see in the north. The logs were covered with strips of bark which gave a distinctive and artistic effect and ruffled curtains at the windows were a pleasing feminine touch. Mrs. Muncaster hurried out to greet us. A little black spaniel and a big husky barked a welcome, standing protectively beside her.

"Dr. Mandy," exclaimed Mrs. Muncaster, "it's a treat to see you again. Too bad my husband's gone away to fetch supplies. Bill liked talking with you last year. I, and all the men on the creek did too. You helped us so much. We can stand more help now. Johnny Fraser just came in with the news you've got yourself married. That's good. A man needs a wife. So, this is the little bride? Bless you, my dear. I'm happy you came. Hear you're from the States same as me. The north will get into your blood, too. I'd bet on that. You're as welcome as all the flowers you see around."

I appreciate your welcome, Mrs. Muncaster, I answered. I've been looking forward to meeting you.

"Well thank you. Say, you look mighty young to be trail travelling in these parts. Don't you worry none. You're married to a fine hubby and he's a good man in the bush. He'll take care of you. Now then, no need to fuss over putting up your tent. The Muncasters have a big tent right next our cabin. That's where you'll stay. It's got lots of stuff in it — nails, hammers, axes, shovels and whatnot but room for your sleeping bags. You'll only be in it to sleep anyway. Dr. Mandy, take the wife there now. Get into dry duds, then come and warm yourselves in my cabin. You'll board with me as you did last year, Dr. Mandy. Good company and paying guests all in one. That's great for me. I'll have a hot supper ready for you two in twenty minutes."

The Muncaster's cabin had the atmosphere of a much loved home. The front room combined a living and dining room, kitchen and a recorder's office. Below a wide, screen-covered window and above a long, sturdy table was a shelf holding mining data and the small scales for weighing gold. A large window was set in each side wall.

This over 46-ounce gold nugget is believed to be from Squaw Creek, found by Ed Peterson and Barney Turbitt in 1937. But in 1987 the creek, below, yielded one nearly twice as big — over 74 ounces.

Madge and Joe on the trail to Squaw Creek. In the background are the St. Elias Mountains, highest in Canada.

Canvas blinds at the windows were rolled up for light and a flow of cool breezes during the day and dropped in the evening to keep out chilly night air. Chairs were round tree stumps and a wooden box provided extra seating. Nails on the wall supported pots and pans and shelves in corners and under the stout table were fronted by printed cotton draw curtains concealing dishes, cutlery, staples of tea, coffee, salt and pepper, soap, wash basin and dish pan. A large range fitted into one corner for cooking and heating. Everything was neatly in place for quick use when needed.

A room at the back of the cabin, with a canvas pull curtain as a door, was walled solid without a window. It was not only a bedroom holding two camp beds with sleeping bags on them, but was a spacious storage place. Clothing hung on the walls, boots and mocassins were on the floor and bags of flour, sugar, salt, many tinned foods, packages of prunes, dried apricots and dried apples were symmetrically arranged in corners. Mrs. Muncaster said camp equipment was assembled there in the winter. Light in the room was adequate with a flashlight or coal oil lamp. This home with its emphasis on necessities was a true expression of pioneer living.

I had expected to meet a large, muscular woman, because of her active participation in mining. Mrs. Muncaster did not resemble such a person. She looked beyond middle age, slim in build, somewhat taller than I, with silvered brown hair and a very feminine, fragile appearance. Her pretty face was lined with character and her outgoing personality had a warmth like a friendly embrace which made me feel that we were kindred souls. After supper, Mrs. Muncaster put on a pair of her husband's trousers and hip boots in preparation for showing Joe her workings in the Creek. I walked with them and Mrs. Muncaster gave information and advice as we followed a worn trail.

"Dr. Mandy, you'd better talk to the Indian miners here about blasting. You know, they're like boys with fireworks when they set off powder. They like the noise and danger that goes with lighting the stuff. I know they have to use dynamite to get big boulders out of the creek. And I know they use too much. Once they blew up sluice boxes along with boulders. Land sakes, splinters of rock and wood went up and came down all over the place. Why, they might have put somebody's eye plumb out. They might have killed someone too. For goodness sake, do tell them how to use dynamite. Don't forget to say if they don't do right, the law will be after them. Here's my claim. I work it myself."

I was impressed at how skilfully Mrs. Muncaster handled a pick and small shovel. Her light pick was especially fashioned to prevent wrist injury. However, she preferred to use a shovel saying, "So much easier. I can put a little bit of gravel on a shovel. Try doing that, Mrs. Mandy. Not heavy, is it? A pick can often strike boulders and pieces flying off are not good. Placer mining keeps me strong and healthy and oh how I love it when I see nuggets in the clean-up. They mean money and are downright pretty."

As we climbed back to the cabin Mrs. Muncaster continued, "Must say the Indians sure like placer mining too. Only they don't work like I do. They go at it in such a slow way. Sit around and talk about where to shovel, maybe for hours. When they find a few nuggets, what do you know? They stop and take the next day off. 'Tain't the thing to do, but they have a clean-up most every day. Never bother with fine gold, only good sized nuggets. Well, they've done better than me, spite of such doings. Jimmy Kane got a nugget this summer worth $171.00, his brother one that fetched $140.00 and other Indians and white miners found nuggets ranging from $5.00 to $50.00. Likely much bigger ones will come out of Squaw Creek."

At the door of her cabin Mrs. Muncaster motioned to our sleeping quarters and suggested, "Why don't you go in there and lie down for half an hour? You've had a long, tiring day. Do that. Then come here and I'll give you coffee with cookies I baked yesterday." We were tired enough to enjoy the rest and refreshments afterward. The miners had quit work by now and some came calling to consult Joe about their problems and to meet the wife he had taken since they met him the previous year. They looked me over and asked, "You, you cross Tatshenshini River?" Their faces and voices expressed disbelief. Joe settled the matter by affirming, "She did."

The men talked mining but my thoughts were of the Tatshenshini River which I must cross again. I certainly hoped by that time it would have a lower water level, be less turbulent and that my horse would not balk in midstream. Mrs. Muncaster had quietly left the room and now joined us, having changed from masculine clothing into a woman's ensemble of skirt, blouse, colourfully flowered scarf and dainty slippers. This change, I was to find out, was a daily procedure and for a very good reason. Mrs. Muncaster had never studied psychology but common sense and observational experience had taught her that a woman in feminine attire had a refining and uplifting influence on men, especially needed and appreciated in a wilderness camp. No wonder morale was high at Squaw Creek.

We met a succession of callers in the Muncaster cabin when going there for breakfast the next morning. The Indian owner of our trail horses, Johnny Fraser, had a share in Squaw Creek claims and had brought gold nuggets from them for Mrs. Muncaster to weigh and appraise. Other Indians assembled to ask a question or two. Also, between serving the Mandys oatmeal porridge, eggs, toast, bacon, flapjacks and coffee, the efficient and cheery pioneer woman gave medication to a sick miner and discussed the gold rush to a neighbouring creek with a constable recently assigned to the Squaw Creek area for the summer. Mrs. Muncaster was mother, friend and an official giving guidance, practical assistance and sympathetic understanding to all miners on the creek. They repaid her with respect, admiration and affection. That remarkable lady even mothered me, remembering how she felt as a young chechako in the golden north.

Finishing coffee after the callers had left I asked, How was Squaw Creek discovered and how did it get its name? Joe tells me you were one of the first here, Mrs. Muncaster.

"Yes, I was," she replied. "You and Dr. have another cup of coffee before you set off to inspect workings. You've been to Dalton Post. 'Twas a busy place when prospectors and Indians traded there with Jack Dalton in Klondike days. An old Indian woman often came to the Post and paid for what she bought with gold nuggets. Nobody knew where she got that gold. Lots of people tried to find out. They couldn't and she died without leaving a clue. In September, 1927, two Klukshu Indians, Paddy Duncan and big Jim Fraser, were hunting. They came to where we are now. Naturally, they were tired and hot and flattened themselves on the bank of the creek and leaned over for a drink. The water, you'll see, is very clear. Well now, Paddy saw something yellow in the gravel of the creek bed. He scooped up a handful of gravel and found gold nuggets in it. Remembering the often told tale of the old woman who always paid trader Dalton in gold nuggets, he shouted to Jim Fraser, "This Squaw Creek!" That name stuck and is on the map today.

"My husband and I were in Whitehorse in '27. Bill picked up packhorses there. We decided to winter them in the Indian village of Champagne nearby. I'd gone to that settlement to make arrangements for this. Paddy Duncan and Jim Fraser came riding in. They were on their way to Whitehorse to get help in recording claims they'd staked on Squaw Creek. Their good news about gold discovery was told to another member of their tribe, George Chambers, who had a trading post at Champagne. He told them about me. When I met Paddy, he had one arm bandaged. I'd had first aid training and asked, What's the matter with your arm? Let me look at it. Paddy brushed me away shouting, 'No you help. Dog bite. Go doctor Whitehorse.' Off he and Jim Fraser went, along with George Chambers.

"The two men and three other Indians hurried back through Champagne, leaving George at the village. As they rode on I asked George, What did the doctor say about Paddy's arm? He told me the truth. 'Paddy no see doctor. Go Whitehorse for telegraph Atlin. Know why?' He finds gold, I said. George nodded saying, 'Find gold in Squaw Creek. Atlin record claim.' I had spent years in mining camps from Dawson in the Yukon to Nome and Candle in Alaska. Right away I knew Paddy was trying to avoid a rush that follows discovery of gold. I decided to get ahead of a stampede and be the second staker on this find. Then, too, I was positive I could help the Indians because of what I knew about mining. George agreed to be my guide and we rode as fast as we could to Squaw Creek.

"There was no trail. What tough going it was! Finally we got there and surprised the men sitting beside a campfire. Were they ever mad at me! Paddy shouted, 'Bad luck you come. This no-nothin' creek. We hunt. Go. Move.' George, who'd had some schooling, stood up for me. He said, 'Mrs. Muncaster be mining recorder Squaw Creek. She knows how mine, how record for law. She smart. Tell what do.' Paddy, Jim Fraser and the three other men talked this proposal over for an hour. Their decision was, 'White woman stay. She help Indian. Good Woman.' I was soon appointed emergency mining recorder for Squaw Creek. Then a special act of the British Columbia government made me an independent recorder so I could stake and work claims. I hear that for quite a spell I was the only woman in your province with such a position. I love it here and I'm busy all the time. Oh, before you go, let me show you something besides mining that keeps me hopping and happy."

Mrs. Muncaster led us to a cleared plot behind her cabin surrounded by a rail fence in which we saw a thriving garden. "Look," she exclaimed, "see what we grow here. I've bordered potatoes, turnips, carrots, lettuce, radishes and chives with a row of nasturtiums. Those bright flowers add a touch, don't you think? Been so dry this summer, I've had to water the garden every night. How do you like my sprinkler? Home made by perforating a gas can. 'Tain't fancy but works. Frost comes at night and would sure get the potatoes if I didn't cover them with a silk tarp. The fresh vegetables help the menu. All other food, except fish and game, has to be bought outside and packed in. Want to nibble on a young carrot? I -"

Joe interrupted with, "Mrs. Muncaster, isn't gardening here a tremendous amount of hard work?"

"Sure it is. Everything one does in a wilderness spot like Squaw Creek is. Still, I learned years ago that hard work is the best tonic a body can have. I get plenty of exercise to keep healthy. It starts when I pop out of a sleeping bag at one in the morning to see if everything is all right in the garden. Have to watch out not only for frost but animals. I check again when I get up for the day at five. It's a great life here, folks."

Paddy Duncan was shovelling gravel from the creek into a sluice box when Joe and I approached him. He was a handsome Indian of middle age and medium height with a large, drooping mustache. He had recently married an older woman of his tribe after the death of his wife. The marriage was required by some tribal custom and was not of his choosing and Mrs. Muncaster had told us, "He's not very happy this summer." Seeing us, Paddy dropped his shovel and straightened up. He nodded to Joe and then stood silently looking at me for about ten minutes before speaking.

"Dr. Mandy, last year you come. Tell Paddy how fin' gold. Now bring Missus. Fine she come. She little. Not good for work. Look good. Nice I see you Missus. Dr. Mandy, come. Show Paddy how fin' much gold."

Moving on after a long conference about and an examination of Paddy's operation, we met Mrs. Paddy, a stout, smiling woman. She came out of a tent beside the creek and like her husband gave me a long, silent scrutiny before asking Joe, "Your Missus?" She spoke English fairly well, her three former husbands having been white men who had contributed to her vocabulary. Mrs. Paddy, so called by the camp, had acquired some white customs and refused to chop wood, carry water and perform other traditional chores of Indian women. Mrs. Paddy's defiant justification for her behaviour was a declaration to all residents on the creek, "Paddy treat me white or me go."

We did not meet Princess Alice, a transient at this location. Local gossip confirmed Frith's comment about her, "She's quite a gal!" Miners told us Mrs. Muncaster had hired her to help with housework and garden and Alice had proved unreliable. She disappeared without notice for days at a time to visit relatives and was so lazy that the Indians on Squaw Creek wouldn't associate with her. All agreed Mrs. Muncaster was too kind to the princess, never criticizing or scolding her and ever hoping to improve her conduct by friendship.

One morning I did not go with Joe on his round of examination and advising because Mrs. Muncaster was staying in her cabin and wanted to chat with me while baking. "I never have time to sit down except when I'm eating, weighing gold or filling out forms for mining," she said, "but we can talk as I whip up a cake, stir up a batch of cookies, make rhubarb pie and get a stew ready. It's so nice to have a lady from the outside with me for awhile. Besides, it'll be good for you to have a rest before you take that tough trail back to Dalton Post."

I wanted to know about her background and northern experiences and questioned, May I ask where in the States you came from and why you came north?

"You sure may. I'll tell you the story of my life. I reckon it's a bit unusual. I was born in St. Paul, Minnesota. Grew up in the state of Washington. A young woman I was in '98. That's when the gold rush was on. My father got gold fever and took me with him to Dawson. There I learned about the north and mining. You might say I fell in love with both. I was sent outside after a year and a half for more schooling. Couldn't stay away from the north though. I went back to Skagway to marry Tom Noyes, a wonderful man from Montana. Mining was his life and it became mine too. We shared everything together. We were in Atlin in '99, had three winters in Nome and lived for ten years at Candle in the Arctic. My husband was with a big company in Candle. We had a comfortable home there and travelled by dog team. I even hunted polar bears and I became a good shot.

"We enjoyed the north but decided we should see more of the world. Took a year off to travel in Europe. Sure was a different kind of life over there. Rome was such an interesting city, full of history. Just when we were getting acquainted with the place, the Panic struck and wrecked Tom's company. In the '30's we call such a happening the Depression. It's the same thing as the Panic of yesterday. Businesses failed and people were out of work. Tom and I lost all our money. Came back to Alaska as quick as we could, Rome to Nome without a stop. Quite a thing to do in those days. Tom took what jobs he could get and when there was a rush to the White River country, he and I were in it. Thousands went on that stampede. Chichini City there became one of the largest log cabin mining camps ever known. We were a part of it from 1913 to 1914.

"Then we went outside where my dear Tom died. Losing Tom was such a blow. I didn't think I could go on. Found I could four years later when I met another wonderful man, Bill Muncaster. He's a civil engineer and had surveyed in the north. We got married, went to the White River country for awhile and have drifted around the north ever since. I've already told you about meeting Paddy Duncan and following him to stake a claim on Squaw Creek. Bill and I are here every summer and his packtrain brings in ready cash. So do my gold nuggets and with percentage paid me as mining recorder gives enough income for whatever we need. And, do you know, in all recording I've only made one mistake. Once I sent in ten dollars too much. Life on Squaw Creek is great. A city would drive Bill and me crazy.

"Oh yes, I should tell you about the artifacts I had a chance to collect, mostly Eskimo. I had one rug made from 17,000 pieces of fur. An Eskimo woman spent her whole life putting it together. The fur used was mink, weasel and reindeer. Right in the centre was an eagle. That bird was lifelike, really stood out. You can understand why it took so long to make when I tell you this. The largest piece of fur in that rug was no bigger than a thumb nail. All those little bits were sewn for strong holding by sinew. I had a very fine bag, too, from intestines of a seal and several jade and ivory tools. A man from the Smithsonian Institute heard about these artifacts. He came to see them. Said it was the best collection of Eskimo art he'd seen and wanted it for the Institute. I knew it belonged in a museum and gave it to the Smithsonian on condition there'd be a special caretaker for it."

What a fascinating and eventful life Mrs. Muncaster had enjoyed and such drama continued. There were no dull days at Squaw Creek and some incidents were very dramatic, like the one related by Mrs. Muncaster while Joe and I ate breakfast just before we left her isolated camp.

"Do I look tired?" she asked. "I sure am. Got up at one this morning, like I always do, to see if everything was all right in the garden. My goodness, it was cold. Didn't want the potatoes to freeze, so I built a fire to keep them warm. A wind came up after I went back to bed. When I got out there at two, the fire I'd set was jumping like mad. The danger wasn't only roast potatoes but a burning cabin. Took me an hour to douse those flames and I've been up every hour since to see whether the fire has stayed out. You can't say we don't have some excitement at Squaw Creek."

It was with reluctance we said goodby to the indomitable pioneer lady, but we told Mrs. Muncaster we looked forward to seeing both her and her husband Bill the following summer. We wondered if she realized her influence in maintaining amiable relations between Indian and white miners who worked side by side in the creek. The miners were unanimous in praise for both the Muncasters. Several told us that when down and out, without provisions or tools, "those good people took us in, tided us over a bad time and helped us get started again." We rode away from this beautiful wilderness setting happy to know the coarse nuggets among the huge boulders of the creek provided a living for those willing to work hard and endure hardships of the wilds. Paddy Duncan reflected the thinking of the camp in a brief summary.

"Dat gold. She hard get. Dat gold lots rock all time over. He good gold. Buy lots things. She — golly, dat good gold."

Leaving Squaw Creek, Joe and I headed up above timber line to trace its source. We had a steep climb with no trail and numerous patches of snow. Two riding problems began to bother me. I had fallen over a log, camouflaged by moss, the day before when looking for wild flowers to press and struck my knee on its hard surface. I hadn't paid any attention to the swelling and soreness that resulted, but after riding for an hour my leg stiffened and pain in the knee became intolerable. I had to cry out for help. Joe, I must get out of the saddle. My left leg is stiff and my knee hurts like the mischief. He had to lift me off the horse, massage that hurting knee and walk me up and down for ten. minutes before the pain subsided. We had to continue doing this all along the way.

The second problem was my horse Jimmy. He was not at all like wise and gentle Polly but instead he was nervous and jumpy. He paid no attention to restraining reins and stopped often to graze and then to gallop and hurdle small ravines. I was experienced enough now to hang on to the saddle but still had a fear of being thrown. Jovial Indian Bobby Kane had an agreement with Joe to supply transportation with his packhorses back to Dalton Post and Jimmy belonged to him. Bobby was a partner of Paddy Duncan and never missed an opportunity for making money to help defray expenses of their joint mining. The Indian youths who had accompanied us to Squaw Creek led the single file packtrain, with Joe next, then me and Bobby last in line. I puzzled over what Bobby kept shouting at me.

"Mrs. Mandy, wish I meet you in fall. Stars shine. No wind. No rain. No nothin'. Wish I meet you in fall."

My horse demanded full attention which kept me from asking for an explanation of Bobby's wish until we dismounted on the bank of the Tatshenshini River. His answer was concise. "I take you hunt. I good guide." Fall was the season when he was well paid for guiding expeditions hunting big game. I didn't tell him I would not shoot any animal, whether a small rabbit or a big moose. It was now midnight, an hour that Shakespeare described as "the very witching time when churchyards yawn and hell itself breathes contagion to this world." Certainly nature had provided a hellish atmosphere with a dark sky and the roar of the Tatshenshini River rushing on its destructive way. Rain had been falling intermittently all day and now became a very heavy downpour. There was not as much light that evening as usual in northern summers although everything was well outlined.

Bobby was our sole companion, as the Indians who had accompanied us had stopped some distance back to camp for the night. He looked speculatively at the still swollen, turbulent river and sat down to debate silently with himself for half an hour before stating his decision about going on.

"No cross river on horse. Horse swim. We go dugout. I pole."

I knew Joe trusted an Indian's judgment when confronting wilderness hazards and when he answered, "That's fine, Bobby. Let's go," I put on a smile and added, I'm ready, Bobby.

Bobby suggested his black bear chaps for comfortable seating. One glance at the bedraggled fur indicated possible habitation by "creepy crawlies" so we pushed them aside, preferring the hardness of the canoe. I sat as close to Joe as possible and the dangerous crossing began. We hadn't gone far when I felt I was sitting in water and I was. We were in a leaking canoe and had to stay in it! The water inched up to form a chilling pool and this was more frightening than Polly's balking when she carried me over the river. I could do nothing but sit motionless, clutch Joe's hand and pray it was not our time to die. Finally, a combination of prayer for safety and the belief that one does not leave this earth until he has fulfilled whatever mission is his had a calming effect. I closed my eyes, tried not to listen to the river's roar of violence and opened them when the dugout scraped to a stop. Bobby leaped ashore shouting, "We here. Come."

Joe rose slowly from a cramped position and helped me stagger out of the dugout. We walked to Princess Alice's cabin, my husband carrying part of our dunnage and Bobby the rest. Joe piled wood into the stove and a hot fire and steaming coffee soon warmed the three of us. Bobby stayed on after being paid for his transporting horses, guidance and successful river crossing. I wanted him to leave so I could remove wet clothing and get to bed. He said nothing and Joe and I were too tired to converse. Twenty minutes passed before Joe thought of giving him a gift, which he told me later was an Indian tradition akin to potlatch. Bobby accepted a tin of corned beef, cheese and rye krisp and left immediately. As for me, my hands couldn't unlace or take off my high leather boots. Joe did this for me and must have smiled hearing me murmur from the sleeping bag, Shakespeare's right a second time tonight. We've proven true what he wrote so many years ago, "All's well that ends well."

Susie cooked breakfast for us early in the morning, minus the mosquitoes, and when Indian George Chambers rode into Dalton Post we were ready to start on another trail. An old prospector and a white teenaged boy, bound for the outside, joined us. Five Indian youths unexpectedly arrived at the Post and tagged along. My injured knee had to be attended by stopping frequently and I was glad for an hour's rest when we stopped for lunch at Desedeash Lake. From here we were to continue our journey with George in a small outboard motor boat on the lake. He was not worried when, ready to take off, the motor didn't function and simply said, "Kicker no kick. I fix." At least three hours later we started and progressed slowly. Several times Joe and the prospector had to row while George struggled with an on and off kicker.

Night came and we passed from Desedeash Lake to Desedeash River. The air grew cold and, though there wasn't much room to manoeuver, Joe managed to zip me into a sleeping bag for warmth. The prospector warmed himself by folded arms across his chest. George and the boy shivered in thin cotton shirts and jeans. Even woolen clad Joe began to turn blue. At midnight George stopped, knowing it was wise to stop for food and to make camp on the river bank. Beside a blazing fire we wearily ate a belated supper of sardines, cheese, hard rusks and honey washed down with boiling hot coffee. Fatigue was better than any pill to give us a sound and refreshing sleep that night.

Some wandering Indians were camped nearby and in the morning I was surprised to see an elderly woman among them sitting on the ground stitching a mooseskin jacket on a portable sewing machine. George told the campers we had no meat left in our supplies and they gave us liver from a moose just killed. Then George fashioned skewers from twigs on which to hang slices of it over a camp fire. I stuffed myself with the tasty food to gain strength for another long day ahead. Some time later I learned that game meat is not as sustaining as that of domestic animals.

George's boat tardily got its five occupants to Champagne Landing. George had an old Ford truck there to take us through the bush where truck tracks had formed the semblance of a road. He had built himself a log house and trading post at the Indian village of Champagne. We stopped there to lunch from tinned food bought at George's store and drink coffee boiled by his wife. The small village was a cluster of log cabins and most of the inhabitants were away fishing. We noted a part of Champagne was on a hill overlooking the flat valley of the settlement and climbed with the prospector to explore it. We found ourselves in a burial place, the tiny cabins erected there were actually tombs. Peering through the window of one we saw pots, pans, food, a mooseskin jacket and beaded moccasins, presumably for the comfort of the departed in another life. This form of burial, Joe informed us, was a contrast to Indian grave boxes in trees on the coast and must have developed from symbolic and practical traditions.

In the afternoon George set out to drive our little group sixty miles to Whitehorse on a bumpy, winding road. Joe thought I should be fairly comfortable seated beside George while he, the prospector and the boy stretched out in the back of the truck. An extra cushion placed under me gave me extra height, enough to hit the hard top above me during frequent jolting. The door on my side of the truck was missing and this caused me to hang on with a desperate grip in order not to be thrown out. George drove without speech and didn't seem to notice the many times he almost lost me. One rest hour during the drive included supper cooked over a campfire which soon appeased hunger and lifted our spirits. On reaching Whitehorse Joe and I went without delay to the Whitehorse Inn where our only wish was for a much needed bath and a restful night of sleep on a mattress covered bed. I was teary next morning knowing our exciting trail days had ended for the season and the Mandys must now return to calm days in Prince Rupert.

The following year my husband said, "We're going again to Squaw Creek. This time, after the coastal voyage we'll fly thirteen miles south from Skagway, Alaska, to Haines, Alaska. From there by truck we go to the British Columbia border and then ride packhorses for sixty-five miles. We'll climb to five summits and cross several rivers in the St. Elias Range area. Mount Logan is there, the highest mountain in Canada. This trail is an endurance test like that of last summer, only longer. You stood up to that. A similar trail will be no problem for you."

The trip north to Skagway on a coastal steamer, fraught with romantic memories, was as pleasant as we'd known it before. On arrival at Skagway we took off on a small plane of the White Pass and Yukon Railway Company, flying over Lynn Canal to land on the beach at Haines. On the way Joe cited a bit of interesting history about this locale.

"I don't suppose many people know there's an Army Post at Haines. Construction was started for the military in 1903. By 1905 it was garrisoned by two companies and named Fort Seward. The name was changed to Chilkoot Barracks in the '20's. I'm glad the world is at peace because the few soldiers stationed at Haines offer the only protection for Alaska, the Yukon and northwestern British Columbia. God help us up here if there's ever a Second World War."

Big Erik Oslund, locally known as "the terrible Swede," was on hand to meet us. He acknowledged me and then turned abruptly to Joe saying, "Can't bunk youse in my cabin. Don't have no room for a lady. Youse walk to the hotel, Me, I'm drivin' your dunnage there. 'Tain't far. Bess'll sign youse folks in. See ya."

Half way to the hotel we met a tall, thin man whose features reminded me of those in pictures of such rugged frontiersmen as Daniel Boone and Kit Carson. He stopped us with, "Hello there, Dr. Mandy. So you've got a wife with you. Heard nice things about your visit to Squaw Creek last summer, Mrs. Mandy. My wife took a real fancy to you. Oh, I should tell you I'm Bill Muncaster. Got your letter Dr. asking for transportation. I've got a full load of supplies to take to Squaw Creek tomorrow. You two can be part of my packtrain, Doc."

"It's good to see you again, Bill," declared Joe. "Mrs. Mandy and I will be having supper soon. Won't you be our guest?"

"No thanks. I ate with the horses," he replied and added after seeing the expression on my face, "at the same time. Not the same food."

"Well, will you join us for a cup of tea or coffee?"

"Dr. Mandy," and there was reproof in his voice, "you should have remembered I don't drink either. No good for the stomach. Tell you what. I'll go with you and have a cup of cocoa. There's just one restaurant in this town and I don't recommend it but, if you want to eat, we'll have to head there."

I understood Bill's aversion when we entered the café. It also housed a beer parlour and adjoining liquor store. Patrons stood at a long counter or sat in booths along the wall in a large room. Soldiers from Chilkoot Barracks had crowded into the place. Several young army men were fraternizing with Indian girls and the racket they created with shouting and giggling made conversation impossible for us. The restaurant served no dinners, only bacon and eggs and soggy sandwiches and that combination could not satisfy our longing for vegetables and fruit. The coffee served was strong enough to taste like bitter medicine. Bill, however, found his cup of cocoa very pleasing.

Mrs. Steve Sheldon, the Bess to whom Erik had referred, presided over the one hotel in Haines to which we walked after our sketchy meal. She asked us to sit with her for awhile in the large lounge where it was difficult to find a seat. The room was filled with trunks, boxes, blankets and Indian and pioneer handcraft piled high on the trunks and chairs. Bill had told us Mrs. Sheldon was known as "Babbling Bess" because she talked continuously and we soon discovered the title fitted her perfectly. She told stories of local residents and military personnel and then reminisced about the historical to which we could relate.

She babbled, "Did you know this hotel was built by Jack Dalton in 1898? He was an honest-to-goodness pioneer. Laid out the Dalton trail about 1893. He intended it to be a supply route for Alaska and the Yukon. That man was a go-getter. Why, he had packtrains, oxen and wagons for long hauls and drove cattle over the Chilkoot Pass. I think that was in '98 when there was the big gold rush to the Klondike. Dalton built several trading posts and road houses. Quite a man that Jack Dalton! My husband and me own his Haines hotel now. It's called Sheldons. Oh, we wasn't northerners. My man came from Ohio and me, a nurse, from Pennsylvania. We got other businesses here — a steam laundry and —."

My husband had to stop her chatter or she would probably have continued far into the night. His interruption was polite but to the point. "Mrs. Sheldon, what you tell us is indeed interesting. We'd like to hear more but must be up by five in the morning ready to start for Squaw Creek at six. Mrs. Mandy and I should get to bed or we'll meet ourselves getting up. Will you please show us to our room? There's something else, too. The restaurant doesn't open until late. Could you give us breakfast?"

"Goodness me, no. I don't serve meals. If I'd been born here in the north I'd do it. These northerners are all out hospitable. Too much I say. You're right lucky I have a room for you."

Joe suggested a compromise. "Could you let us have some food to take to our room?"

She was agreeble to that. "Reckon I can. Let's see — I'll give you a box of cornflakes, a loaf of bread, butter and milk. I'll even dig out an old percolator so's you can make coffee on the oil burner in the bathroom."

Carrying our breakfast, Bess escorted us to a room above. To get there we crossed a front porch, with a sagging floor, to a rotting board walk leading through a tangled growth of weeds to a stairway standing beside the hotel but detached from it. Steps of the stairs were rickety and the whole structure shook as we climbed to a roofed, attached landing. A door with loose hinges opened into a narrow hall with papered walls gray from the grime of years. The bedroom was functional with bed, straight chair, top-heavy small table and crookedly hung old looking glass which hazily mirrored anything reflected in it. Curtains, from their shabby, yellowed appearance, must have been those originally there and one window was held open by an empty whiskey bottle. Nothing additional could be put in a wardrobe filled to the ceiling with empty liquor bottles of all shapes and sizes but clean linen on a solid mattress promised a good rest and for that we were grateful.

I took one look at the bathroom and squealed, Incredible! Enamel was almost worn off the bathtub to make it unsightly and discourage any thought of a bath. The wash basin was chipped and discoloured, the floor bore unwashed soil from tramping boots of yesteryear's gold rushers and papered walls were the grimy gray of those in the halls. How much soap and water and a coat of paint could have transformed that room! The toilet flushed only when water was poured into the bowl from a bucket sitting in the bathtub and no water came out of the tap for the wash basin. A hotel without water was as incredible to me as the condition of the bathroom and facilities and I looked around for the reason. It was a notice above the sink, "Because of water shortage in Haines, water will be turned off at ten p.m." The solution for a little personal cleanliness was found by sharing with Joe some cold cream from a jar in my kit bag. With it we "washed" our faces and hands.

Joe went into the bathroom in the morning to brew coffee and I heard him explode, "There's no oil in the stove here! Such service can't be tolerated. I'll get oil if I have to search the place and wake up the whole family downstairs."

My husband's scouting was successful and he returned to percolate coffee which was stimulating, though breakfast was not even nourishing. Hot weather, and no refrigeration, had soured the milk, caused the butter to turn rancid and the stale loaf of bread was mouldy. Our breakfast was reduced to half a box of corn flakes moistened by gulps of coffee. This was certainly not a sustaining meal for a long trail ride. However, the humour of the situation made me giggle and say, Joe, such a breakfast isn't very funny but the thought of it will be in time. Let's anticipate this by laughing now. That's what we did and laughter enabled us to greet Erik and Bill cheerily at the outset of a forty-two mile drive in Erik's truck to where Bill's horses ranged. We travelled a road of sharp turns parallel with the Chilkat River, its bed made up of sand bars, many of them covered by seasonal high water which spilled over onto the road. The ride ended at Pleasant Camp on the border between Alaska and British Columbia. Bill rounded up and packed his horses and Mr. White, who was renovating Dalton's old roadhouse there, prepared a hot lunch for us.

Those horses of Bill's were powerful, one capable of carrying three hundred pounds. Joe rode Sonny. I was seated on Doll. Bill walked and the horses Molly, Flax and Dick followed. We soon passed into an avenue of giant Devil's Club, a shrub studded with sharp, stiff thorns on both stems and leaves. I didn't need anyone to tell me a fall among the plants would be disastrous. Two years later I met a man who had lost an eye from a thorn on that devilish bush. This remote segment of British Columbia was usually open for packhorses from

Joe and Madge enroute to Squaw Creek from Haines, Alaska.

the first of July until mid-September and the Muncasters travelled the route in early spring and late fall via sled and dog team. Thinking of summits and rivers to cross, I hoped we wouldn't encounter fog which Bill said often clouded the way. We climbed until fatigue and hunger demanded a camp. Bill unpacked the horses while Joe built a fire and showed me how to cook a quick camp meal. My, it was nice to rest and a supper of bacon, eggs, corned beef, rye krisp and jam tasted like a gourmet's dream and was supplemented by strong coffee.

Bill said it wasn't necessary to put up our mosquito tent because a frosty night would keep insects away. He formed a shelter like a tepee for himself from a canvas tarpaulin which mosquitoes could not penetrate. Joe and I threw our sleeping bags on the ground and hurried into them. Cold air did not discourage the mosquitoes and they attacked us viciously. Joe quickly unpacked our mosquito tent and draped it over our faces but those pests put their stingers through the netting spaces. He tried propping the tent above us with firewood, but it didn't give any support and the tent fell down. Tired out, I fell asleep and didn't know until early morning that Joe, afraid of disturbing me if he put the tent up properly, built a big fire by which he sat and dozed. The heat from it and his frequent fanning with a leafy bush branch kept the mosquitoes away from me. What a considerate man I had married! I prayed I might ever be as kind to my husband as he was to me.

We now rode for eight hours with only an occasional ten minute rest. Bill considered stopping for lunch but decided that could show a weakness of character. It was his packtrain, so we conformed to his decision, lunching in the saddle by nibbling a bit of rye krisp and cheese stored in Joe's jacket. I also acquired almost instant vitality by chewing on a square of bitter chocolate Joe had advised me to stow in my shirt pocket. Mosquito Flats, covered with low bushes and honeycombed with furrows tramped by Dalton's cattle, was our camping ground for the second night. How very appropriate that name! The mosquitoes here were bigger and stronger than any battled before. They must have been having a convention, assembled in hundreds, and with them were black flies, horse flies, yellow jackets and no-see-ums which I began to call you-feel-ums. Joe put up our mosquito tent before eating, knowing from last night's experience, that protection was required for successful sleeping. The tent had a canvas top and netting for sides and stood firmly tied to a bush at each end by attached cords, the height below my shoulder. Protected from noxious mosquitoes, our sleep was sound until Bill's crackling fire woke us.

An early morning start was possible through the cooperation of the horses. Grazing was so good on the flats that there had been no need for them to roam. Joe decided all in the pack-train would benefit by stopping for a rest and lunch at noon and discussed the matter with Bill. He reluctantly agreed in a few words to do so. "Not necessary, but I suppose we could spare a few minutes on the trail." Several streams were forded coming up over a divide before we halted at the Gold Run Creek camp of Derud and his associates from Seattle. Bill devoted himself to the care of his horses, Joe and I quickly ate a supper of canned food and then my husband went off with Derud to examine showings while I called on a lonely woman of my mother's age in a nearby cabin. She had come north from Seattle to cook for and generally look after Derud and his partners, as her son was one of the company's prospectors.

I knocked at a partially closed door and hearing a weak, "Come in," walked inside to see a woman lying on a bunk holding a towel compress against a swollen cheek. She jumped up, discarded the wet cloth, and after shaking hands seated me on a stump chair with a cushion on it and began talking rapidly.

"You're Mrs. Mandy, aren't you? Bill Muncaster told me you was coming. I must look a sight. I got an awful toothache. The nasty thing is driving me up the wall. There's no dentist around here so I have to grin and bear it. Let's us have coffee and a cookie while we're sitting here. My dear, you're a tonic. Didn't think I'd mind being with just men. But, you know, when a woman's sick she needs a woman. The north isn't what I thought it'd be either. I expected a place like the movies show with big he-men rushing around with gold nuggets in bar rooms sweeping women off their feet in square dances, a place for a real good time. What did I find? Pretty scenery, men working like mad, nobody to talk to, me stuck with hand washing filthy clothes and cooking three big meals a day. Oh, how the men can eat! And there's nothing to do after working except cards at night for a little while. The men goes to bed early. I was brought up with bright lights of the city, lots of people around and lots of amusements. And how deadly quiet it is here! What I call creepy.

"Good land, how can a little girl like you rough it around in this lonely country? Forded flooded rivers, too, I hear. They'd scare me to death. I'm old enough to be your mother and I couldn't do what you're doing. Ought to be able to stand up to things, but this isn't my kind of life. Guess being young and in love are on your side. Say, won't you be more comfortable tonight in my bunk bed than lying on the ground? You're welcome to it. Your husband can bunk across the room and I'll go up in the loft. My tooth'll ache wherever I am."

Joe had sized up camp facilities and thanked my hostess for the accommodation she offered but assured her, "Mrs. Mandy and I will be comfortable in a tent vacated by a prospector who has gone to a strike on Silver Creek. I understand you have a toothache and I know what that suffering is. I've brought you aspirin from my first aid kit. It should keep the pain bearable."

Joe concluded, after an evening and morning on Derud's claims, that Gold Run Creek was mis-named, for there were few nuggets in it. Advice given, we headed for Squaw Creek Canyon. Once there, the friendly spirit of the camp made me feel as if we were celebrating old home week. We renewed acquaintance with the miners we had met the previous summer and were introduced to newcomers. Many consultations kept Joe busy, but mining on Squaw Creek was suspended on Sunday in favour of laundry and "visitin'." A message on that day from a small crew of prospecting Americans from Seattle, at the mouth of Squaw Creek, asked the Mandys to lunch at their camp. We were met on the trail by one of the group, young Brown, with a particular request for me.

"Mrs. Mandy, I prospected here last summer. Never met you but heard how much you liked roughing it in the north. You and my wife are both from the States and I think about the same age. You've both been teachers, too. I brought her up early this summer. Thought she'd take to everything like you did. Seems I was dead wrong. She don't like it at all. Could you talk to her? Maybe you could change her mind."

Brown was construction trained and with help from other men in the camp had built a log house for his wife. It comprised a long, wide room that combined the kitchen (including a built-in cabinet beside a large range) and living area at one end, a dining nook with table and backed benches along the middle of one side wall and a sleeping space fitted with a bed instead of a bunk at the other end. In a semi-populated area this sturdily constructed, roomy and well planned building would have been an unusually desirable summer home but here it was an isolated log house in virgin forest without the amenities found in rustic retreats near settled communities. I met Mrs. Brown inside, an attractive brunette wearing a pretty summer dress and high heeled slippers, perfect attire for an afternoon at a bridge club in the city. She graciously served a delicious lunch enhanced by a bowl of wild flowers on the table. Joe discussed mining with Brown and his crew and shortly after eating they left to inspect workings. Mrs. Brown wasted no time in sitting down beside me and pouring out her frustrations.

"Mrs. Mandy, I can't stand it here. Do wish I'd never come. What shall I do?"

She laid her head on my shoulder and cried. I patted her arm and waited until she could speak coherently and more calmly.

"It's awful here. No running water. A bath in a washtub where I do the laundry. Plumbing is outside. No entertainment. My husband is gone most of the time looking for gold he doesn't find. I'm so lonesome shut up in this cabin and too afraid to go out. I might meet a bear or a wolf. I - I can't go on."

I was sure her dislike and fear were too deeply entrenched to change and merely tried to console and suggest something to help her. Mrs. Brown, I said, you're only here for the summer. Could you think of yourself as a temporary pioneer and enjoy adapting briefly to wilderness ways like our ancestors did? Her answer was a negative shriek.

"No, I couldn't. I don't like being a pioneer for even a day. I hate everything here."

When I told Joe about Mrs. Brown's reaction he sympathetically replied, "It's understandable. Not everyone can adapt to pioneering. That's true of men as well as women."

Mrs. Muncaster talked of needed change for Squaw Creek on our last night there. "Mining on this creek won't go ahead till we get better transportation. Cost of plane and train, coming and going, is too much for prospectors. Of course it's cheap to walk in from Haines as some have done, but that takes too much time. We can only mine for a short summer season. Then, too, equipment and food must come from the outside. We can't afford all we need because freight rates of the White Pass and Yukon Railway are too high. George Chambers packs in supplies from Whitehorse but isn't too dependable. He sells things to trappers and prospectors along the way. Often has nothing left when he gets to Squaw Creek. Our camp just couldn't get along if Bill didn't pack from Haines.

"To make matters worse, the government has a constable at the camp this summer. He's a nice man but not very long out of England. Doesn't understand conditions in the Canadian Northwest. Part of his job is being customs officer. He says he doesn't like to collect duty on goods from Alaska, but the law is the law. Boloney, I say. What nonsense to charge thirty dollars for a broken down horse not worth five! You know what else he did? Took mining tools from an old prospector who didn't have money to buy any more. Poor fellow! He'd have died if we hadn't all pitched in and helped him. There's something else I want to tell you, Dr. Mandy. A stupid government regulation tells us we can't leave our property for more than seventy-two consecutive hours without losing rights to it. That's all very well if you're near a trading post. All the miles we have to travel to even get a moose or fish takes more time than that. With all these problems, don't you wonder why I keep on mining at Squaw Creek?"

I answered that question. You stay because you're a pioneer. Tell me, do you ever get lonesome?

"My gracious, no. Too busy for that. Besides, after all these years I've spent in the north, I belong to it. Couldn't live anywhere else."

We were getting ready to leave the camp in the morning when Paddy Duncan and his wife came to say goodby. They had honoured us by dressing in their best. Paddy wore a white shirt, black trousers, sleeveless brown sweater, brown felt hat and beaded mocassins. Mrs. Paddy was glamorous in a mail order brown satin dress, blue silk

Mr. and Mrs. Paddy Duncan, Mrs. Muncaster, Madge and Joe at Muncaster's cabin. Mrs. Muncaster's big husky, though protective of her, accepted the Mandys with restrained friendliness.

scarf, cream cardigan and beautiful mocassins embroidered in intricate, colourful, beaded design. We posed with them and Mrs. Muncaster for a memorable picture. Then Paddy, holding out a sizeable gold nugget inlaid with quartz, delivered a presentation speech.

"Dr. Mandy good man. Tell Paddy where fin' gold. His Missus we give. Take. Tell everone — Paddy Duncan give. Paddy fin' Squaw Creek. Paddy big chief."

Rain was falling when we started off for Haines with Bill Muncaster and his packtrain. We were told the trip would take a day less than when we came to Squaw Creek since the horses were free from packs until they picked up supplies in the Alaskan town. Peggy, recently from New York city, left her husband mining on the creek while she rode with us for personal shopping in Haines. My husband soon detoured to look over a reported gold prospect and rejoined our party on a narrow plateau just as my saddle and I fell to the ground. Shaken and shocked, I wanted to lie there, but the direction I had so often given when producing plays in Kansas, "The show must go on, no matter what," brought me to my feet before Joe could assist me.

Joe quickly dismounted saying, "Your saddle is too big for you. Let's exchange."

We did what he thought wise and rode on. Intuition warned me that what had happened to me would happen to Joe and it did. I looked back to see him kicking free as he fell. The saddle problem was a weak cinch which unfastened to throw me and broke under Joe's heavier weight. Resourceful Bill managed a repair and we continued on the trail, often hampered by the horses leaping into the air when stung by yellow jackets. I determined not to let those disturbing wasps unseat me and though it was difficult I stayed on my attacked horse. An abandoned cabin was shelter for Peggy and me that night. We were so tired we hardly noticed the discarded belongings of transient occupants strewn around the room and slept soundly on wooden bunks in the windowless refuge. Bill retired to a tarpaulin tepee and Joe to an unprotecting frame which once supported a tent. With morning came a clear sky and we resumed travel.

Riding steadily we came to Mosquite Flats by mid evening. We were all dead tired after the long hours of riding and very hungry too. In spite of Muncaster's protests (that man never seemed to want or need food), Joe insisted on a hearty supper, his special five course wilderness meal. It consisted of soup made from oxo cubes dissolved in water which came to a boil slowly in a pot suspended over a crackling campfire, boiled rice as a second course, a third course of canned corned beef, then rice with tinned honey as dessert, the whole topped by a crunchy rusk with cheese and a cup of strong coffee. We felt invigorated after this sustaining supper and lingered around the cheery fire, enjoying its warmth in the cool night air of the St. Elias Range region. The men entertained with trail tales and we had a good laugh over Joe's story of a trip in the Atlin area of British Columbia.

A prospector asked Joe to accompany him for an examination of an outcrop of gold "high up in them big hills." It was a very steep and exhausting climb to an elevated ledge which was a golden yellow. "Look Dr. Mandy," exclaimed the man, "pure gold for the takin'. Ain't it jes' tremenjus?"

My husband realized the chap was geologically ignorant and paused before saying "Let's sit down and rest a bit. Certainly takes a fellow's breath to climb up here but the view, well, it's worth all the sweating we did. Now let's talk about gold, which is generally hard to find. Prospectors have to count on being disappointed over and over before striking it rich or striking it at all. I must tell you, we're not sitting on gold but a splendid showing of sulphur. They're both yellow so I can understand your mistake. Don't give up. Keep on prospecting and read about where and how gold may be found. Get pointers from other prospectors who've discovered it. You may unearth another Klondike."

Rain started now, so the men constructed a lengthy lean-to from

Dave and Rosie Wing
hauling logs with
their dog team.

canvas and stretched it over our four sleeping bags placed close together. A roaring fire, which Bill replenished during the night, drove mosquitoes away. The tireless man was up at four-thirty cooking breakfast and the tantalizing scent of bacon and coffee brought three sleepers out of our sleeping bags to eat and hear Bill's schedule for the day.

"Thirty miles to go, folks. Got to be at Pleasant Camp by supper time. That'll be six o'clock. Erik'll be there to drive us to Haines in his truck. Plenty tiring, I know, but we're tough enough to make it."

The sun was hot and eventually made me drowsy. Just as we were entering the remembered avenue of Devil's Club I cried out to Joe, I'm sleepy. Can't keep my eyes open.

Joe called back, "You mustn't go to sleep. That would make you fall off your horse into those devilish bushes. Keep thinking how close we are to Pleasant Camp. Just three miles to go. That's not far."

I began talking to myself and repeating aloud, Three miles. Only three miles. Joe helped me fight dozing by singing loudly, "Onward Christian Soldiers". I was still in the saddle but drooping when we reached the border roadhouse. That inspiriting man of mine lifted me down from Doll with words of commendation.

"What a trooper you are! The three miles were really six."

Erik jolted us to Haines in his truck and the following morning we crossed Lynn Canal by plane to Skagway and booked a passage on a steamer bound for Prince Rupert. In my pocket was Paddy Duncan's gift of a gold nugget and stored in my mind were priceless memories of hardy pioneers and the hardships they endured to placer mine at Squaw Creek. I recalled Mrs. Muncaster's prediction that much bigger nuggets than those found in the '30's would be discovered at Squaw Creek and she was right. I saw in the Vancouver Sun newspaper of July 11, 1987, the headline, "Gold Nugget as big as a baked potato," and read the report beneath it of the 74.5 ounce discovery in a Squaw Creek sluice box. The nugget's owner can claim, according to records, the second largest gold nugget ever found in British Columbia. How happy the late Mrs. Muncaster would be if she knew her prophecy had so richly come true. Perhaps she does know.

## HISTORIC ATLIN THE BEAUTIFUL

Joe called out to me from the study one evening in late spring when poring over maps, "Come and see where we're going soon. To Carcross, where you've been and then on to Atlin, one of the loveliest spots anywhere. It is always spoken of as Atlin the Beautiful."

Tell me about this enchanting place. From this location I presume it must be associated with mining.

"It is, and knowing the history of Atlin will give you a better understanding of how and why boom mining towns develop. Take yourself back to 1897. At that time a man named Will Miller was the owner of a hotel in Juneau, Alaska. One day a young chap came there who had been prospecting in northwestern British Columbia. There, he said, the mountains were high and held many glaciers. He also reported seeing a creek running into a large lake from the east near three islands, a conspicuous location mark. The prospector was sure the creek carried gold. Miller's brother Fritz and this Canadian prospector, Kenny McLaren, who was on his way to the Klondike, decided to search together for the possibly gold-bearing creek.

"The prospectors must have jumped up and down and shouted upon finding gold in the mouth of that creek. They named it Pine Creek because of adjacent pine trees. The find was in January, 1898. Shortly, the two went back to Juneau for supplies and other prospectors sensed 'they were on to something' and followed them to the rich creek. By summer, news of their discovery had spread and a rush started, people coming from all over the world. Between 1899 and 1900 an estimated ten thousand were there, mostly living in tents and for miles along the trail to the boom town of Discovery on Pine Creek called Pine City. Atlin, the main town for the area, evolved six miles from the gold camp on the Atlin Lake front where it still stands today.

"I'll read you some data I've compiled from a report by C. L. Monroe, Gold Commissioner in Prince Rupert in 1929, about recovery of gold in the Atlin camp. 'It was about $75,000 in 1898. In 1899 it increased to nearly a million and for the eight years after that averaged around $500,000. Then through the war years the average fluctuated between $500,000 and $200,000. During the last few years it has diminished to approximately $50,000 but accounted for more than half the placer gold produced in British Columbia during 1928.' Lack of transportation and now the Depression have severely curtailed Atlin mining, but both optimistic prospectors and companies carry on hopefully. You'll find in Atlin and vicinity friendly, kind and hardy pioneers and some characters whom Charles Dickens would have immortalized in novels. En route, we'll stop for mining consultations and you'll meet the Lawsons and Brooks family on Tagish Lake."

On arriving at Carcross we boarded a small plane waiting to speed us to Lawson Landing. How fitting it was in this northland that Fred Lawson, standing on the sandy lakeshore watching our descent to the Landing, should look like Santa Claus. I almost said, Santa, how nice to meet you. What are you bringing me for Christmas? The man was certainly Santa's double in appearance. He was tall, big framed, and had a rotund body, large blue eyes, white hair and flowing white beard. Mrs. Lawson beside him was a decided contrast — medium height, thin, fragile looking and wearing facial lines depicting hardships.

Mr. and Mrs. Fred Lawson at their home on Tagish Lake.

The Lawsons led us to their log house which held one large room with a front window facing Tagish Lake and two smaller windows on the side viewing forest. A thin wooden partition, centred halfway across the middle of the room, fronted a double bed with space between forming a narrow aisle. Along its wall clothes hung on nails with boots stacked on the floor beneath them. The bed fitted tightly into a corner position and a few feet from it in the opposite corner stood a stove flanked by a small counter-topped cabinet holding cutlery, pots, pans, dishes, salt and pepper shakers and tightly capped jars filled with flour and sugar. The kitchen section stretched frontward into a dining nook where benches were seats beside a rectangular table. The living division of the room offered some comfort in a sagging couch, splitting leather armchair, straight chair and a small table on which rested a coal oil lamp and a little battery radio.

The Lawsons cleared a space for the Mandys in a big, recently constructed log cabin a few yards from their home, which could have been divided into two large rooms. It stored their mining and trapping equipment. We were left to settle in and I wondered why the Lawsons had not moved to this spacious place. The reason was obvious when we rejoined the couple for coffee and cookies. Fred lounged in the armchair while Mrs. Lawson packed heavy buckets of water from a distant spring, carried in armfuls of wood for the stove and attended to other chores which should have been her husband's. He was the ruler of his domain who demanded and got service in all things from his meek wife. Moving into the other cabin would have been an impossibility as frail Mrs. Lawson would bear the brunt of it.

Fred got up slowly when we entered, shuffled to the door and called loudly, "Barney, come in here." When his mining partner appeared he introduced Joe and me. "This man's Dr. Mandy, government minin' engineer. He's agoin' to 'zamine our Atlin Pacific showins. The girl's his wife. Recon she don't want to look at no diggins or ore samples. Say, little lady, I got me somethin' you'll like to see. Mrs. Lawson, bring out that fur catch I'm atakin' to Atlin.'" Mrs. Lawson trotted away to do what was ordered and came back weighted down with the pelts and arranged them where they could best be inspected. Fred proudly displayed the yield of his trapline — beaver, lynx, wolverine, bear and wolf while stressing their importance in his wilderness living. "Don't 'zactly like trappin' animals but them furs brings in most of the cash I gotta have. My minin' so far don't bring me much."

Joe, who was well informed concerning fur, complimented Lawson on the quality of his catch. "You should be proud of what you offer for sale. These are prime pelts."

Fred snorted, "Course they be. Ought to bring a might fair price. Don't trust nobody but meself to take them in for atradin'. I gotta go off with them furs come mornin'. Barney'll show you our claims. You can tell me your findins when I gets me back from Atlin."

Fred was away early next day after eating stacks of flapjacks and swilling several cups of coffee. Joe and Barney stoked themselves with much food, including a whole jar of Mrs. Lawson's wild strawberry jam, in preparation for a long day on the trail and intensive inspection of claims. I remained with Mrs. Lawson at her request.

"Won't you stay with me?" she had asked. "Don't often have a woman to talk to. You bein' from the outside makes our talkin' really somethin'."

Mrs. Lawson had baked the day before but decided company deserved a special pudding and a tin full of cookies. She wanted to talk as she mixed ingredients together for the baking but was too timid to start a conversation. I tried to help her overcome her shyness by saying, Your home has a beautiful location here on Tagish Lake. When the wind whistles across it and through the tall trees around, lovely music is in the air. You don't need entertainment of movies outside when you can see live moving pictures from your windows as moose, deer, caribou, bears and other animals pass by. Then, too, the air is clean and fresh, so different from that in the city. How lucky you are to live in such a pretty place.

Mrs. Lawson's reply rushed forth in a torrent of suddenly released emotion. "'Spose it's purty hereabouts. I ain't had time to look at it. Busy, busy all the time. Guess you're tryin' to figger out how I come to be in this here neck of the woods. I wuz American. Me an' mother, she wuz a widow, lived in the U.S. northwest. Mother run a boardin' house. Didn't pay much. I helped her an' worked awful hard. Never had no time for play. Schoolin' 'nuff for learnin' readin' an' writin'. Fifteen I wuz when long comes a good lookin' French Canadian. That man sweet talked me into elopin' an' marryin' him. We set up housekeepin' in Spokane. He wuz a builder. Made good money. Got us a nice house, nice furniture an' nice clothes. But he wuz downright mean an' stingy. Never give me money 'cept for groceries.

"Guess I might have put up with him. When three kids come 'long, two boys an' a girl, things wuz different. His temper wuz terrible. He throwed things at me. I knowed such goin' ons wuz bad for the young 'uns. Bein' Catholic, I didn't hold with divorce an' asked the priest for a separation. He says no, go home an' stay married. Honest, I tried to do what Father says an' that man of mine kept gettin'worser. One day I can't stand no more. I walks out of my house, gives the kids to the church an' starts a boardin' house. I wuz too green to make a go of it.

"Then I goes to visit folks I knows in Revelstoke, British Columbia. I'd been thinkin' of goin' to Fairbanks to get me a job but Canada wuz closer than Alaska. My friends set up a meetin' with Fred Lawson in Revelstoke. He wuz goin' to a gold rush in Atlin, B.C. That camp had work for the likes of me he said. So, in a little while I goes to Atlin. That boom minin' town skeered me half to death an' when I run across Fred Lawson there it wuz like meetin' a angel. He don't like noise that goes with so many folks millin' round, or gamblin', drinkin' an' sportin' women no more than me. He says, 'I've got me a homestead where a man can prospect, trap an' hunt for a livin'. Come with me.' I wuz right glad to come. We been here most thirty years now.

"Allus done my share. Fred can't read or write, so I does that for him. He's smart 'nuff to figger some. Tough times we've had. Summers we prospect. Winters we trap. I've allus been sickly an' it's been hard to keep goin'. One time I wuz terrible sick on the trapline in a cold winter. They wuz lots of snow an' we wuz four miles from Tepee. That's a old log tepee some prospector put up in rush days. Me an' Fred uses it when trappin'. We gets there an' I crawls in a bunk an' stays down three days. Fred goes on checkin' traps, eatin' sandwiches an' drinkin' thermos tea we brung from home. Never thinks of feedin' me. Oh, Fred's a good man. He don't drink, smoke, gamble or run 'round with women. Sometimes I think it 'ud be better if he'd do some of them things. They's somethin' here I hates — no privacy."

No privacy in the heart of the wilds? I asked. I don't quite know what you really mean.

"I means privacy in livin'. Look at this cabin. The bedroom ain't really a room. All open on one side so's I can't close it off. If'n anyone's here, I can't go to bed till they goes. One room I'm stayin' in. See how I can put out my hand an' purty near touch the stove from the bed? Another thing, Fred don't think of savin' me steps. We come here in 1905 an' Fred's been intendin' to put a door in the back so's I don't have so far to carry flour, sugar an' other food stuffs from the storage cabin behind. He ain't got 'round to it yet. I carries water from the spring. Fred's promisin' to pipe it to the cabin don't get done. Shouldn't be complainin' but a woman gets lonesome for 'nother woman to spill out to."

For two days Mrs. Lawson talked on and on, finding relief in expressing years of repression. Fred did all the talking when he was home and this opportunity to speak freely to sympathetic ears was a tonic to her. Northerners met later, who knew the Lawsons, told me Fred was "plain lazy" and his survival depended on his submissive and hard working wife. One prospector summarized their life bluntly.

"Manys the time I met them on the trail trappin', huntin' or prospectin'. That weak wife does all the doin' an' that big ox of a husband comes along an' he don't do nothin' but Lord it over her. Fred looks like Santa Claus but, by gosh, he don't act like Santa.

Can't understand how Mrs. Lawson has lived so long with nobody to rightly look after her. Must be good old grit keeps her goin'. Yessiree, grit's what she's got."

We stopped en route to Atlin, travelling on the lake steamer Tutshi, at the site of the famous Engineer Mine on Tagish Lake. Since closure of the operation, there was no longer a docking facility. Consequently, watchman and caretaker Reggie Brooks rowed out to meet us and take us ashore. He was a powerfully built Englishman of more than medium height with thick, gray hair, a skin roughened by the elements and a strong, commanding voice, apparently well suited to the challenge of an old mine. According to the Lawsons, he had been a friend of Captain Alexander who had staked lapsed claims and brought the Engineer Mine into production. Reggie had been with the company since its inception and was very knowledgeable about the location of veins and pockets of rich ore. He believed there could be a profitable re-opening. Meanwhile, a lease permitted him to carry out mining on his own and his gold recovery gave him a good income.

Reggie talked while leading us across a grassy meadow to the ghost community. "Glad you've come, Dr. Mandy, as your letter said you would. I need your examination of the mine and technical advice. I can tell you all about mining carried on here. I can show you possibilities for the future, too. I'm so glad you've come along, Mrs. Mandy. You'll be company for the wife. She and the boys are with me for the summer. They've been putting the deserted but habitable manager's house in order for you folks. I'll take you there. It's really deluxe housing in the isolated Northwest. My family and I are in an equally choice house and my boys will call for you at six and escort you to dinner with the Brooks family."

Of course we had to thoroughly inspect the highly praised dwelling we were to occupy. On the first floor were sitting room, dining room, kitchen, breakfast nook and bedroom with bath and upstairs we found two bedrooms and another bathroom. A basement included a laundry and from a small back porch and front verandah one could feast on the majesty of mountains. A lone prospector would have been overwhelmed by so much space and the luxury of electric lights instead of coal oil lamps. Our main floor bedroom boasted a full length mirror as a panel of the door leading into an adjoining bathroom. I laughed over my reflection in that glass for it made me, dressed in layered, masculine, woolen clothing, look like a stuffed boy.

Joe was away to the mine before I woke in the morning. He left me a note suggesting I enjoy a hot bath, not possible on former trails we had followed, and a leisurely day with Mrs. Brooks. He also left data about the Engineer Mine and its storied past which I decided to read before breakfast and from which I summarized interesting facts.

The history of the Engineer Mine dated back to discovery of gold on the Tagish lakeshore in 1899 where twelve claims were staked. The original company allowed the claims to lapse and they were relocated and staked in 1908 by Captain James Alexander. Litigation soon started because the old name of Engineer was retained. A lawsuit decided in favour of Captain Alexander and his associates and they were permitted to continue the use of the name. In 1909 the

Aerial view of Atlin on Atlin Lake and, below, the famous
Engineer Mine on Tagish Lake. This northwestern region
of British Columbia is appropriately called "The
Switzerland of North America."

Company began open-cutting and stripping and made enough shipments to more than pay expenses. By 1910 several miners were employed and a stamp mill utilized. Mining was carried on spasmodically for a few years and in 1916 the stock of the Engineer Mine rose to $100 per share on the New York stock exchange and approximately three million ounces of gold and forty-one thousand ounces of silver were mined.

The mine was located on a slope back from the lakeshore, the land forming the footslopes of Engineer Mountain. All around, heavily wooded mountainous country provided pine, fir and spruce for mining and heating. Easy access from Skagway to Carcross was available throughout the year and steamer transport by lake, some seventy miles from Carcross, in the months of June through October. In winter, transportation and freighting was by dog team over frozen Tagish Lake. During spring break-up of lake ice, the mine was completely isolated. Outdoor work for the company stopped when temperatures dipped to forty or fifty below zero. Remoteness of the site did effect employment of miners, many men refusing to take any job there because they didn't like being cut off from the outside for seven months yearly.

I read with increasing interest that there was appreciable silver as well as gold in the ore and that free gold carried in quartz veins characterized it in this historic mine. There was, though, a problem in mining here which kept predictions of results inaccurate. The gold content was erratic, appearing frequently as high grade in pockets, bunches and sometimes in shoots. On the other hand, good values had been obtained in diamond drilling and profit realized from shipping ore and qualified mining men reported the Engineer Mine had not been given a "fair show". I tended to agree with this opinion and began dreaming of a future for it and the re-establishment of a thriving community. The power plant was still in operation and there remained accommodations for some two hundred men, cottages for married miners, spacious quarters for management, warehouses, office building and stores. All had been somewhat neglected during the irregular operation and closure for litigation but could be made habitable again. My optimistic thoughts were interrupted by a knock at the door and the voice of Mrs. Brooks.

"Mrs. Mandy, are you up? The boys caught fish for your breakfast. They can hardly wait for you to come and praise their catch."

The lively young boys, Reggie and Billy, told me of adventures in the north which would give them hero status when in school outside. Mrs. Brooks, a pretty, little and feminine woman frankly said, "I came from Missouri, a city girl, not the pioneer type. I never will be that kind of person. Oh, yes, we have a really nice house to live in with conveniences in this deserted place. But there's no movies, concerts, clubs or even churches to go to. We're so alone. Most of all, I miss having other women around. Wish you could stay here a long time. I suppose the historical Engineer Mine seems romantic to you. It sure isn't to me. I wouldn't go a step into the dirty old mine if you paid me to do it. Of course the mine is our living and it doesn't cost much to be here in summer. Reggie and the boys like this roughing sort of thing. I don't, not one little bit."

I was with Mrs. Brooks and the two children during waking hours for the two days spent at the ghost settlement and saw little of my husband whose examination of the mine was intensive and extensive. My hostess talked constantly and mostly about her childhood in Missouri and the wonderful city of St. Louis. She was delighted I had some happy memories associated with her state. A restful interlude for me and an informative one for Joe ended when Reggie walked us to a cabin down the lakeshore where he kept supplies and mining equipment. From this point he rowed us to the incoming steamer Tutshi en route to Taku Landing. The meadow that framed the cabin was a mass of colour from a plant bearing purplish flowers closely resembling clover blossoms which reminded me of the clover fields in Indiana. Caught up in remembrance, I picked a bouquet of them and couldn't understand why Joe and Reggie smiled broadly when I held out the pretty posies for admiration.

From the deck of the lake steamer we saw a panorama of beauty surrounding us with snow capped mountains on a vast scale, their glaciers, forested slopes and green valleys blended into a magnificent picture of varying colour and contour. We disembarked with a group of tourists from the Tutshi at Taku Landing. There a very little train on a narrow gauge track consisting of a coal-fired steam engine and two coaches waited to carry us across a portage of 2 and ¼ miles to Lake Atlin. Jovial engineer Bill proudly told us, "This here's the shortest railroad in the world. It was built way back in 1898. White Pass and Yukon Railway Company got it in 1900. They've been runnin' it ever since. The locomotive's called 'Duchess'. A right good name, ain't it? Now then, if the load's too heavy for our little engine, I just know you'll all get off and help it along by pushin'. Fare one way's only $2.00. Pay up, if you don't already have tickets and we'll chug along."

The motorship Tarahne waited at the end of the railway to ferry us six miles across Atlin Lake to the town of Atlin. It had been especially designed for sightseers who could view spectacular scenery from a glassed-in observation lounge or wide, open decks. A well educated and much travelled tourist from New Zealand started a conversation with us upon learning we were British Columbians. He expressed enthusiastic praise as we neared Atlin.

"I came here to see for myself if the title in travel brochures, 'Atlin the Beautiful' is merited. Mind you, I'm prejudiced in favour of New Zealand as the loveliest country in the world. In fairness, I must now admit the beauty of the Atlin area in Canada's province of British Columbia cannot be surpassed. I understand this eighty mile Lake Atlin is the largest lake in British Columbia and the water in it is like a mirror. The reflections in the lake are so clear and perfect that one can hardly tell whether he is standing on a deck or a mountain peak. I've read, too, that one of the largest ice fields on the continent of North America is the massive Llewellyn Glacier, extending from the south end of Lake Atlin to Juneau, Alaska, ninety miles long and thirty-five miles wide. The lake and glacier are indeed symbolic of the bigness and grandeur of your northland. I shall certainly encourage friends to come to 'Atlin the Beautiful'. I cannot adequately describe this superb scene to them."

The Alpine setting at an altitude of 2,200 feet of the lake-fronted town of Atlin compared so closely with Swiss settings that travelled tourists lingered to comment on the likeness when the Tarahne docked. Joe and I went on to the Atlin Inn, a large summer hotel owned and operated by the White Pass and Yukon Railway Company. Nature's own green painted on the frame building was accentuated by a white trim, and windows and a wide verandah overlooked Lake Atlin, Atlin Mountain and the range opposite in all their splendour and mystery. Mr. and Mrs. Bill Garrett, a middle-aged couple from the outside, managed the Atlin Inn in a friendly and efficient way. Mrs. Garrett presided at the desk in the lounge and husband Bill combined fellowship among the guests with fishing expeditions to supply grayling and trout for meals. Mrs. Garrett had met Joe the previous year but was not prepared for my appearance and the flowers I was holding.

"You must be Dr. Mandy's little boy," she surmised.

Joe laughed and introduced me. "Boys seldom gather bouquets, but this lad is special and different. At dinner you'll see a transformation into a lovely lady. Evidently you've not heard I was recently married. May I present my wife?"

"Pardon my mistake," replied the embarrassed woman. "She looked like a boy in her masculine get-up walking across the lounge with a big man like you. Now, close up and hat off I can see the boy is a bonny girl. All the best to you love birds. You both look mighty happy. Anything I can do for you, Mrs. Mandy, say the word. I can tell you your flowers don't need water. They'll dry well."

Like clover, aren't they? Do you know their name? I asked.

"Yes, I do. Wild onion. Excuse me for wanting to laugh when I saw you holding them as if they were orchids. Something tells me you and I are going to be great friends, Mrs. Mandy."

The three story Atlin Inn was to be the headquarters for most of our stay in this part of Joe's district. It had comfortably sized rooms, shared bathrooms strategically located, a large dining room bright with light from many windows and a homey lounge in which a huge fireplace of native stone, with antlers above it, supplied warmth on cool evenings. Pressed and framed wild flowers on the wall were the artistic achievement of Martha Louise Black, wife of George Black, the member of Parliament in Ottawa for the Yukon Territory and Speaker of the House of Commons. The spirit of the north dominated the hotel and Atlin town which had a pioneer atmosphere and appearance. On our first evening there, friendly Atliners talked at length to Joe and me as we strolled about, shopped in stores for northern artifacts or discussed the mining which had brought us there. What I learned in these conversations condensed into the following information:

"Our Atlin was built by gold. Goes back to 1898 when Fritz Miller and partner Kenneth McLaren staked claims on a creek they named Pine. We've put a monument in the cemetery to honour the late Fritz Miller. McLaren's still mining. Too bad his pay streak didn't hold out. He's now working for a company near where he and Miller first discovered gold. Atlin was a boom town and thousands were here during the rush. It'll boom again. There's been mining ever since that first gold discovery in '98 and there's still lots of gold in creeks hereabouts. There's Pine, Birch, Otter, Boulder, Fourth of July, McKee, Ruby, Spruce and other creeks for placer mining. Then there's O'Donnell River south of Atlin where gold is found.

"Atlin is a wonderful place to live, pretty as a picture, away from the troubles of the world and everyone here is a good neighbour. Our climate is good, too. We have a long, dry summer and a winter in which below zero temperature can be mighty stimulating. Our gardens grow well and there's plenty of wild fruit to can or make into jelly or jam. Raspberry, black and red currants, gooseberries and blackberries taste fine. Atlin has two churches, St. Martins Anglican and the Catholic, a hospital, a Government Agent and the police. Sometimes we have a doctor in residence and we can always go to the one in Whitehorse, a town in the Yukon not very far away. We could do with better transportation but that will come. Why shouldn't we be proud of Atlin?"

A large building with a tower housed the government office on the ground floor and living quarters in an apartment upstairs for the Government Agent who was also the Mining Recorder and Gold Commissioner. The Agent, Mr. Wright, was a busy man with many responsibilities. He had to record mining claims and assessment work on claims, collect taxes, act as public administrator and magistrate and was authorized to marry and bury people. I met the affable Agent when Joe conferred with him about mining operations to be inspected and the hiring of an old, open Ford touring car owned by the government to carry out his work. I looked at that vehicle doubtfully for it had seen better days. Noisily the car took us to the Atlin Inn from where we would drive each morning on gravel roads to gold bearing creeks fanning out from Atlin.

"First on the agenda," Joe informed me, "is examination of Carl Lykkergard's one man operation. He's exploring an old mine in a bench area of Spruce Creek. Going into a tunnel there will be another adventurous experience for you."

Carl had come to British Columbia from Denmark ten years before our meeting and spoke English quite well. He had a cabin near the entrance of the mine and lived there with his wife and small baby. While he and Joe studied sketch maps and reports, Mrs. Lykkergard drew me aside to talk about the outside and give me a bit of advice.

"You're not going underground, are you?" she asked.

I answered, Yes, I am. I want to learn as much as possible about my husband's work.

"Don't go, Mrs. Mandy. It's terrible dangerous. I'm scared all the time Carl's in that dark, old place."

Carl heard her warning and said, "Don't listen to her. She's what you call a scaredycat, afraid of everything. I've been in that old mine hundreds of times and never got hurt. Proves it's safe, don't it? You'd better put on my extra pair of hip boots, Mrs. Mandy. Your husband and me has carbide lamps on our hats and here's one to fasten on yours. That's good, Dr. Mandy, to give your wife a waterproof jacket. It's wet and cold underground. Have to go slow, so we'd best start."

I followed Carl and Joe into a black cavern feebly lighted by our small lamps. Joe whispered, "Don't talk. Vibrations can dislodge

Lykkergard and Madge at entrance of old Spruce Creek Mine, Atlin.

loose rock and even tumble walls." I waddled in Carl's big boots but found they were needed. Drainage had been lacking in the tunnel for so long that in places we had to wade in water which came up to my knees. Many cave-ins from rotting support timbers made us stoop so low as to be almost crawling and the air became dank and foul the farther we went into the crumbling adit. How long we shuffled at a snail's pace, with the men stopping frequently for examination and notes, I don't know. It seemed hours before we reached a cross-cut where a part of the wall ahead of us fell with a terrifying reverbera-tion. It did not entirely block the passage but Joe whispered. "We must get out." I tried not to think of movies I'd seen where one cave-in was followed by others which prevented an exit. This did flash through my mind as we slowly inched our way to the entrance of the mine. When at last we staggered out, I gulped fresh air and thought the sky and sun had never looked as beautiful as at that moment. Mrs. Lykkergard herded us into a warm cabin for sandwiches and coffee and they revived us.

Soon after our visit to his property, Lykkergard became a lucky man. He took out, from 500 feet below the surface of his placer drifting operation, a gold nugget weighing 43 ounces. It was valued at $1200 in cash and considered worth more as a specimen. Joe and I were in Atlin when Lykkergard came into the town with his find. He let me hold the heavy nugget in my hands and feel the thrill of a prospector who has "struck it rich". I was so glad this optimistic man was rewarded for his hard and dangerous work in an old, abandoned mine. I was also glad I didn't have to enter that mine again to scare both my mind and body. Well, I concluded, gold is hard to locate, hard to get out of the ground or creek and, judging from what I'd seen and heard in mining camps, hard to keep after one has mined it.

Joe headed us toward the creeks early each morning, continuous daylight allowing him to work far into the night and this gave me a chance to meet many miners. One chap I shan't forget was Bill Kennedy, a well read, expressive philosopher. He and a partner had called on a fellow prospector into whose old workings on Pine Creek Joe and I were about to enter with him at eight one evening. After introductions Kennedy declared, "Mrs. Mandy, you don't have to go into that gloomy tunnel. Stay here in the cabin with my pard and me. You'd be doing us an honour. Forgot my manners. Should say, please stay."

Of course I remained with the two men and a coal oil lamp was lighted to brighten the dark log walls of the cabin where we sat. Kennedy talked while his partner made sandwiches of thickly sliced sourdough bread with two inches of cheese between them. Northern hospitality required serving coffee or tea to guests and it was quickly brewed by adding to the beverage still in the pot and soon brought to a boil on the stove heated by wood. It was then I learned why prospector's coffee and tea were so strong and dark. Two pots, either granite or aluminum, were constantly on the stove. The contents boiled and simmered and built up a heavy ring of caffeine in one and of tannic acid plus caffeine in the other. Prospectors worked off the effects of the potent brews but I had to resort to milk for two or three months after a season of drinking their coffee or occasional cup of tea before my system returned to normal.

Conversation was started by Kennedy. "Hear you came from Indiana, Mrs. Mandy. That means you're a Hoosier. I know something about your state and your state poet, James Whitcomb Riley. Why, I've read lots of his poetry. He wrote some mighty fine verse. Where do you think I come from? Same town as the woman who wrote 'Anne of Green Gables'. You've read that book? My, wasn't it funny when Anne dyed her red hair and it turned green? I've got to laugh just thinking on it."

Kennedy stopped talking and laughing heartily rocked back and forth on a box seat slapping his knees. His partner and I laughed too, but not as long as he did. Kennedy was enjoying Anne's predicament so much that it was fully ten minutes before he was calm enough to speak sympathetically about another of Anne's problems.

"Wasn't it sad when Marilla wouldn't let Anne have puffed sleeves? That was a shame, making her feel she didn't fit in with the other girls. Poor Anne. My, my - very, very sad. Brings tears to my eyes," and he wiped away a heavy flow of them with a red bandanna. "Anne spelled with an e was quite a girl. I'll never forget her, not ever."

The prospector related incident after incident in his favourite book, 'Anne of Green Gables' which he had practically memorized from numerous readings. The characters in it were as real to him as if they had actually lived and he shared equally all of their joys, sorrows and achievements. I was trying to down a second cup of extremely strong coffee without choking when Kennedy changed the subject and surprised me with a thought provoking question.

"Do you believe in fatalism?"

I reflected for a moment and answered, No. I believe in a Divine Power stronger and wiser than we are who guides and directs, a God in whom we must have faith and with whom we must co-operate for a happy and successful life.

"You're no fatalist, my girl. I am, for I do believe everything is mapped out for us and we have no choice in the matter. Fate decides when and where we're born, then what we do and how we do it, where we go and when we must leave this earth. I've got me a lot of books on the subject and — here comes your husband. Fate protected him in that old mine he's been checking on. It isn't his time to die yet. I'm glad he's come back to you this night."

McKee Creek was eight miles south of Atlin where a hydraulic operation was in progress under the direction of George Adams. We arrived there one day shortly after lunch and were cordially welcomed by brawny, mining-seasoned George and his matronly, hospitable wife. The property was well equipped with a roomy residence for Mr. and Mrs. Adams, several cabins, a cook house, bunk house, store rooms, carpenter shop, stable, garage and sawmill. As George, Joe and I started off for a survey, a sudden deafening noise sounded. Joe quickly grabbed and threw me face down on the ground and himself over me. Adams hit the ground at the same time and a shower of gravel came flying over, around and on top of us. I lay there surprised and motionless until Joe pulled himself up and lifted me to my feet. Then he shouted angrily to Adams.

"Whoever set off that blast of dynamite didn't shout the required warning. My wife might have been severely hurt or killed and so, George, might we two. That's a serious offense."

George was equally furious and shouted back, "Wait till I get my hands on that - that stupid idiot. He'll pay for this. What an awful thing to happen to you, Mrs. Mandy. I'm taking you right to my house. The wife will look after you."

Making sure I was not injured, the men went off to censure the man who did the blasting and to examine mining results under George's direction. Motherly Mrs. Adams sat me down beside the kitchen stove, my feet on a stool, a cushion at my back and a blanket covering most of me. She soothed shivering me by saying, "My dear, you must have a cup of hot tea. It'll warm you, and I'll cut a piece of this cake I just baked to go with it." I chatted with her drowsily, tired from long days at mining operations and shock from realizing that the unexpected blasting could have taken my life. I could hardly keep my eyes open while trying to eat a little of the delicious supper Joe and I were invited to share with George and his wife. Mrs. Adams was very tactful in what she said when the meal was finished.

"No wonder you're tired. You've got a new husband, a new country and the excitement of things that happen in mining. Dr. Mandy says he'll leave your car here for about a week. During that time he'll examine showings on O'Donnell River. The Murphys will be here this evening to drive you there. You'd better lie down and rest till they come."

By this time I could hardly sit up and staggered when I tried to walk. Understanding Joe carried me to a couch in the living room where I instantly fell asleep. Later, Joe aroused me enough to say goodby to Mr. and Mrs. Adams and assisted me to the Murphy's car. I must have acknowledged introduction to Mrs. Murphy and her son

Melvin but my blinking eyes did not properly see them nor did I hear their response and ensuing conversation. I slept all the way to O'Donnell River where we were housed in the cabin of Herman Muller, a neighbour near the Murphy's. Herman was away but the Murphy family acting as caretakers declared visitors were welcome whether he was there or not. Such hospitality was the unwritten law of the Northwest.

Our temporary log home had three rooms and everything in them was neat, clean and useful. A battered table, old range, essentials for cooking, cutlery, dishes and box chairs were in the kitchen-dining room. The living room had a tiny table, three straight chairs, shelves filled with magazines and books hiding behind a printed cotton curtain, a grizzly bear pelt on the wall, a black bear rug on the floor and a small stove. Joe was pleased about the bedroom and pointed out why.

"Look! The heavy door leading into it will keep mice out. Those little creatures like to scamper about old cabins, but they don't make good roommates. See that half size bed in the room? It has a firm mattress on it. You'll sleep comfortably there and I'll bed down across from it on the little cot with flattened springs."

That arrangement won't work, I said. You're too big to fit on the little cot. At bedtime he found I was right and was disturbed about my being uncomfortable. He should not have worried, for I was so tired I would have slept soundly on a bed of hard, solid rock.

The Murphys were early morning callers and stocky, sentimental Nate Murphy was their spokesman with these words of cheer: "Good morning, folks. Still in honeymoon days, I hear. Found me a wife in Atlin gold rush days, some thirty years ago. Marriage has been great! A happier couple than the Murphys you'll never meet. We've had us the luck of the Irish. May the same good fortune be on the Mandy's trail."

Mrs. Murphy, of Scandinavian ancestry, was of short stature, like her husband, and sturdy build. Her smile welcomed us as she said, "You Mandys is to make yourselves to home in Herman's cabin and in the Murphy's house. Family with us you now are."

Joe mapped out plans for the day — seeing part of Nate's claims that morning and in the afternoon going with him to inspect his entire operation. On following days other prospectors along the O'Donnell River would have his attention. Mrs. Murphy spent most of the morning with me, chatting and showing me how to operate the kitchen range which required wood for fuel. She also filled the woodbox and baked a pan of biscuits to demonstrate her instructions. Joe came back for lunch and Mrs. Murphy reappeared just as we were finishing the meal to say, "Mrs. Mandy, while your man goes off with Nate, you come with me. Nate's got a new tunnel started not far away. Maybe me and you can dig out some nuggets there."

I followed Mrs. Murphy up a steep slope with a young husky named Buller Mahatma, Buller for short, in the lead. It was necessary, I thought, to keep quite a distance between this huge, wolf-like dog and me. Mrs. Murphy had warned he was only friendly with the Murphy family. We puffed our way leisurely to the tunnel but Buller ran ahead to disappear into its darkness, but not for long. There was an agonizing cry as he rushed out and down the slope toward the river. Mrs. Murphy hurried after him shrieking advice to me as she raced away.

"Don't move. Stay right where you are till I get back."

She needn't have told me to remain on the spot. I couldn't have moved for I was frightened into temporary paralysis. There must be a dangerous animal in that tunnel, I thought. Was it a bear, a wolf, a wolverine, a -? Fear blanked out further speculation and I stood motionless for what seemed hours until Mrs. Murphy speeded up the hill to explain her behaviour and that of the husky.

"Mrs. Mandy, what an awful woman I am to scare you half to death! You see, I had to act plenty fast. You know what happen? Buller meets a porcupine in the tunnel. Gets his nose full of quills. If them sharp things don't get took out quick, well, they works up to the heart and kills. Buller ran off to put his nose in cold river water. That helps pain some. Prpich, he's a prospector, sees us and comes to help. I holds on to Buller and Prpich pulls out the quills. Guess my scream was pretty loud. Nate and Dr. Mandy must have heard me because here they come. It's all right now, fellows. Buller and a porky tangled in the drift. Quills is out and you better drive that porcupine away. You Mandy folks'll have supper with the Murphys. Think I'd best start getting it ready. Come to the house with me, Mrs. Mandy. I'll get you hot coffee. That'll settle you down."

The Murphys grew an extensive vegetable garden, raised chickens, canned or made wild berries into jam and cultivated very tall, sturdy rhubarb plants. Joe and I enjoyed their produce in a supper of stewed chicken and dumplings, potatoes, carrots and peas supplemented by a wilderness fireweed salad, homemade bread and rhubarb pie. The crust was so good that I asked, What makes it very flaky?

Mrs. Murphy hesitated before answering, "You're a pioneer kind of girl, so I'll tell you. I renders down bear's grease. Best shortening anywheres. Terrible strong. You use a wee bit and has flaky crust. Another piece of pie? Melvin, you're piggish. That's the third pie slice for you."

Melvin Beckman was Mrs. Murphy's son by a former marriage. His father had died when he was very young and the penniless mother had to find work to support herself and child. She heard of the Atlin mining boom in northwestern British Columbia where there would be jobs and travelled there with her son. Shortly after reaching Atlin, she met Nathan Murphy and their happy marriage had been blessed by a completely compatible relationship between Melvin and Nate. Melvin was a slim, nervously active, boyish looking fellow about thirty-four years old but acted like a teenager because his mother treated him like one. He never sat on a chair except at the dining table, stretching out on a bear rug in the living room when in conversation. He participated equally in Nate's mining of placer gold and all chores necessary in isolated living and said as Joe and I were leaving after supper, "We're going after a moose tomorrow. Then, fresh meat for everybody."

Can you go hunting and get a moose any time you want? I asked skeptically.

"Sure we can. Those critters feed regularly at the same place.

Hunting for one here is like going to a meat market."

The hunting was successful as predicted and a big moose was stored in a cache on stilts adjacent to the Murphy home. From then on during our stay at O'Donnell River, a contribution of moose meat was on the Mandy's menu every day. It was pre-cooked by Mrs. Murphy because I was away with Joe daily and had little time to prepare meals. The continuous summer daylight of the north allowed us to stay in the field until late and many times we did not get back to our cabin until ten or eleven at night. Nate, who was a big game guide as well as a mining man, provided us with horses for transport in this remote area where Joe mapped, surveyed, explored and gave advice to prospectors. No matter how late our return, the Murphys were always on hand to refresh with hot coffee, cookies and tales of pioneering while we ate a belated supper. I laugh heartily every time I recall one of Nate's experiences, as he told it.

"One snowy winter I was out trapping and hunting for meat. Found me a moose and followed it to an Indian cemetery. Up here Indians puts their dead in little houses. By golly, a man was looking at me out of the window of one of them cabins. He had a bushy, black beard and looked fierce. I tell you I was scared and jumped back ten feet, snowshoes and all. I stood still. So did the chap inside. Pretty soon I sneaked back. When I see what's going on, I let out a whoop and most laughed my head off. The fellow I'd seen was me in a looking glass on the wall. Didn't know myself 'cause I'd never seen me with a beard. That bush on my face growed while I was on the trap line and hunting. By George, that chap in the mirror was an ugly looking customer. I've never had me a beard since that day when I almost scared me out of my skin."

Mrs. Murphy told us a funny yarn, what she called true and nice. "I knew a young Indian couple who was to get married. The bride wanted everything to be right, just like what a bride would have in what we northerners call 'the outside'. So, she picked out a white wedding dress from a mail order catalogue and sent off for it. Now then, the bride pictured in the catalogue had a bokay that the girl thought was made from paper. Bless me, if she didn't order paper flowers for her wedding! I wanted to make her a bokay of wild flowers. They're so pretty and don't cost nothing. She said, 'No. Like book. Paper flower.' Guess she had the laugh on me. Her paper posies lasted for years. Wild flowers would have died on her wedding day."

The Murphy family represented the spirit of the north, summed up in a poem nailed above the door of their cozy home:

> The lintel low enough to keep out pomp and pride,
> The threshold high enough to turn deceit aside,
> The doorbands strong enough from robbers to defend,
> The door will open at a touch to every friend.

Each person passing by, in the tradition of the Northwest, was a potential friend and therefore welcomed by the Murphys.

Spruce Creek, the leading gold producer in the Atlin area, had been worked continuously since discovery and in the '20's and '30's attracted the attention of companies. Joe told me one of them was developing a profitable operation which came into being through the ill fated Mitchell Exploration Expedition. Mining promoter Tom

Mitchell had combined samples of gold from around Finlayson River with a charming personality. His prediction of "another Klondike to lead the country out of the Depression" interested Jim Eastman, designer and builder of airplanes in Detroit, Michigan. Eastman was suffering from the market crash of '29 and became so enthusiastic about the possibility of a Klondike deposit of gold, waiting to be staked and mined, that he persuaded owners of the Detroit News to back an exploratory flight to northwestern British Columbia. The newspaper even had headlines, "Second Klondike", ready to accompany an article about the discovery.

Optimistic Eastman guided five Eastman open-cockpit bi-planes to Tulsequah and Atlin, the selected headquarters in the gold field. The Expedition did extensive prospecting and found only colours instead of the bonanza predicted by the promoter who kept saying, "The gold is here and in time we'll find it." A mining engineer had accompanied the flyers and after a disappointing search wrote a report advising against further expenditure of time and money. The disillusioned Detroit backers withdrew their support.

Meanwhile, Eastman and some associates had discovered Atlin was still a promising gold camp. Hand working by old-timers had scraped the surface and left countless nuggets to be mined by more efficient methods. The pilots formed Columbia Development Company which was financed by Kaufman rubber interests of Kitchener, Ontario, and their steam shovel dug into gravel banks on Spruce Creek from which they were producing a profit. Joe and I met the clever Eastman when inspecting his workings and he commented, "The steam shovel is an improvement on hand shovelling isn't it? You've heard how I happened to come here. Things didn't work out as I was led to believe they would. My show isn't a second Klondike but it's good and you couldn't mine in a more beautiful place than Atlin." Mitchell had faded quickly from the scene in the manner of typical promoters. I came across the captivating dreamer three years later, in the Cassiar section of my husband's district, heading another expedition financed by substantial eastern men in the United States. It, too, founded on mere speculation, was soon called off and Mitchell disappeared leaving no address.

Mr. Colpe, a man from California who boasted of having been a classmate of Herbert Hoover at Stanford University, managed another productive mine on Spruce Creek. He looked ready for golf with his plus fours, belted jacket and cap when Joe and I met him in his office at the mine.

"You're on the dot for your appointment, Dr. Mandy," he approved. "I believe you want to look over what I've been doing and write a report about progress. I'll show you everything. This is Mrs. Mandy with you? It's unusual for a wife to accompany her husband in our type of work. Helpful to her, though, in understanding the problems he encounters. You're welcome, Mrs. Mandy, but I can't let you go underground. Walking through the adits is too tiring for a woman and the technical talking in which Dr. Mandy and I will engage would not be interesting to you. Sit down here in the office. You'll find magazines to while away the time and chocolate bars should you feel hungry. When we come back, I'll let you see part of a clean-up."

I not only saw the clean-up but held it in my hands — a pan of gold nuggets worth about $1700. Looking at them, I felt the powerful pull of the metal and recalled the explanation of a prospector's wife when asked why men travel far, exhaust themselves and endure tremendous hardships to find gold. Her answer was, "I asked my prospector husband that question. He said it's because of a clean job, for there's no blood or tears on gold that comes out of the ground or the creeks, and may pay off well." I've often thought of that interpretation and wish all gold seekers could say the same but I've learned that most are motivated by what gold can buy.

Jenny Bender was a colourful character who had set up a laundry business in Atlin's gold rush days, really a front for other activities which included "sporting women". At that time she had staked claims on Wilson Creek and still held them in the '30's. Jenny sent a note to the Atlin Inn for Joe asking him for advice about her "mine". He read the message written on a scrap of brown wrapping paper and said, "We'll call on this Jenny. An interview with her should be interesting." Jenny's apartment was above a barber shop on the main street of Atlin. A huge husky barked and lunged toward us as we neared the building. I could only hope the chain restraining him was strong. The entrance at the back required a climb up a shaky ladder and the crossing of a sloping tin-covered roof between an avenue of boxes to reach her living quarters. Joe knocked four times before an elderly woman opened the door a fraction and peered out.

"You are Jenny Bender?" inquired my husband.

"'Course I be. Who be you?" she asked.

"I'm Dr. Mandy, government mining engineer. You wrote me about your claims on Wilson Creek."

"Why didn't you come alone? Who's that with you?" she demanded.

"My wife. She goes everywhere with me."

"Oh! You can both come in. Hate to have you see my place. Ain't got round to straighten up. Have a seat, Mrs. Mandy."

Jenny removed an old coat and cap from a battered rocker for my seat, cleared a straight chair for Joe and a rickety armchair for herself. While she whined out her problems with mining, I studied her and her surroundings. She had a multiple-lined face with squinting eyes, stringy, gray hair pulled into a tight knot at the back of her head and her clothing was ingenuous. A once white blouse peeped at the neck from a faded, green silk pullover patterned by runners. Her sleeveless dress, made from soiled gunnysacks, was sewn together on the sides to an arm opening and fell to ankle length. The sacks had been rounded at the neck for easy pulling over the head and hemmed with big stitches of white string. Instead of a hem for the skirt, the finish was a deep fringe which Jenny must have considered a stylish touch.

Jenny had much to tell Joe and I half listened as my eyes took an inventory of the long, wide room in which we sat. The ceiling was decorated by tops of boxes with shipping labels on them of well known firms such as Nabob, Swift & Co., Woodward's and Hudson's Bay. Crowded around, higgledy-piggledy, were small tables, a piano, writing desk, double bed, two stoves, cupboard, kindling, small lengths of stove wood, pots, pans, dishes and heaped articles of unrelated junk on chairs and trunks. Clothing hung on a rope attached to the wall from a bedpost. The floor was covered with pieces of carpet, linoleum scraps and gunnysacks and excelsior was scattered all about. The room was dark, with tiny windows at each end. I knew that even if lighted by the three coal oil lamps displayed, it would not be very bright. Overwhelmed by the sight of such living conditions, I began to listen closely to Jenny's complaints.

"Them Wilson Creek claims, theys worth millions. A man comes by this summer as wants them. He looks right nice. But you know what he's a-doin'? Tryin' to make an unfair deal, that's what. Read this here yourself, Dr. Mandy."

Jenny put some papers in my husband's hand and he read the documents carefully. They did not contain anything to support her accusation. Moreover, she had no reports of proven worth or potential of her holdings. The interested stranger was relying on hearsay of value and Joe had to tell her this. She became very angry when he refused to agree that the man was a "crook". Joe was, however, diplomatic in outlining a course for her to follow and the interview ended pleasantly with Jenny praising him and giving advice to me.

"You 'pears to be a right honest man, Dr. Mandy," she declared. "I wants to say this to your wife. Don't do nothin' to lose him."

Joe and I were usually too tired to engage in many social activities after long days at the placer creeks and retired early to bed. Some Atlin residents thought we should have a little recreation and urged us to see the town's highlight of entertainment. This was a silent film shown in a hall owned by druggist C. Pillman whenever the film arrived, slowed by lengthy transportation of coastal steamer, railway and lake boats. The date of presentation was advertised by a boy walking around the town ringing a bell and shouting, "Show at 8:00 o'clock," and word of "Movie tonight" spread in various ways to mining camps nearby.

One Saturday night Joe and I joined a large group of people eager to see the movie and we filled every seat in the hall. Admission was seventy-five cents and the audience sat on folding wooden chairs, some of which buckled under weighty viewers. Projectionist Pillman was not too adept and required several intermissions to adjust the projector and change reels. We Mandys didn't mind these interruptions because the assembled crowd was more entertaining than the picture — rough miners, hopeful prospectors, tradesmen and dressed-up townspeople rubbed shoulders amiably. Actually, the feature of that evening was not the film but a four weeks old baby attending with his proud parents who had recently come to the community. During intervals, when lights were turned on, comments and demands from both men and women echoed through the hall such as:

"My, my, what a sweet baby!"

"I say, let me get hold of him."

"Gosh, such a little feller. Ain't he cute? Pass him over."

"Lay off. I ain't passin' him yet. Had me a youngun' and I likes babies."

"Yes, indeed, quite an adorable baby. What is his name?"
During the evening the tiny tot was handed around the hall to a chorus of "Oh", "Aw", "Gee", and "Ah". After the show, admirers treated "mom" and "pop" to ice cream at Pillman's drug store while their baby son slept peacefully through further admiration in many cuddling arms, tired out from all the "passin'". I don't know what the baby grew up to be but he was the star performer that night, charming an audience into sincere emotional response which kept everyone in it delighted.

An important member of the Atlin community was Corporal Ronald Stewart. When Joe had to consult him about infractions of mining law there, I went along. The Corporal was a big, impressive, stern man whose house combined living quarters, office and jail. He kept prisoners constructively occupied in cleaning the premises daily and to facilitate this chore let them have a key to their cells. At the time of our call, Corporal Stewart was embarrassed by an incident that week which had set the whole town laughing. He was away on official business for a couple of days and was gleefully told on returning that his lone prisoner had cleaned the house and then gone to a local bar to get disgracefully drunk, staggering back to lock himself in his cell. Knowing we would have heard this true story, the Corporal started Joe's interview with a terse comment.

"What happened when I was away won't happen again. I must tell you, too, the prisoner had nothing to do with mining."

An indispensable man in Atlin was the carrier of water from Lake Atlin. Major Neville, a proper English gentleman, was the water man in founding days of the town. He delivered with dogs pulling a tank of water on a sled and later changed to a horse-drawn load, charging five cents a pail to fill cans in which buyers stored the water. Eventually, the Major sold his business to Walter Rasmusson, whom I met in the '30's. Walter started rounds carrying water in a wooden, metal-lined box with a tap at the back. In winters he hauled it in forty-five gallon barrels from which a tap poured the water into galvanized buckets. Three full pails were required to fill a purchaser's container, usually a cleansed gasoline can, and his price rose to ten cents a pail. Cold months necessitated breaking through the ice on the lake, but this did not disturb the water man whose essential deliveries were always welcomed. "I like my work," he told me. "It's a steady job. I'm my own boss and folks smile when I come round. They need me."

Atlin fills a large space in my treasure chest of memories. The town and surrounding area enriched my life with unsurpassable scenic beauty. I also acquired knowledge there about mining in many gold-bearing creeks of boom days and those of the '30's and best of all developed lasting friendships with many courageous and interesting men and women. I hope the inspiriting characteristics of the pioneer founders will continue in the years ahead to bless Historic Atlin the Beautiful.

# THE SCENIC STIKINE RIVER AREA

"You'll love the Stikine River Area. It's a northwestern part of our province called the Cassiar," said Joe as he planned for our trip there.

Another big river? I asked. Do we ford it on horses as we did the flooded Tatshenshini?

"No, my dear. We'll go by coastal steamer to the mouth of the Stikine at Wrangell, Alaska. Then by river boat to Telegraph Creek, crossing the boundary thirty miles upstream into British Columbia. This off the beaten path voyage will take us one hundred and sixty-three miles through spectacular scenery of the Coast Range. The boat can accommodate forty passengers, but I discovered last year that it carries few now. People have little money for travelling in these Depression days. The friendly informality on the river boat is as memorable as the surrounding scenery.

"I must tell you a bit about Wrangell. It is one of the oldest settlements in Alaska, named for Baron Wrangell, governor of the territory in 1830. A minor gold rush from the community started in 1861 when a small amount of gold was found in sand bars of the Stikine River. The first real boom for the town came in 1873 when gold was discovered in the adjoining Cassiar district of British Columbia. The stampede was good for both Canada and the United States, promoting commerce and settlers. Wrangell still has a frontier aspect with board walks and old buildings. The friendliness of those living there is typically pioneer. They'll make you feel you belong among them."

Joe was right. I had an immediate feeling of kinship with the many residents waiting at the wharf to watch the steamer drop anchor in their harbour. A short walk took us to an old, rambling hotel presided over by "sourdough" owners, Mr. and Mrs. Johnny Grant. The proprietor welcomed us with a hearty backslap for Joe and a gripping handshake for me and a very loud greeting.

"Dr. Mandy, great to see you again," and his voice boomed out to include everyone within hearing range. "Didn't think when you was here last year you'd be back with a bride. You've got a tip-top man, Mrs. Mandy, and from the looks of you I'd say he's got a tip-top wife. A fellow slipped up from the boat to tell me you was married and coming here, so I'm prepared. A box of cigars for you, Dr. Mandy, and a box of chocolates for the little lady. You're to have the best room in the hotel. Mrs. Grant will take you to your room and I'll send up your luggage. Get settled, then take a walk around. Folks'll want to meet you. Whatever you want in Wrangell, I'll do my best to get it for you."

Mrs. Grant was a short, dark-skinned, quiet woman. She silently led us up a long flight of stairs to a large, homey room with flowered slip covered chairs and a colourful patchwork quilt on a brass bed. Before leaving us she shyly said, "Me and Johnny — we marry long time. Like we, you be happy. I know."

The lobby of the hotel featured a large bay window overlooking the main street. It was centered by a huge hanging basket from which lovely white blossoms of the Star of Bethlehem plant cascaded to the floor. Everyone passing, both inside and out, gave an appreciative glance at this floral beauty. While stopping to admire it, Joe and I were approached by a tall, thin, white-haired, elderly man with a clerical collar. He extended his hand and spoke to us in a gentle voice.

"Do you remember me, Dr. Mandy? I am Rev. Corser. It was my good fortune to meet you last year. Now it is my privilege to meet your dear wife. I have been told you have recently embarked on the sea of matrimony. May the waters on which you sail be for the most part calm and may you be given strength to withstand inevitable storms through which you must pass. God bless you, my Mandy friends. If I may assist you during your stay in Wrangell, do not hesitate to call upon me. I am always ready to serve."

The minister's good wishes brought brightness to a rainy day and so did the friendly folk of Wrangell who smilingly "hello'd" us when we walked to the office of the Barrington Transportation Company. Joe had time to tell me, "The two brothers you'll meet there are the owners and navigators of the river boats which transport freight and passengers up the Stikine River to Telegraph Creek. Sid is a tall, graying man, tough mentally and physically. His younger brother Hill is stocky, husky and somewhat brusque. They are men of integrity, strong character and very kind, helping everyone along the river. Northerners refer to them as 'straight shooters with warm hearts'. You'll like them."

The Barringtons, seeing us coming, rushed out of their office to meet us. Sid grasped my right hand and Hill the left, the latter expressing the sentiments of both.

"Welcome to Wrangell, Mrs. Mandy. Met Dr. Mandy last summer. Now we find you're smarter than we thought, Dr., you've taken a wife. We've heard she's a Hoosier of pioneer stock from Indiana. That means you've got it in you, Mrs. Mandy, to follow wilderness trails. You couldn't have a better man to do it with than your hubby. We Barringtons are from the state of Washington, spend winters there and summers in the north. Our next river boat sailing is in two days. Sid and I'll get to know you as we go along the river."

I told the brothers about meeting Rev. Corser and his offer of any assistance we might need. This launched Hill into an eulogy of the minister.

"That dear old man! Everybody in Wrangell respects and loves him. You know, he's spent his life doing things for others. He has what the church calls a mission post and is paid a pitiful pittance for his work. Would you believe he's given most of that salary away? That's what he's done. He's old now and has almost no money. I'm right glad to say he's being looked after by the Grants. A non-paying guest he is at their hotel, with all needs supplied. That's only fair. Still, it's a fine thing for the Grants to do. Just shows the real northerner has a heart as big as all outdoors."

While waiting to go up river, we were entertained by several residents of Wrangell and Rev. Corser asked us to attend his Sunday morning service in the First Presbyterian Church, Alaska's oldest Protestant church. We joined a large congregation and were seated in the front row with Mildred, Hill Barrington's wife. The clergyman announced his text, the Beatitudes. Instead of turning to the Bible to read these declarations of the Sermon on the Mount, Rev. Corser began to recite them in a firm voice:

"Blessed are the poor in spirit; for theirs is the kingdom of heaven. Blessed are they that mourn; for they shall be comforted. Blessed are the meek; for they - shall -- inherit the earth. Blessed are they --- blessed are they --- which do hunger and thirst --- after righteousness; for they --- they ---."

A now quavering voice trembled into silence and the minister looked helplessly at his listeners, many of whom were silently mouthing familiar phrases in an effort to help him. Five minutes went by before the fifth Beatitude came to his mind. Remembering was slow but exact words and a strong voice tripped out when he reached the last Beatitude:

"Blessed are ye, when men shall revile you and persecute you falsely for my sake."

Rev. Corser concluded the recital of his text with a comment of relief. "I knew if I stayed with it, God would help me recall every one of those Blesseds, and He did." This man of faith then spoke conversationally, though scholastically, and applied the guidance of his text to daily living. The congregation had not been disturbed by his lapse of memory. He was a thoroughly good man doing his best at an advanced age and was supported by members of his flock with understanding empathy and devotion. At the end of the service, he stood at the door smiling and all who were there stopped to shake his hand. Mildred Barrington summed up the feeling in Wrangell about the minister.

"People remember what Rev. Corser has unselfishly done for so many for so long. We all know he is not only a good but a great man."

The Barringtons operated three boats on the Stikine — Hazel B1, Hazel B2 and Hazel B3, named for Sid's semi-invalid wife. We sailed on the Hazel B1 for a leisurely cruise of one hundred and sixty-three miles to the head of navigation. The only other passengers besides Joe and I were hunters, business men from Wrangell and a shy, middle-aged woman bound for Telegraph Creek to become a housekeeper for a rancher in the vicinity. The boat had a broad deck for walking or reclining in deck chairs to view the loveliness of the Coast Range and winding river. Cabins were large and a round table for dining encouraged togetherness. Jack, the cook, called us to meals by marching around the deck blowing a tune on his whistle and in leisure moments entertained with his accordian.

The Barrington brothers were like hosts at a house party and, though busy piloting, found time to mingle with the passengers. Their colourful career dated back to Klondike gold rush days bucking the Yukon water course from Whitehorse to Dawson. They had learned the hard way to "read rivers" and they skilfully navigated the tortuous, canyoned, sand-barred and rapids-filled Stikine. Boyish Dar Smith competently combined the roles of purser, room steward and dining steward. He gave me a brochure of the Barrington Transportation Company and cited some facts it featured.

"Mrs. Mandy," he informed, "look for the hundred glaciers and canyons you'll be seeing. I know there's that many because I've counted them. No wonder this trip up the Stikine is called rugged glory off the beaten path. It's short but thrilling. Takes four days to get up to Telegraph Creek, as we have to tie up at night when it's too dangerous to run the river, and only one day to come back downstream to Wrangell. The booklet tells you, too, 'The Cassiar is the greatest big game country in North America. We have moose, caribou, mountain sheep, mountain goat, black bear and grizzly here, a sportsman's paradise, and hunters come for them from all over.' Comfortable on the river boat, isn't it? You're travelling civilized and not 'roughing it' like Dr. Mandy says you've been doing."

This is a luxury way to travel in the northern wilderness, I answered. I love it.

"Don't get spoiled," advised Joe. "You'll be on tough trails again."

Progress of the boat was slow while wending its way through channels, riding rapids and dodging shifting sand-bars and snags. The depth of ever-changing water had to be constantly pole-tested, and I never tired of watching Dan, a Stikine Indian, handle this manoeuvre expertly. Dan's knowledge of rivers had been handed down by ancestors wise in the way of the wilds. On constant watch at the prow of the boat, Dan's fingers signalled the depth of the river. High up in the pilot-cabin, Sid or Hill responded by hoisting or lowering a hinged propeller mounted in a tunnel. To me the journey up the Stikine on the flat-bottomed river boat was one of the most enchanting in the Northwest, where time stood still and the quietness in a majestic, mountainous setting was deeply soothing.

For many miles the only sign of habitation was that of prospector's and trapper's cabins and mink, marten and fox farms. Then, suddenly around a bend, after crossing into British Columbia, Clearwater Landing appeared with a large log house on a wide flat high above the river. Hill was at my elbow to say, "I'm taking you Mandys to meet the English settlers here — Fred Hallas, his wife and son Ken. They've lived in different parts of Canada but Fred, well he talks and acts as if he just came over from England, sort of stiff and proper. Mrs. Hallas has changed, as folksy now as all northerners. She does most of the talking, too. Gangplank's up. Follow me."

Hill led us to where the Hallas's were waiting for delivery of freight from the boat. "Howdy!" he called out. "I've brought Dr. and Mrs. Mandy of Prince Rupert to meet you. Show them what you grow here."

The family walked with us to a large, semi-circular plot which was colourful and fragrant from a display of candytuft, pansies, dahlias, summer cypress, sweet peas and nasturtiums plus a number of heavily laden berry bushes — all blending into a background of evergreen and deciduous trees. We saw in an extensive vegetable garden on the right of the flowers, cauliflower, carrots, cabbage, turnips, green beans, spinach, onions and experimental watermelon and peanuts. At the left of the flowers stretched row on row of potato plants almost as tall as my five feet, crowned with enormous white blossoms. I had never seen such a potato patch and asked, Do these extraordinarily tall plants produce big potatoes?

Hill was quick to answer, "You can bet your boots they do. There's some on the boat. Ask Jack to give you a feed of honest-to-goodness spuds. Your Indiana can't grow giant potatoes like these plants do, little lady."

My husband had eaten some of Hallas's potatoes on a trip up the Stikine the previous year and added, "You've never really known the goodness of potatoes until you've eaten some grown by Fred Hallas. I'll tell you the secret of his produce. It's moose manure, hard work and continuous summer daylight."

Look! I exclaimed, pointing to huge, very red strawberries of equally huge ever-bearing plants. They make my mouth water.

Mrs. Hallas laughed appreciatively and took my arm saying, "You and the men come along into the house and have yourselves some strawberry shortcake. I always have cakes ready on boat days when Hill brings visitors. Sure is nice to meet people from the outside. You summer callers gives something to think and talk about during the long winter when we're alone and frozen in. We're here. Dining room and kitchen is all one. Ken, you got that whipped cream ready? The cake will be flat without it."

Whipped cream? I echoed. Do you have a cow?

"No dearie, just tins of condensed milk. We tie a long cord around a can of it and drop it over the river bank. In no time the water chills the milk enough to whip. You need to add lemon juice if you've got a lemon, which we don't often have. Sour berry juice does just as well."

Hill suggested, "While we're eating, Ken, tell the Mandys your wolf story. It's true and one of the best you'll ever hear."

Ken grinned and began, "Well, I grew up in a city. Didn't like school and didn't go far till I quit. Then I come up to my folks who'd taken up a land claim along the Stikine River. Course I didn't know nothing about the north. You know, I'd never thought of killing an animal but right here furs is the only way to make money 'cept for summer vegetables and fruit we sell to Barrington for the river boat. We've got to have cash for things like sugar, flour, tea, coffee and clothes. That's why dad learned me to trap. Two days every winter I cover our trapline across the river.

"My wolf story happened one morning last January. I started out to pick me up my catch. Gosh it was cold — 32 below. The Stikine River was froze solid. Believe me, I didn't walk over. Just sat on the sled and let our husky team pull me. From a ways off, the big animal in the first trap looked like a horse. Great Scot, I thought, a packhorse must have trotted down here from Telegraph Creek and got hisself caught. There'll be the devil to pay if it belongs to old Bill Elder.

"When I come closer, I let out a yell. There with one foot in a trap I'd set under a tree was a whale of a wolf. He was growling and panting, trying hard to get loose. I got real near and he jumped at me. I jumped several feet back. Oh brother, was I ever scared! I knew a mad animal would attack and he was sure mad. I had to kill him. It was either me or him. Couldn't chance his downing me. Besides, he must have had an awful pain and putting him out of his misery was the best thing to do. I had to think quick how I could do it. Didn't have a gun with me. Had to use what I had, an axe. I lifted it to strike the wolf but the darned thing was too short. Looked around and saw the chain on the trap. It was long and that told me what to do. I cut me a five foot pole and used it as a prod to chase the wolf around the tree next the trap till the chain was wrapped tight about the trunk. That held him. He couldn't jump no more. Then I hit his head as hard as I could with the axe handle. I hit fifteen times before he gives up and falls down dead.

"I had to go on to the other traps and found the catch wasn't nothing to brag about — one mink, one weasel and a few squirrels. Then I backtracked the line to pick up the wolf. When I got in sight of him the huskies started yelping. No wonder. The wolf I'd killed wasn't dead! No, he was standing up howling, still chained tight to the tree trunk. I hit him on the head with the axe handle again, thirty times before he fell down. To be sure he was a goner, I poked him with the pole I'd cut. He didn't move, so I loaded him onto the sled, sat on him and rode him home. The ice on the river cracked just as we came to the other side. Lucky me, the dogs ran fast enough to keep us from breaking through.

"I pulled up in front of the window where Mum sat watching for me. She ran to open the door and I shouted, See what I brung? She screamed, 'That wolf's not dead!' Sure he is, I says, I killed him twice. She screamed back, 'He's not dead! He's winking at me. He - he isn't dead.' Darned if she wasn't right. One eye was moving. This scared me and I screeched, Dad, come out here and take over. My dad knew what to do and put the wolf out for good. He was so big and heavy we had to use a block and tackle to hoist him off the sled and up to rafter poles in front of the house. Almost froze our hands skinning him. His pelt measured eight feet one inch from tip to tip when it was fleshed and stretched. They say he's the biggest wolf ever seen in the Stikine River country. Must have been king of the pack. Would you like to see him? I'll bring him out to meet you."

The big wolf was laid across the kitchen bench and I knelt beside him to stroke his thick fur and cuddle his head. He was very beautiful, a creamy white with a broad, black tipped stripe

Ken Hallas and "The King of the Stikine Wolves."

symmetrically extending from head to bushy tail. How powerful he must have been I thought and how sad he could no longer roam throughout his wilderness domain. While I was admiring him, Ken and my husband held a whispered consultation. It ended when Ken laid as much of the huge wolf as possible in my arms. I was surprised and pleased at what he now had to say.

"Mrs. Mandy, I ain't the one for making speeches but your husband wants for me to tell you something. Seems he met you on August tenth heading north. That date will pretty soon be here and he wants a gift for it. He says, because you really enjoy trailing with him up here, my wolf would be the best anniversay present he could give you. I think that's right. I told Dr. Mandy I'd let a city girl, who fits into the North like you do, have the wolf as a gift from me, but he's made me take some cash for it. I hate to part with this 'beaut'. I know, though, you'll take good care of him. Hang him on the wall and tell the story of why what I call King of the Stikine Wolves had to die."

Over coffee Mrs. Hallas enlightened us about her nearest neighbours. "You'll meet the Jacksons coming back downstream. They're on t'other side the river. Jackson's called Groundhoç Jackson 'cause he discovered the Groundhog coal fields. Got lots oi money for his claims, he did, from a German Company. Yes, a down payment with more to come when a mine developed. That foolish man! He got married, took his wife on a trip to California and the sillies spent all their money. They expected a fortune and that didn't happen. World War started and Groundhog never got another cent more from the Germans and our government took over his property. The Jacksons are northerners and they come back to live on the Stikine. They prospect, hunt, trap and don't work very hard. They're good neighbours and the eatinist folks you'd meet up with. Don't know how they get down a case of eggs in two weeks, six to ten at a meal. Sometimes they get up at two in the morning to cook a moose steak.

"You'll meet Charlie Span when you go to Barrington's mine. He lives near there. Charlie's a prospector, fine old man who was in the Klondike gold rush. Must tell you the Christmas story about him. He was to have dinner with us and never showed up. Two days later, neighbour Clarence snowshoed in to find out about him. He wasn't in any trouble. No, he's getting a meal ready. He says to Clarence, 'You're in time to eat Christmas dinner with me. Too cold and too much snow for me to traipse to Hallas's.' 'Why Charlie,' says Clarence, 'Christmas was two days ago.' 'Can't be,' says Charlie. 'I marks off the days.' Well, Charlie had counted wrong and lost out two days. That's easy to do when you live alone in wilderness places."

The river boat was a delight and necessity for several Indians and a few white settlers who seemed to materialize out of nowhere when a stop was made for the night. They built glowing campfires on the river bank to help them have a comfortable social time while waiting for the freight carried by the boat. On the fourth day, twelve miles below Telegraph Creek the boat passed by Glenora and Dar Smith rounded up passengers to tell us about the deserted site.

"I'll bet," he began, "few people know that in '98 Glenora was a boom town. It was the administrative centre of this big, northern wilderness part of British Columbia called Cassiar which is drained by three great rivers — the Stikine, Dease and Liard. There were fifteen to twenty buildings here with ever so many tents of hundreds passing through on their way to the Klondike. The Cassiar Central Railway had plans to start a rail line at Glenora which would connect with Dawson in the Yukon Territory. After the gold rush ended, tight money and the World War stopped construction. There's nothing here now except a few miles of grading for a track. The place looks like a moose pasture. The whole north would be different today if that railroad had gone through. Well, as the poet Whittier wrote in a poem I had to study in high school, 'Of all sad words of tongue or pen, the saddest are these — it might have been.' I'll fill you in on more history when we're pulling into Telegraph Creek."

Two rapids had to be navigated between Glenora and Telegraph Creek. The worst of the two was Little Canyon, where the river narrowed to one hundred and fifty feet between granite walls. I remarked to Dar as we approached the little village of Telegraph Creek, It looks like the picture of a frontier settlement in a book.

"You're right," he replied. "I'll tell you why it happens to be located just here. There's two reasons. It's the head of navigation on the Stikine River and the centre of several Indian communities. Those factors made it the Western Union Telegraph Surveys headquarters for Cassiar back in 1866 - 1877. The company was constructing a transcontinental line which would go through British Columbia, Alaska, across Bering Strait and on to Europe and Great Britain. Those telegraph line men were real toughies. They had to be to slash and tramp through this mountainous land. I'm sure they started swearing when the project had to stop, all because the Atlantic cable was laid and their telegraph line wasn't needed. Most of those fellows stayed in the north to help develop the country in other ways."

Why is the village named Telegraph Creek? I wanted to know.

"That's easy to figure," he explained. "A little creek flows into the Stikine at this point and the telegraph men headquartered here. The name of Telegraph Creek fitted. The river, you can see, is wide now, four hundred and fifty feet across in a gorge between high mountains. Look up at that steep hillside. Not a likely place for living, is it? The hill had to be terraced before the double row of houses and buildings could be put on it. Telegraph Creek is small and away from the world but it has a constable, an Indian Agent and, like Atlin, a man who is Gold Commissioner, Magistrate and Government Agent. You'll find here the historic Hudson's Bay Post and its adjoining hotel, Anglican and Catholic churches. Hear me being called to help unload freight? I'm off and I say have yourself exciting fun in the Cassiar and I'll see you when you come back down the Stikine."

Most of the village's population comprising whites, Indians, two Chinese and big, handsome huskies, had gathered for the great event of the river boat's arrival. I was somewhat embarrassed by the group's penetrating stares in appraisement of the government engineer's wife. Joe and I immediately started to climb steep and shaky steps leading to the street above when we were halted by a shout.

"Hey, stop! Go the long way up by the path. There's a hornet's nest under the stairway."

We almost fell down hurrying to distance ourselves from the hornets. The shouting man had collected our luggage and joined us talking loudly as we walked.

"Nice to have you back in the Cassiar, Dr. Mandy. Prospectors here need your help. By golly, getting yourself married was a surprise. My name's Joe Morrison, Mrs. Mandy. Say, you're a little lady, not the big, husky gal I thought you'd be. Hear tell you take to the trail same as the bush man your husband does. Come along to the hotel and meet Mrs. Morrison. Between us, we run it, right next door to the Hudson's Bay Post."

Mrs. Morrison was a rather faded but vivacious blonde who shook my hand with a squeeze and spoke softly.

"Mrs. Mandy, Ahm glad you cum. Youall are maghty welcome."

You're from Texas, aren't you? I asked. She answered me with a question.

"Mah goodness. How youall know Ahm from Texas?"

Because I lived in Dallas for a year and recognize Texas speech.

Mrs. Morrison gave me a hearty hug and babbled, "How much Ahm gwine to talk to youall, honey! Not many folks lives heah and we gets fed up with ouhselves shut in by ace and snow in wintah. Maghty nice to see sumbudy from outside. Why, youall havin' lived in Texas, you'll be lak a sistah."

Joe was off after lunch to interview Indian Agent Harper Reed about Indian mining claims and took me with him for the conference. I learned that Joe knew him from official correspondence and personal contact the previous year. Harper was an Englishman (a gentleman of the old school), had served in the army during the World War, was well educated and had a high and idealistic standard of behaviour. He had the reputation in the Cassiar of being a superman in the bush, travelling with dog team in winter and on boat and packhorses in summer. Indians and whites respected him as a man of character and as an efficient Indian Agent.

Suddenly Joe stopped and whispered, "We've come at an inopportune time. I see Harper is busy with a necessary chore. Let's call anyway."

The cultured gentleman was bending over a galvanized tub in front of a fairly large residence and office building. He was so engrossed in vigorously soaping and rubbing heavy underwear on a washboard that he did not see us until he heard Joe's voice and looked up.

"Harper, I'm here to discuss mining with you. I've brought my wife along. Meet Mrs. Mandy."

Harper straightened, smiled, bowed and declared, "It is indeed an honour to meet you, Mrs. Mandy. I congratulate you on your marriage, Dr. Mandy. Looking upon the bride, I must say you are a very fortunate man. I wish for you both many years of marital bliss."

I have something to tell you, Mr. Reed, I said. The wedding gift you sent us is unique. I had never seen a smoked moose skin before. The floral designs embroidered on it, I understand, were the handwork of Indian girls under the direction of the Anglican minister's wife at Telegraph Creek. It attracts everyone who sees it hanging on a wall in our home. Thank you for a present so fitting for two who love the north. Sorry we interrupted your chore. Go ahead and finish."

Harper, with great dignity, continued with the washing and at the same time gave me some advice. I can still remember what he said and I can hear him speaking in his formal way.

"Mrs. Mandy, you are a bride and cannot be expected to have much knowledge of laundry. For your guidance, I must tell you of something important regarding that necessity which I have learned from experience. This is a delicate subject to discuss with a lady but, as the wife of a man who must travel in the wilderness, you will have the problem of cleansing his underwear. Woolen garments, commonly known as longjohns, require much soap in their washing. Do not rinse out all the soap for they will wear longer when some is retained by the material from which they are made. It would be wise to remember this when you attend to Dr. Mandy's woolens."

After the men concluded their mining conference, Harper announced, "We shall now have tea and English biscuits, Peak Frean, which I recommend as the best on the market. Mrs. Mandy, I have learned that your husband will be occupied tomorrow outfitting for a journey into the hinterland and that leaves you alone. Consequently, I should like to help you pass some of that solitary time in mutually rewarding conversation. You are, therefore, invited to come here for tea at three o'clock tomorrow afternoon. You will be accompanied by Mrs. Morrison to insure our meeting is perfectly proper."

I accepted the invitation and was amused and yet impressed by the note he sent to Mrs. Morrison, which she read to me. "Will you kindly bake an especially desirable cake for a tea at three tomorrow afternoon in my residence when you and Mrs. Mandy will be my guests? I shall pay whatever price you ask for doing so. Thank you in anticipation of a very pleasant afternoon." The tea party was pleasurable and informative as Harper was a gifted raconteur and his stories of happenings in the wide district he covered were preparation for what I might meet in future days. I admired his doorbell, the like of which hung on horse's necks in the Squaw Creek and Atlin areas. He took a duplicate bell from a shelf and pressed it into my hands. "Please," he requested, "place this in your collection of northern curios. It was once the property of a now defunct mining company headquartered at Telegraph Creek."

Joe set off soon for the Dease Lake country, leaving me at the Telegraph Creek hotel because of an especially tiring trail he must follow. Through Mrs. Morrison I met several local residents. All were courageous examples of pioneering and eager to hear about the world outside, though assuring me they did not want to live in it again. Mrs. Morrison talked to me continually and fed me so well that my clothes became uncomfortably tight. The river boat arrived at the end of my second week in the village. Among the passengers were Mr. Murdoch, a wealthy Wall Street broker, and his wife. The typical, socialite easterners had arrived to hunt big game. Their interest was in acquiring antlers of moose, caribou and mountain sheep. They asked numerous questions about my wilderness travel and invited me to accompany them the following day to Dease Lake, from which point they would start hunting. I happily agreed to go along as my husband was scheduled to be at the lake on that date.

We travelled in Joe Morrison's creaky, old, open touring car. Morrison said we were driving on the Dease Lake trail of 1874 which, with some re-location, had become a road. What a rough road it was! Joe had told me it was in poor condition as the government couldn't afford much for upkeep. He and fellow travellers, during the previous rainy year, had to reconstruct it so often that three days were required to go seventy-two miles. I was glad a dry season cut the time to one day for the Murdochs and me. The couple were not used to being jolted up and down, through and across deep ruts and loudly insisted, "Such a condition should not be tolerated."

At noon Morrison stopped at a camp he maintained for supplies of gas and oil. An old Indian couple in charge brewed tea for the four of us and we hungrily ate a lunch of sandwiches and cake prepared by Mrs. Morrison. The New Yorkers snapped many pictures and I suggested they take one of moose meat strips drying in the sun while laid across and suspended from horizontal poles supported by vertical poles at each end. This was an example of Indian food preservation. Mrs. Murdoch's eyebrows went up and her aristocratic nose registered disgust as she exclaimed, "Oh, no! Those strips look like dirty stockings. I couldn't show a picture like that to my friends in New York."

Morrison was adept at driving on the old trail road which clung to the hillside above the Great Canyon of the Stikine and then climbed until it reached a high plateau before crossing the divide and descending to the level of Dease Lake. I jumped quickly out of the car when we reached our destination saying cheerily to the Murdochs, Thanks for bringing me here to meet my husband. I know he'll want to make your acquaintance. Then I tripped forward a few steps and stopped in disturbing astonishment. There was no settlement at Dease Lake Landing, only a lonely Hudson's Bay Post with adjoining factor's house, two small cabins which I later learned belonged to nomad Indians and there was no husband. Where was Joe, I silently asked and where was I to find shelter? Before I had time to seriously worry about the situation, a tall, smiling young man came out of the Hudson's Bay Post. His was the leisurely stride of the north where the pace of everything was slow, but what he said was characteristic of northern friendliness.

"Mrs. Mandy, how nice you could come to Dease Lake. I've been expecting you to arrive at about this time."

Surprised, I asked, How did you know I was coming?

"My radio keeps me in touch with the constable at Telegraph Creek. He reported you were on your way with big game hunters. Oh, I should tell you I'm William Crisp, Hudson's Bay factor at the Company's Post here. I saw your husband off to some of our gold creeks. This is the day he hoped to get back to Dease Landing. Don't you worry none because he hasn't. A man can't have an exact schedule in the wilds as he can in an office, a factory or a school. While you wait for Dr. Mandy's return, my wife Jean and I will look after you. Come into the house and we'll arrange for your stay."

I followed Crisp to meet pretty Jean, a very feminine woman who, though much younger, reminded me of Mrs. Muncaster on Squaw Creek — fragile in appearance but with great strength of character. The living room of the Crisp's home had ruffled curtains at the windows and grizzly bear rugs on the floor. Shelves were filled with books to help happily pass long months of snowed-in winter. The radio kept them in touch with the outside world and they shared living quarters with Wendy, a little, black bear dog prized by Tahltan

Indians. Wendy mothered another occupant, Dinah the cat, and they all lived together in complete contentment.

Crisp told me enough about him and Jean to assure me we were akin. "Jean and I were city folks like you, Mrs. Mandy, but I was born at Dawson in the Klondike. I grew up in Vancouver and always remembered the north was in my blood. So, I spent three years as radio operator on a schooner in the Arctic, a wonderful experience. Now I enjoy keeping shop for the Hudson's Bay Company at this isolated Post. Customers are Indians, prospectors, trappers and hunters. What I learn from them could fill a book. Jean and I both love the peace and beauty of the Cassiar and — here I am gabbing away when I should be getting you settled in our tent next door. That's your temporary home and you'll board with us. Hello, who's at the door?"

The visitor was George Ball, big game guide and outfitter for the Murdochs. He came in and stayed just long enough to tell me, "The New Yorkers, 'lowin' they brung you here, wants you to come to their tent for supper. They says dinner. Half an hour, it's ready."

I wondered as I walked a few feet away to join the hunters, if Mrs. Murdoch dressed formally for dinner in this wilderness setting. Even if she didn't, I smiled over the contrast between her expensive, tailor-made riding habit and my bush clothes. Their tent was very large, half for sleeping on folding cots with mattresses and the other half for dining at a long, folding table while seated on sturdy, folding chairs. I did not see a portable bathtub but it must have been in the camp. The cook for the expedition had set the table with a white linen cloth and silver cutlery and the dinner he served was excellent. I tried to picture my host and hostess throwing sleeping bags on the hard ground and cooking over a campfire beset by hordes of mosquitoes and other insects and couldn't. Yet, Mrs. Murdoch kept saying, "Oh what fun it is to rough it!"

After dinner we sat on cushions around a campfire while Ball described the terrain where the hunt would take place. His wrangler was asked why he was living in the Cassiar and his reply had us laughing.

"Ah wuz a cowboy. Cum up heah from Texas yeahs ago. When the fust chilly days nigh frize me, Ah dun tole mah padnah to git anotha. I wuz goin' back to the wahm, sunny south. He sez wait till he looks roun' sum moah. The snow cum an' Ah couldn't git out. Ah've been heah evah sence."

I happily spent the time waiting for Joe by watching colourful, northern lights at night, chatting with the Crisps and hiking with the little bear dog Wendy and a roaming, friendly, half-husky Jimmy. Coming back from one ramble, I met a lanky, grizzled prospector sitting on a log by the lake. He asked me to stop and have "a bit of talkin'." I sat beside him and listened to an interesting and informative monologue about life in the Cassiar.

"Crisp told me 'bout you, Mrs. Mandy. Met your husband last year. Good man that. Knows what's what an does his darndest to help prospectors. Name's Dan Kean an' I'm an old-timer. I come here from Ontario in 1918. Great country this Cassiar, but pioneer livin' an' that means tough times. Summers is plenty good. Winters is turrible.

You'll know what I means when I tells you some things what happens to me.

"One winter I'm comin' round a bend in lots of snow an' I meets a moose. The big bull rushes me. He knocks me clean off my feet, hurts my side an' makes my head bleed. Then he has to stop, caught up in a hold 'twixt two trees. The hand of God was protectin' a shorn lamb, maybe. Yessiree, that moose is held long 'nough for me to shoot him. Couldn't rightly see with blood comin' down in my eyes but I hits him in the head an' side. Knows I got him. Ain't takin' no chances though. I hobbles up an gives him three shots in the back of the neck. Then I goes to my cabin an' lays on my bunk for ten days, stiff an' sore.

Madge and old prospector Dan Kean at Dease Lake Landing.

"That tangle with the moose takes only a few minutes. Worser was the time a big boulder rolls down an' strikes my leg. Knowed it was broke, binds it up best I could an' starts crawlin'. Three days I crawls over ice and snow, stoppin' to build a fire once in awhile. Only food I has is linin' of my boots to chew on. Marion from Telegraph Creek comes 'long an' saves my life. He's travellin' with his dog team, missus an' kids on the sled. They takes me to my cabin an' fixes my leg. Too late to set it proper, so I limp. 'Spose I allus will.

"When I kills my last moose, has to stand all day in water to dress it. Plenty tired I goes home to sleep. Back next mornin' an' finds a bear has et a lot of the meat an' spoiled the rest. More bad luck is on the way. I'd loaded me a raft with grub an' prospectin' gear. The thing lets loose an' floats down river. Whatever's on it is washed off. This happens after I has a bout of 'flu. All of them things I'm tellin' you don't worry me none. I'll be all right soon's I get cash owed me for gold turned in at Telegraph Creek. That'll buy me grub and new tools. Got to get goin' now. Sure pleased to meet you, Ma'am."

Old Dan shook hands and limped off on a lone trail. Another old-timer sunning himself on the lakeshore said to me, "Dan's worse off than me. Old fellow lived on rabbit all winter and got scurvy something fierce. Dan's a real man, lady."

Joe's guide, Al Ritchie, came ahead of him on the afternoon of his return to Dease Lake Landing. Al said they'd been delayed when his horse was mired in a swamp and injured a thigh. Al then had to walk and lead the horse on the rest of the trail. Joe had lingered to examine claims but came along shortly after. Seeing me he hallooed, "Madge, you're here!" The joy in his voice and in my heart sent me running to meet him. Upon dismounting, he gave me a vigorous hug and then turned to help old Bill Elder off his horse. Later Joe told me about his trail companion.

"The man is so crippled by rheumatism he can't get on or off a horse without some assistance. I was riding one of his horses. Bill has several packhorses and insists on accompanying all who hire them. He is a cantankerous hindrance on the trail and an embarrassment to Cassiar settlers because he has debts which will never be paid and depends mostly on the Indians to support him. The chap is no longer an honest, commendable pioneer and should be sent back to Texas."

The following day Joe and I were taken by Al Ritchie in a small boat with a kicker along Dease Lake for consultations with prospectors. It was interesting to hear from talkative Al that the Lake and its Dease River outlet were named for Peter Warren Dease, an explorer of the Cassiar in 1837. We stopped at Porter Landing and asked Al to come back for us there in the afternoon. Joe told me we were in a ghost settlement, the site of a Hudson's Bay Post in the rush of the 1870's. Gold was mined extensively then on Thibert and Dease Creeks which flowed into Dease Lake. The thriving mining centre had dwindled to a few old-timers living off the land and on dreams of the golden past. We met them hobnobbing with Billy Noel in his cabin, a man nicknamed "Pea Soup". The men showed us a few gold nuggets and Joe advised them for a couple of hours during which we were served cheese sandwiches and boiled coffee.

We then set off hiking on a one mile trail through the bush to meet Joe Jackson who was also called "The Millionaire Kid". Does he really have millions? I asked. Joe replied, "He has them in his promoter's dreams." The prospector-promoter saw us coming and strutted forward to slap Joe on the back and shake my hand.

"Dr. Mandy," he assured, "Am I ever glad to see you? Of course I am. I was forewarned of your call. Everything is ready for your inspection. And Mrs. Mandy, I do welcome you, the first lady to visit my camp. You must be tired. That trail you walked is not like the smooth pavement of the city. Do sit down," and he waved me to a stump seat as if it were a gilded throne. "You rest, dear lady. Dr. Mandy and I will study my hydraulic operation and gold recovery machine which must be very good because it cost a thousand dollars. Help yourself to coffee and biscuits in the cook tent. For entertainment you'll find there a stack of western magazines. Come along, Dr., and see the best mining show ever."

Left alone I read Jackson's promotional brochure which Joe had given me. I even memorized some generalizations such as, "Mining has transformed more poor men into millionaires and raised them to positions of honour and trust than any other business. Eliminate mining and you wipe out civilization. Extensive mining should do more to return prosperity to this country and the world than any other industry and those who participate in that industry should reap far the greater profits."

Reading on I learned the Three J's Placer Mines Ltd. had a lease on approximately eighty acres of placer ground. It had been prospected in 1932 and the drill holes showed promising gold recovery. Of course better results were expected in the present year of 1934. Joe Jackson was depicted as a successful miner who had discovered rich deposits of silver in Alaska and lead and copper in British Columbia.

He encouraged speculation in his company by stating optimistically, "I've never seen better looking claims than these on Thibert Creek." His prospectus glowed with optimism and this combined with his outgoing personality assured purchase of company shares by those ignorant of mining reality and the unreality of promoter's promises.

Joe and I relished a stick-to-the-ribs supper with the enthusiastic Jackson and his miners before hiking back to Porter Landing. We found Al Ritchie drinking tea with "Pea Soup" and deep in discussion about a possible gold rush to a nearby creek. He told us there was plenty of time to stop at prospector's Blick's place to give him needed advice about his placer mining on Dease Creek. Mr. Blick was an affable man who shook hands with us and immediately started off with Joe to have a look at his operation. His friendly wife took my hand and squeezed it before expressing her delight at having me there.

"My, my," she said, "You just can't know how nice it is to have a woman visit me. The Cassiar has mostly men. Come along. My old man shows gold. Me, well, I got something better to show."

I followed plump Mrs. Blick on an inspection tour of her flower and vegetable garden which presented vivid colours against a background of trees. Then we went into her three-room log cabin, starkly outlined as a lone habitation in the forest. She brought out vari-coloured aprons of her own design and proudly turned my attention to a patchwork quilt drawn up on a frame stretched across the ceiling of the living-dining-kitchen room.

"See," she said, "my quilt's almost finished. Them pulleys drop it when I wants to add more squares. Blick's right handy fixing things like that for me. Ain't it downright pretty?"

I sat down and stared upward at a startling brightness and disharmony in the composition above. The quilt blocks were in brilliant and harsh tones of red, yellow, green, purple and magenta which formed a background for floral and geometric patterns printed in black or brown. They had been ordered from a mail order catalogue and surely must have been cut from material impossible to sell to the general public. Mrs. Blick beamed with honest pride and pleasure as she looked at her handwork and her face showed that what was garish to me looked beautiful to her. With empathy I could see the unblending colours fuse prettily to brighten the dark brown of her cabin's log walls, especially in the long shut-in days of winter.

A magnificent Star of Bethlehem plant, in a large pot, stood on a roughly hewn table in the tiny parlour of the Blick home. The white flowers on it descended almost to the floor and Mrs. Blick looked at the beauteous blossoms triumphantly. They were her constant joy and she spoke of them with reverent affection.

"The stars in the sky ain't any prettier than them posies. When it gets right cold in winter, I set up nights with them. Have to keep piling wood on the fire to keep the room warm. Darsn't take chances on a freeze. I think I'd plumb die if that plant died. The Star of Bethlehem means more to me than gold. Bet you wonder how we settlers can stand what the outside calls isolation. Don't you believe we're loners. We're not alone. Got good neighbours in deer, moose and other animals and friendly prospectors, trappers and Indians pass by from time to time. 'Course it's a hard life. I'm up at six every morning and I works till midnight 'cause there's so much to do. But there's so much to learn, so much to see, so much to think about and so much to laugh about. Goodness me, I likes living in the Cassiar."

Al Ritchie commented as he sped us back in his boat to Dease Landing, "You've seen what kind of person Mrs. Blick is. She makes everyone who meets her feel good. Wonderful woman! She's right for the north."

A good night's rest prepared us for enduring that terrible Dease Lake road of potholes. Chris, an Indian employee of Morrison, had come to drive us back to Telegraph Creek. We were hungry on arrival at nine in the evening and the dinner kept for us in the warmer was eaten with gusto. We were also tired and dirty and wanted the refreshment of a hot bath. Mrs. Morrison thought there would be enough hot water for two in the tank connected with the kitchen range. The water was heated by a wood fire which had almost gone out and no more fuel would be added that night.

My husband insisted I bathe first and I gratefully went into the kitchen where the bath facility was located. The tub, in a corner next the stove, was partitioned from the room by a thin wallboard which stopped a few inches from the ceiling. This cubby-hole was entered by a narrow door and was just big enough to house the tub and a narrow aisle beside it. As I turned on the water, I heard the sound of something pushed against the door. It was apparently a chair with someone plumping down on it. This surprising happening was followed by the voice of Mrs. Morrison.

"Ah thought, honey, we'd bettah get in all the talkin' we can, 'cause youall go down the rivah maghty soon."

Mrs. Morrison's voice was soft and low and her conversation mostly a monologue. It was only necessary for me to say Yes, or No or Really occasionally but I had to keep the tap at a mere trickle in order to hear her. To get enough water to bathe in, during which time the temperature of the water dropped from hot to lukewarm to cold, took an hour. By then Mrs. Morrison was tired and said goodnight. I emerged from the bath exhausted, yet elated in spirit like a Boy Scout after a good deed, and dragged myself upstairs to the bedroom. My husband was dozing on a mattress which was an uncomfortable, pulpy mass of sagging lumps from the many heavily clothed and booted men who had thrown themselves and their packs on it through the years.

"What took you so long?" he asked sleepily.

Mrs. Morrison was talking to me.

"Was she taking a bath too?"

No, but she was sitting beside the bathroom door talking to me. I could only hear her when the water was barely turned on and she sat there a long, long time. Why did I listen to her? To do anything else would have been unkind. She desperately needed to pour out frustrations and hopeful dreams. I had to let her do it. Sorry you've had to wait so long for your bath.

Joe sat up and sympathized. "Poor dear," he observed, "she must not have a kindred soul in this pioneer village and found one in you. Of course your bath wasn't refreshing but it is one you'll always remember. I don't doubt you've helped a lonely woman more than you'll ever know. Do you think Mrs. Morrison will talk to me while I have my bath?"

She won't, I replied. Like most pioneer women she hungers for talk with women from the world she no longer knows. Men don't interest her at all. How's that for your male ego?"

A message was waiting us from the local priest. He requested a call for an examination of ore samples brought to him by Indian parishioners. Joe and I went to his home and, after mining discussion, Father Allard served us tea and biscuits. Joe asked if his native church members became good Catholics. Yes, he assured, though in the remote Cassiar their culture made it difficult for them to completely understand Catholicism. Many Indians in his district knew only their own language and translation of the Bible to them was not easy. However, he stressed the fact that he taught the essence of religion, "Do unto others as you would have others do unto you." We commended the dedicated priest for his beneficial work among the Indians and wished him many more years of inspiring instruction and service in the Cassiar.

The next day Joe hired Morrison to take us in a small boat down the Stikine River to Clearwater Landing. I huddled in a sleeping bag since it was cold so close to the water. I could not only see swirling rapids but feel chilling spray and quivered with apprehension of possibly being thrown out of the boat when roughly tossed about. What a relief to arrive at our destination and enjoy a reunion with the Hallas family! Mrs. Hallas warmed us by the kitchen stove and hot coffee and then prepared a meal for us of moose mulligan, fresh garden vegetables and rhubarb pie. Our next stop was to be at the Barrington mining operation on the north fork of the Chutine River and Mr. Hallas agreed to drive us there in his old Ford truck. As we rattled away Mrs. Hallas called out. "Dr. Mandy, that little wife of yours fits into the north. Why, she's already proved herself a pioneer!" Her praise was heartwarming. Perhaps I was becoming the "trooper" my husband expected me to be and my dream of being a part of the north was close to reality.

The road on which Hallas drove us was like a rough bush trail and the delapidated truck carrying us moved so slowly that we could have made better time walking. Several times Joe and I had to wait hopefully beside the truck when the motor threatened to fall out, but Fred Hallas tinkered it into temporary stability. Tired and sore from jolting, we finally reached the camp around nine in the evening. Sid Barrington was there, having taken leave from the river boat for a few days to supervise mining. He knew we must be hungry and insisted on cooking supper for us. The cooking role had been forced on him when the camp cook had suddenly left three days before.

Sid laughingly admitted, "I'm the world's worst cook. The miners here groan when I dish up what isn't fit for man or beast. How would bacon and eggs suit you?"

The arrival of guests caused Sid to seek competent kitchen help. That night he called on a neighbouring prospector and begged him to take the cooking job. Charlie Span, about whom Mrs. Hallas had told us, wasn't really interested but decided a lady visitor deserved decent meals. The man was a loner who lived by a rigid schedule in an ultra-tidy cabin. He moved into the camp cookhouse, carefully planned meals a week in advance and laid down rules of punctuality and no extra service. Joe and I ate with him and Sid after the miners had finished eating in order to linger over discussions of mining problems.

Charlie sat beside me at the table and gave me unwanted second helpings. He considered his rice pudding a gastronomic achievement on his first day in camp and described it as "a very good pudding with raisins, currants, spice and bear's grease in it, prepared especially for you, Mrs. Mandy." The pudding was served hot and I eyed it with averson, seeing the inch of liquid grease on top. Oh, Charlie, I gasped, I've eaten much more than usual. You're kind to make me this special pudding, but I don't think I can eat more than a spoonful. Charlie thought I should have a liberal portion and heaped a bowl with the pudding topped by hot grease "to make it more flavoursome."

Fortunately, I was able to conceal my dislike and ate all Charlie spooned out for me. He was delighted and said, "Have some more," giving me a duplicate serving. I could do no less than make him happy by forcing myself to consume it. Charlie concocted the same pudding each day of the week I was in the camp and I downed two bowls of it daily. I never told him I hated grease of any kind and the hot, oily substance of his specialty gave me a severe stomachache. After many years I can still say Charlie's rice pudding was the most outstanding dessert of my life.

Joe and I were certainly comfortable in Barrington's camp. We were provided with a floored tent and smiled at Sid's apology for "rough" accommodations. It was downright luxury to have two cots with mattresses, a small stove to warm us on chilly nights and a basin of hot water placed at the entrance of our tent in the mornings. The outhouse was deluxe, the only one I had ever seen furnished with a lighting fixture. The coal oil lamp, attached to the wall, brightened a small room enough to easily read magazines piled on the floor. Provision for the welfare of all in camp was apparent. There were roomy tents for the crew and additional sleeping quarters in the cookhouse. Mining was carried on by a large dredge brought in during 1931 and I hoped as much as the Barrington brothers did that the gold recovery from gravel it dug up would yield a profit.

I spent my time in this camp happily watching the dredge at work, typing letters on my portable typewriter, writing notes about the Stikine River area, taking long hikes and chatting with Charlie in his few leisure moments. Charlie reminisced about his days prospecting in the Klondike and spoke well of the dance hall girls in Dawson saying, "They were, using a slang term, straight, and became better wives than a man finds in many other places." Charlie's correctness of speech and excellent vocabulary, like that of many pioneers of his time, came from reading such classics as the novels of Charles Dickens and the Bible. He was observant and had learned much from his wilderness environment and its animal inhabitants, some of which knowledge he shared with me. I especially liked an incident noticed in his ramblings and tell it as he did.

The picturesque Stikine River. Between Wrangell at its mouth and Telegraph Creek were 100 glaciers and mountain valleys.

"One evening at dusk I saw a mountain goat go to a ledge and start climbing a steep cliff. She had a kid with her and he tried to follow but failed each attempt. The mamma goat watched him, wanting him to succeed. Finally, she knew he could not yet climb. Do you know what she did? She came down fifty feet and pushed him up. The father wasn't there to help, off on a rampage I suspect. Mothers in all nature know how to take care of their little ones and they do take care. God bless them."

Barrington's river boat took us back to Telegraph Creek. After tying up, thirty hours would elapse before it sailed downstream to Wrangell. Waiting there was big game hunter, F. Carrington Weems, a Harvard graduate associated with the J. P. Morgan Banking House in New York. He had met Joe the previous year when hunting in the Cassiar and had been informed of Joe's marriage by mutual friend, Indian Agent Harper Reed. Weems conveyed a message from Harper that we and Weems were invited to tea in his home that afternoon. Though from different backgrounds and professions, we all had a common bond in our love for the wilderness which Weems expressed poetically.

"The fascination of the Cassiar is what it proffers in the tranquility of solitude and communion with nature in all its natural beauty. We four are kindred souls and fate is kind to let us meet in this lovely mountainous segment of British Columbia where spiritual thoughts soar to the sky and those of stress, predominant in the outside, fade away."

The Hazel B started downstream with very few aboard. The passengers were three men who had taken the trip upstream from Wrangell for a holiday, a young doctor considering a first year of practice in Telegraph Creek, a French Canadian priest, a Hudson's Bay factor, Carrington Weems, Joe and myself. We left early in the morning but were slowed around noon when the boat struck a sandbar. Later, a strong wind blew the boat off course and the pilot decided to tie up briefly at Jackson Landing where Groundhog Jackson and his wife lived. The couple were watching our approach with lively interest, the river being very low at the Landing.

Groundhog saw me and shouted, "You're Mrs. Mandy, ain't you?

Hallas said you'd be along. Know that man of yours. Been in mountains with him. Right good man he is. Now, don't you be skeered havin' to stop here. The boat can't sink. 'Tain't more'n two or three inches of water 'neath it."

The northern spirit of friendliness prevailed between passengers with the exception of one. Purser Dar Smith told me that the aloof Englishman had lost his job as a Hudson's Bay factor. Apparently his personality clashed with that of Indian shoppers and made dealings with them impossible. I watched the reserved man sit or stand on the deck by himself, so detached he appeared to be living in another world. I tried to converse with him and was answered curtly by five words, "I have been in Patagonia." I met many eccentric types in the Cassiar and he was one of them whose life story I should like to have known.

At the coast we had to wait for a steamer sailing south and were entertained during the delay at homes of hospitable residents in the frontier town of Wrangell. An experience there, in the Bear Totem Store of Walter C. Waters, acquainted me with a true connoisseur of artistic, historical treasure. Walter was an old friend of Joe's, a big, very masculine, florid faced man. As a merchant, he specialized in Indian and Eskimo artifacts, and he carved unique jewelry from mammoth and mastodon ivory tusks found by traders on the Diomede Islands. Walter was looking very depressed on the afternoon we called at his shop.

"What's the matter with you on this sunny day, Walter?" Joe inquired.

"I'm terribly upset," he responded. "This morning I bought a little basket brought in by an old Indian woman who said it had been made by her grandmother. It's been sold."

Why should you be upset about selling your merchandise? I questioned.

There were tears in Walter's eyes when he answered. "That small, finely woven basket was a beauty and a real antique. I'm sure there's not another like it. I put artifacts like that on display with an outrageous price tag on them. If some rich tourist wants to buy anyway, I pretend a marking mistake and put up the price. So, in that way I've been able to keep what I prize. My regular clerks know this practice, but today a new sales girls didn't and sold that basket when I was out to lunch. No. I wouldn't have let anyone have it for any amount of money. I'll never get over losing it, never · never."

On the coastal steamer bound for Prince Rupert, my thoughts travelled back to Wrangell, the Stikine River, Hallas Landing, Telegraph Creek, Dease Lake Landing, Porter Landing, Joe Jackson's camp, the Blick's home, Jackson Landing and the Barrington mining operation. I recalled memorable incidents linked with people I met in those locations. Joe promised a return to deeper penetration of the Cassiar and I looked forward to further exploration there. A constant reminder of that northern sojourn, the King of the Stikine Wolves, is prominently displayed in the Mandy home. The very big and beautiful wolf silently repeats from the wall the story of Ken Hallas's encounter with him in the Scenic Stikine River Area.

# THE HEART OF THE VAST CASSIAR

When Joe asked, "Would you like to go to Atlin again?" I answered, Nothing will please me more.

"Glad to hear you're so fond of Atlin. We'll go there, stop a few days while I examine some workings and then fly to McDame Landing."

As usual when getting ready for a trip to the unknown, I asked, Where's McDame Landing?

"It's near the junction of the Dease and Liard Rivers in the heart of the Cassiar. From this centre we'll trail to Quartz Creek where a pioneer couple are mining. We may have some exciting adventures in that area for you to write your folks about."

Joe found mining development on the creeks near Atlin was quite encouraging. Of special interest to me was a day on Nate Murphy's claims on O'Donnell River. After an examination of mining progress, the hospitable Murphys treated us to a chicken dinner and dessert of blueberry pie with bear's grease crust. Then Mrs. Murphy showed us a collection of gold nuggets, each forming a letter of a partially completed alphabet which she hoped would some day be finished. She promised us the next uniquely shaped nugget found in a clean-up. Her promise was kept when at Christmas we received a greeting from the Murphys. Their card was made from a small, rectangular piece of white paper with a gold nugget resembling a bulging Christmas stocking glued at the top above a penned message — Wishing you a Merry Xmas from "The Murphys". That was the most original and expensive card ever sent to us and I had it framed to treasure through the years.

Joe set a date for flying to McDame Landing saying, "An isolated Hudson's Bay Post is there. Our flight will be with Frank Barr, owner and pilot of North Canada Air Express. I've met an old Atlin prospector who wants to tell us about safety in the air with a man like Frank Barr. Let's call on him and listen to what he has to say."

Said the old-timer, "I want to tell you somethin' about Frank Barr. Frank was in the Yukon flyin' a little biplane. Let's see — that was November of '32. Was gittin' purty dark when he comes down on Wolf Lake near a old cabin. He goes to it after tyin' his plane to a tree stump. Come mornin' an' that plane is upside down in snow. Wind done it, blowun ninety miles a hour. All sorts of damage was done to the plane — wings ripped, propellor tip is off, gas tanks is leakin' an' — don't know 'nuff 'bout planes to tell you all them things that is broke. The wreck don't faze Frank none. No, he jist uses what's 'round for repairin' — axe handle, pieces of old tin cans an' other junk. Bein' winter, they was only four hours of daylight for workin'. Fifty below it was. He most froze his hands, usein' 'em a few minutes at a time. Took six weeks to git that plane flyin'. But he done it. That's one smart flyin' feller. He'll git you anywheres you wants in one piece."

Joe and I flew away with Barr in late morning into a sunny sky and mountainous terrain. When we sighted the silvery gleam of the winding, treacherous Dease River, we started to fly above it. After a short time, Barr began preparing to drop down on the water and Joe, who was snapping pictures, exclaimed in surprise, "I don't see the

Hudson's Bay Post anywhere yet." Barr disregarded him and down we went, landing with a jolt just beyond dangerous rapids. More than a little frightened I cried out, Is - is this a forced landing?

Barr grinned before calmly answering, "Yes, but you needn't be afraid. My plane has a minor problem, no gas. Most people think when you run out of gas in the air, you die. You know now that isn't true."

Barr quickly gave directions for a change in our mode of travel, speaking gaily as if conducting a leisurely excursion. "Weather is perfect and flight on a river unique. Dr. Mandy, you and I will provide power sitting on the pontoons and rowing. You'll paddle with the only oar aboard and I'll row with an axe handle. Mrs. Mandy, you'll take my pilot's seat and keep us in midstream so wings can't be damaged by overhanging branches of big trees. Are you two ready? Take positions and let's be off."

The responsibility of steering was both exciting and alarming and I asked in a weak voice, What do I do? I don't know anything about planes, absolutely nothing.

Unruffled Barr replied, "Do what I tell you. I'll shout directions. Who knows? This may lead to a new career for you."

The men rowed and I piloted for seven long hours, my eyes barely conscious of the forest on both sides of the river, so intent was I on listening for and carrying out Barr's instructions. I kept thinking, Wouldn't my parents be surprised and terrified if they could see me piloting a plane on a rushing river in the wilderness? We had all breakfasted early and it was well past lunch time when Barr decided to speak to us about a meal.

"You Mandys must be hungry. I sure am. Of course I have emergency rations, but it would be foolish to touch them. There'll be plenty to eat at McDame Post."

We had been on the river for two hours before I remembered the box of chocolates given to me by friends at Atlin. I opened it and formally announced, Boys, lunch is served. They laughed in disbelief until I handed down the candy which they insisted must be divided equally between us. The sweet meal relieved our hunger and supplied some energy and all those chocolates disappeared in a few minutes. Occasionally, wandering Indians along the river bank looked at us quite puzzled and two rowed out in a dugout to question.

"Plane on river? Not fly in sky?"

Our pilot was quick with a response. "This plane fly in sky sometimes. Fly on river now. Gas costs too much."

This answer amused them. They went away shaking their heads and laughing to tell their camped families about the men flying a plane on the river with a woman sitting in the seat where a man should be. The story and speculations about what they saw must have been told repeatedly for we could hear the audience's loud vocal reaction echoing through the forest. Barr accounted for their appreciative response with, "We've put on an entertainment for these Indians. They'll talk about it around the campfire for maybe years. 'Good show', as the English say. We're unusual performers."

I heard Joe ask, "What type of plane is this?" and Barr's description.

Transportation methods in the virtually roadless Cassiar-Stikine were very basic, ranging from dugout canoes chopped from a tree to pack horses and crude rafts such as the one below on Bowser Lake. One mile an hour was considered good progress.

"It's a model "S" Stinson, four place with a 215 h.p. Lycoming engine on Edo floats."

My husband declared, "Your terminology is Greek to me. Looks like a good plane."

Barr decided to tell us why he had been forced down. "There's nothing wrong with the plane. It's new though, and that's why I didn't know all it's idiosyncrasies, especially those of the gauges. We had a stiff wind on the way and used all the gas in one tank. Then I noticed the cork float in the other gauge was almost at the bottom. I edged over the river and about two minutes after, the engine quit. You may not know that running out of gas is a no, no. This is a blot on my record. I'll be disgraced among flyers when they hear about it. I'm finished as a pilot."

Joe cheered him. "They won't hear about it. At McDame Post I'll say I saw an interesting formation and you dropped down to let me take a close look. The Mandys will not talk about what actually happened."

I recently wrote to Barr, asking if he remembered my husband and me and our forced trip down the Dease River with him and Joe rowing and me as pilot of his plane. I quote from his answering letter:

"I remember you Mandys very well. I have made so many trips with so many passengers that most of them have faded from my unreliable memory. It might be hard for you to believe, but that was the only trip during my twenty-five years in the north that I ran out of gas. I had heard of Dr. Mandy before I ever saw him. He was well thought of everywhere in the north and on that trip I found out why. Thank you for keeping my secret but now tell the incident as it was."

A young constable, Jack Meek, had recently come to McDame Landing to police the Cassiar. He and two Indians saw us coming and, presuming trouble, rowed out to offer assistance. "What happened?" asked Jack and Barr quipped, "I wanted to give you a surprise." Before Jack could question farther, Joe extended his hand and voiced appreciation of our pilot.

"Barr is not only a skilled pilot but has such an accommodating service. When I couldn't see a formation for mineral exploration, he was willing to come down and give me a close-up from the river. I'm Dr. Mandy, government mining engineer for the B.C. Department Of Mines. Meet my wife. She's had the fascinating experience of piloting Barr's plane on the Dease River."

My legs were very wobbly after sitting tensely for hours at the controls of the plane and I needed Joe's strong arm to support my staggering steps after descent from the aircraft. Joe and Barr must have been affected in the same way from their restricted position on the pontoon seats but, as hardy bush men, concealed their unsteadiness better than I did. We were so thankful to have safely reached McDame Landing that we could almost forget aching muscles and mental strain. I recall thinking that I had experienced a unique and hazardous adventure to tell my grandchildren, if I ever had any, and I've wondered since if anyone else has piloted a plane on the Dease River in the isolated Cassiar.

Barr refuelled and took off at once for Atlin where another flight was scheduled. Joe and I were escorted by Jack Meek to the company-provided log house of Mr. Glennie, Hudson's Bay Company factor for McDame Post, whose quarters he shared. The cabin was quite large for northern wilds, having a spacious living room flanked by a kitchen and bedroom. Floral printed cotton curtains formed partitions between the rooms. Jack introduced us to Glennie who said, "You're just in time for supper. Moose steaks are in the pan." I was very tired but so hungry that my intake of food was disgraceful. The combination of Joe's, Glennie's, Jack's and my appetites cleared the dishes entirely. Jack's cake was delicious and he became such a good cook that in future days he shared original recipes with me.

After supper Glennie took us to the nearby trading Post. The standard Post building of the Hudson's Bay Company was white-washed log with green trim, a red roof and a porch extending across the front. Indian men and boys lolled outside seated on the porch with legs dangling or stretched out on the ground in front of the building. We inspected the store and Joe bought supplies to take on the trail. Coming out of the shop we saw an old Indian woman in front of a tent close to the Post. She walked slowly toward us, her back bent far forward. Her face was such a mass of criss-cross wrinkles that guessing her age was impossible. My husband spoke to the woman in Chinook, "Klahowya Tillicum". She began to moan and her voice conveyed pain.

"Me Polly. Sick tum-tum. All time sick. Cough, cough, cough." The last three words were expressed by the act of coughing.

Joe offered her a cigarette and she took the whole pack, pulling one out and chewing it. She pointed to her tent mumbling words we didn't understand, but her finger implied following her and we did, right into her tent home. She motioned to a wooden box for my chair and the ground floor as Joe's seat. The tent was filled with clothing, skins and mocassins and a stove stood at the back. Polly was a jolly person in spite of her aching stomach, persistent cough and crippled body. She laughed and chattered in her native tongue trying to prolong our visit. We conversed with responsive laughter, brief words, smiles and gestures. Glennie told us later that Polly lived in the canvas shelter all year and he, Jack and passing Indians cut wood for her stove and provided her with food and clothes. These men had praise for her indomitable spirit.

Jack and Glennie said they'd sleep on the living room floor that night and Joe and I could occupy their bedroom. We didn't want to inconvenience them and put up our tent on the river bank. Jack provided army cots for our sleeping bags, thinking they would be more comfortable than the ground. The night was cold with a touch of frost and frigid air rose under the cots to completely chill us. We put on two pairs of woolen socks and a heavy sweater over a woolen shirt and longjohns, but they didn't warm us at all. We were extremely cold and practically sleepless until dawn when we thawed ourselves beside Glennie's kitchen stove. We didn't tell Jack about the uncomfortable night. I've often wondered if he, in the course of being a constable and later an Indian Agent in the north, ever had such an experience. Sleeping bags spread over waterproof canvas on the ground had always kept us warm and that army cot was the only "arctic" bed we had on the trail.

Joe had bargained with an Indian to guide us to Quartz Creek and his dogs would carry our dunnage. The big huskies were able pack animals, seemingly strong as horses, and could carry their own weight or more. They appeared to welcome the loads Joe and Jack placed on their backs. Just as we were ready to hike, a plane landed in front of the Post. Pilot McDonald leaped out and hurried to speak to us before we could start on the trail.

"Wait a minute, Dr. and Mrs. Mandy. I heard you were en route to Quartz Creek. I have freight for camps there and I land on a lake nearby. Why not fly with me? Prospector Lynch Callison is a passenger. He has claims where you're going and wants you to examine them, Dr. Mandy. You can talk about his workings on the way."

Joe consulted Jack Meek, who was familiar with the locale, and his advice was practical. We could go on with the huskies and Indian guide, following an old wagon road almost to Centreville, a long deserted gold camp, and then walk a good trail to Quartz Creek about thirty-two miles beyond. The hiking would be lengthy and tiring, the trip comfortable and quick by plane. Joe decided we'd fly and save both time and energy. McDonald and I entered the plane first and I shivered in the chilling atmosphere of disaster as he waved me to the only seat available. My intuition about a plane problem strengthened when I saw the pilot quickly and nervously fasten a seat belt tightly around himself. There were no safety belts for Joe, Callison and me. McDonald was tense waiting for the men to find a place to sit among boxes and bags. I could see the man was scared and his fright scared me so much that a fearful pain knotted my stomach.

McDonald started a take-off on the river and made two runs unsuccessfully on the water. The plane lifted enough with the third take-off to bump the river bank and then fly upward, but not very high. Joe asked, "Why so low?" and was answered irritably, "Downdraft." I surmised our lack of elevation was due to the plane being underpowered and weakened by years of service. More fright was mine when I sighted the lake for landing. It looked like a tiny dewdrop from our location in the air, much too small to accommodate our aircraft. My body stiffened and I bit my tongue as the plane grazed tall trees at the end of the lake when descending. Of course the pilot knew that an accident had been barely avoided. However, on the ground and intent on developing his air service he asked, "Will you Mandys fly back with me to McDame Post? I'll be here again in three weeks."

Joe's reply was given without hesitation. "No, Mac. We'll be walking the trail out to the river. That will give me a chance to advise a number of prospectors between Quartz Creek and McDame Post." Joe then turned to me and said for my ears only, "What I told McDonald is true, but there is another reason for not flying back with him. I'm sure his plane is doomed and you and I are not going to be on it when the crash comes."

Dave Wing, his son Walter and Lynch Callison's brother and two partners were waiting with huskies to carry freight and our dunnage from the plane to Quartz Creek. We followed the packtrain on a good trail until we came to a long bridge swinging high above a rapids-filled creek. I had discovered before that northern creeks were mini-rivers and not the narrow, shallow and gentle streams I'd known in Indiana. One glance at the bridge filled me with apprehension. It was constructed of three narrow poles with widely separated cleats beginning half way over and it rose steeply upward to a higher creek bank on the other side. Oh, I thought, if I were only a cat, crossing

Approaching McDame Hudson's Bay Post on the Dease River by air.

would offer no difficulty. I watched the railless bridge swing violently with the weight of the men and packed huskies. Then it was my turn to cross, realizing that this was another test on wilderness trails which I had chosen to follow.

Joe had been cutting walking sticks and now handed me one saying, "Take this for support. I shall walk ahead with one hand extended back to you. Hold my hand tightly, put your stick and feet down firmly and walk slowly. Off we go."

I set my eyes on the goal of the elevated bank, stepped cautiously on the poles, held my husband's hand in a vise-like grip, carefully planted my feet and cane on the precarious flooring and forged ahead at the speed of a tortoise. Had I stopped at length to consider what I had to do, such a crossing would have been impossible. Common sense told me that deliberation increases anticipated danger tenfold. A group of long-time prospectors were waiting for their flown-in supplies at Quartz Creek. Both their eyes and mouths opened wide when they saw a woman approaching. One man was spokesman for all.

"Ma'am, you had to come by plane and trail to get here. But the bridge! You never footed it over that there swingin' bridge, did you?"

Yes, I answered, I flew in, hiked by trail from the landing lake and crossed the creek on the swinging bridge.

"Reckon that's so. But how did you cross the bridge?"

I thought that a rather silly question as I replied, The way one crosses any bridge. I walked over.

"Gosh lady," and his quavering voice was respectful, "us old-timers, we crawled over."

Dave Wing and his wife Rosie shared their supper with us in a cozy cabin above Quartz Creek Canyon from which they were extracting gold with an hydraulic operation. Their living-dining-kitchen room was an adequate nineteen feet by twelve feet and Dave told us a room of eight feet had been added for a bedroom. Four small chairs hewn from wood of surrounding trees were supplemented by a large, square, mooseskin-covered box which provided seating for three. A dominant feature of the cabin was a combination heating and cooking stove comprised of a metal drum with a Dutch oven set into the stovepipe which did not go through the drum or oven. Stove dimensions were eighteen inches outside diameter, twelve inches inside diameter and the drum itself twenty-four inches in length. Four loaves of bread could be baked at one time in the oven and a flat top attached on the round drum provided space for general cooking and room for tea and coffee pots.

The Wings gave us a brief resumé of their mining in Quartz Creek while we ate Rosie's moose stew, fireweed salad, homemade bread and dried apple pie. Skinny Dave showed the effects of hard labour by a bent back. Chubby Rosie's face was as weathered and wrinkled as her husband's and that was not surprising for she had helped Dave in every phase of mining except whipsawing and blasting. She admitted, "When it comes to huntin' for food, Dave does shootin' and I does cookin'. I don't fancy firearms myself." Dave was a quiet man whose work was sure and steady but his mind moved slowly and his speech was hesitant. His slowness of thought was in contrast to that of quick-witted, loquacious Rosie.

Joe knew the Wings were Americans who had come north to establish a home in Wrangell, Alaska, where they usually wintered. He encouraged conversation by inquiring, "When did you come to Alaska and then to the Canadian Cassiar?"

"We come from Babcock, Wisconsin, to Wrangell in 1911," Dave began. "Some fellers from Wrangell was comin' to McDame Creek in 1916 an' wants me to come along. Don't know as Rosie was fussy 'bout that."

The conversation shifted to an informative and captivating duologue between the couple. Rosie voiced disapproval of her husband's first entry into Cassiar mining and her subsequent joining him in the venture.

"Now, Dave, you knowed we wuz to have a family addition."

"Yeah, I knowed. But you wuz leavin' to have it in Wisconsin so's you'd be with your ma."

"Course I wuz. Had the youngun and brung little Walter back to Wrangell," and she beamed at her eighteen year old son who couldn't speak because of a swollen jaw due to a painful toothache.

"Let's see," continued Dave. "It wuz -"

"1919," prompted Rosie.

"Wuz goin' to say that. I come to Quartz Creek with our oldest, Harvey, an' uh -"

"Don't fergit our other boy Joel wuz in some years."

"That's right, Rosie, but he had to stay outside to git schoolin'. A real bright boy. He never took to minin' like me, you an' Walter. We three come to Quartz Creek in - uh -"

"1922," interjected Rosie. "Say, Dr. Mandy, did you know Chinese 'long with white men discovered gold in our Quartz Creek Canyon in the '70's an' '80's? Then, a negro found a gold bearin' creek up north here. It's named McDame fer him. I hear tell he was goin' to bring some of his folks to settle in the Cassiar. Don't know why he never done it. Winters too cold mebbe. Guess -"

"Now Rosie, let me tell 'bout us. We stakes claims on Quartz Creek an' times they wuz when we don't have no money for assessment work an' has to pay penalty. My gosh, that wuz tough."

"Hard times we had, Dave. Don't mind that none. We'll hit pay streak one of these days. Aw, look! We'd best git Mrs. Mandy to bed. She's plumb tuckered out. Ain't surprisin' after crossin' that awful swingin' bridge. You Mandys is to stay in our old cabin. 'Tain't but a few yards away an' you'll be dry there if rain comes. Dave, git them settled. Walter, you an' our hired help, Lester Anderson, can put up in the Mandy's tent. If youse need anything, Dr. and Mrs. Mandy, jist holler."

Our cabin was one large room with a bed in it constructed by pulling a mooseskin taut and anchoring it to a wooden bunk frame with wooden slats across it. There was no yield to this covering and it felt much harder than any ground on which I had slept. Like all old cabins, it was overrun with mice and the Wings kept a bush mousetrap in theirs to catch them. The ingenious trap was a gasoline can partially filled with water. A narrow board leaning against it became a gangplank from the floor to the top. Inside, a small can with a bit of bacon tied across its upper surface was suspended by a wire passing through it which was attached to each side. A mouse running up the gangplank and jumping down to get the bacon would start the little can revolving and consequently dump himself into the water below.

We expected a number of mice that night and in preparation I knotted a bandana around my head, having been warned of rodents pulling hair. Shortly after the wood fire in the stove was banked and a lamp blown out, playful mice began racing about the room. We heard some of them run up the gangplank of the trap and squeal when the rotating tin plunged them into the depths of the large can. They struggled in the water and tried to scale the wall of their metal prison unsuccessfully until drowning silenced them. One mouse determined to survive and lashed himself repeatedly against the side of the enclosure. At first, his attempts were quick and frantic but slowed to rest periods and then became a faint splashing. Compassionate Joe couldn't stand this prolonged suffering and jumped out of bed. He hurried to the trap and picked up the dripping, almost dead little mouse, stroked him gently, dried him with a gunnysack and crooned to him.

"There, there, mettlesome mouse, you deserve to live. I'll put you under the stove where there's enough warmth to revive you. When you recover, go back to your family and stay away from baited traps — sound advice for both mice and men."

Joe kept watch until the little fellow recovered enough to scamper away. For the rest of the night relatives and friends of the rescued rodent, having witnessed the near fatality of that fellow mouse, did not go close to the trap. They continued, however, to circle the cabin, run around and across Joe and me and cause my husband to sleep fitfully. I was so exhausted from an adventure filled day that I slept soundly until early morning and woke to hear the sound of a cornet and then a flute playing lively melodies. No, I wasn't dreaming, Joe said and explained.

"One often hears music in the wilds near waterfalls and we are just above those in Quartz Creek Canyon. I've often listened to symphony orchestras in such a location."

The day was spent in Quartz Creek Canyon. Joe took samples, notes and pictures and conferred with Dave. I watched his procedure for awhile before turning to study Rosie's part in this mining operation. She skilfully manipulated a big monitor (hose) which cut with a forceful stream of water into and washed down gold-bearing gravel from both walls of the canyon. It was not surprising Rosie was muscularly well developed. She showed me how fine gold could be panned from the canyon floor and from crevices in veins and even let me pan a little gold to take home. The sturdy woman spent more energy in one day than most people do in weeks and the output combined with optimism kept her healthy and happy.

"Shucks," said Rosie, as we climbed to our cabins to prepare a lunch for our husbands, "ain't this a great life? We is free, me an' Dave, to work when we wants or take a day off any time. Some day we're gonna strike it rich!"

Prospector Pat McNamara called at our cabin that evening to discuss his mining problems and, since Joe was still busy advising the Wings, invited me to his home for lunch the next day. I walked there on a three-quarters of a mile trail, bypassing several waterholes. This was a test of my ability to adventure alone. Pat was watching for me and saw me stop at the one-log bridge over a small creek and make no attempt to cross it.

"Stay right there," Pat shouted, then cut a walking stick from a tree and came over to my side of the creek. "Now," he directed, "I'll hold one end of the stick and you follow me holding the other end. That'll make you feel safe. You'll be in my town of Quartz City before you know it. I'm the whole shebang there, the only resident."

Three other guests greeted me at lunch — a mining man from Salt Lake City who was investigating prospects in the Cassiar, prospector Joe Neddeau and prospector Hennessy. The latter was deaf, toothless, partially blind and spoke in a high cracked voice. We carried on a lively conversation while enjoying moose mulligan, potatoes, Pat's sourdough bread and apple sauce. Discussions were of such diverse subjects as queer characters in the Cassiar, the Depression and the kidnapping of the Lindbergh baby. Pat's dessert was a mixture of dried fruits and the men licked their lips in anticipation of something special. Intuition told me not to indulge in the concoction and I refused a serving saying, I've already eaten too much. Pat was disappointed at my refusal, so I tasted a teaspoonful of the fruit, almost choked and had to wash it down with strong coffee. The men had three helpings each and became increasingly animated. This reaction was rather disturbing and I left shortly with Pat's gifts of a freshly baked loaf of bread and a new walking stick.

Pat escorted me over the log bridge and cautioned about possible danger on the trail. "This is bear country. If you see a bear with a cub, drop down and play dead. Do the same if you come sudden on a bear. Don't you scare the bears and they won't bother you none, except them unpredictable grizzlies."

I set off at a fast pace on a trail which seemed longer than it was in the morning. My eyes were alert but I didn't meet any animals except scurrying field mice. Joe laughed when I told him about Pat's dessert and said, "I'm glad you had only a teaspoonful. If you'd had more you'd have staggered your way back. That dessert is the prospector's home brew to which his male guests and he were accustomed. He served it as something special with never a thought of an adverse reaction for you."

Joe Neddeau had invited me to come with my husband the next day to his headquarters, about four miles from our cabin. His partner, Al Chenard, came to backpack our sleeping bags as we intended to spend a day and a night with these prospectors. Quartz Centre was inhabited solely by Neddeau and Chenard. Their tent was pitched close to a stream with a table and bench a few feet away in the open. Viewing the camp, Joe quickly transferred his packsack to my shoulders and when Neddeau saw us shouted, "My wife carries the heavy loads."

The big, husky man answered, "No, no. You joke. I hear about you. Never do you burden your little wife with such. A gentleman are you and she a lady. Madame Mandy," and he bowed gallantly, "Mayor of Quartz Centre I am and I present to you a bokay from the wild flower garden of the Cassiar."

An artistic arrangement of pine cones in a coffee tin was beautiful and I centred the "bokay" on a dining table of two top-flattened logs pressed close together. Lunch was ready and we sat down to it on a rough log seat. The meal cooked over a campfire was good but swarms of mosquitoes hovered all around. I had to keep a net draped over my face from a hat band and tied at the neck, lifting it slightly for slipping food into my mouth to avoid facial stings. Mooseskin gloves protected my hands from the mosquitoes. Neddeau entertained with a fund of tall tales, beginning with one that made us laugh.

"Folks, I knew a white man once who wanted to marry an Indian woman. She asked, "You got trap line?' 'No.' 'You got pension?' 'No.' 'Then I not marry. White woman good enough for you.' That's a true story."

After an afternoon of strenuous hiking to look at gold prospects, and a sustaining supper, we were ready for bed. Neddeau led us into a roomy tent which was shelter for him and Chenard and consigned to Joe and me that night. He and his partner retired to a tarpaulin teepee. Twin beds of balsam boughs, properly laid by an expert woodsman, combined fragrance with comfort and we were lulled to sleep by rhythmic raindrops on the canvas roof. A mound of pyrethrum powder, smouldering beside one wall of the tent, kept mosquitoes outside. Before leaving his camp I praised Neddeau's restful, scented beds and added, We slept peacefully because of them and the absence of mosquitoes and mice. I shan't forget you and your camp, Mr. Neddeau.

"Talking about mice," observed the prospector, "I was once at a lumber camp that had a trap like that of the Wings. So many was the mice and too small the gas can. We uses a washtub and comes to it seven hundred and fifty mice. Tell you I must. Rows of dozens was in that tub. Graves special big was dug for them danged mice. Don't go till I tell you another story. I was out with a man who don't mind when flies and mosquitoes gets in his food. He says if they was big like moose they'd get hunted same as that critter and wild ducks and geese. So, why not eat them mosquitoes and flies? Leaves them in his grub and smacks his lips, he does. Them insects for my stomach? Never, never."

I stayed in the Quartz Creek cabin on days when Joe travelled long distances with prospectors and busied myself with laundry, typing notes for my husband and recording experiences in the Cassiar on my little, portable typewriter. Such intervals gave me a chance to become better acquainted with Rosie and Dave Wing who often invited me to share their meals with them. The couple had different personalities but were compatible and relied on each other as this typical conversation indicates:

"Rosie, what I wuz spoutin' about to Mrs. Mandy wuz in '29, weren't it?'

"No, 'twarn't, Dave. '30 I'd say."

"Now honey, I thinks -"

"'30, Dave. I know 'twas '30."

"Well, gosh darn it all, I know it wuz '29 'cause - Well, I'll be provin' me right."

Off Dave would wander into a mass of dates, interrupted by interjections from Rosie until he hauled out his diary. The two would pore over pages until they came to a satisfactory entry and then assert, "We both thought that was the right date." Their friendly bickering covered a deep respect and affection for each other which was inspiring to me. Joe and I were delighted when some seasons later the Wings sent us a picture of a four and a half ounce gold nugget. They had found it in a clean-up of their claims and it must have been a deciding factor in the profitable sale of their Quartz Creek operation. It was fittingly named, "The Rosie Wing Nugget."

Joe and I had noticed a large, white spot on a distant mountain, clearly visible from Quartz Creek. Prospectors who had not crossed the valley to inspect the outstanding outcrop said, "That there's a big quartz showin'. 'Tain't worth lookin' at." Joe was interested but his time was limited and he couldn't spare the hours required to investigate, travelling by packhorse or on foot on trailess miles in that mountainous region. The white spot was eventually examined and exploration proved that it fronted an enormous deposit of asbestos which became a mine in 1951 and developed with it a town called Cassiar. Roads, planes and money available after the Second World War helped to promote and develop the profitable mine. The deposit was worthless in the '30's because transportation to and from it was lacking and speculation from investment capital unobtainable.

Now, products of Cassiar Asbestos Corporation find a market throughout the world and indicate the mineral potential of the Cassiar.

When Joe's work around the Quartz Creek section was finished, we required assistance for packing while hiking back to McDame Post. Luckily, we met Dr. Hansen and his university students from Ottawa. They were on a field trip for the Geological Survey of Canada and had arrived at Quartz Creek with horses. Hearing of our need Dr. Hansen advised Joe, "Your little wife shouldn't be walking trail all those miles to the Post. Neither should you. My boys and I are doing leg work for a few days so I'll loan you four horses and a good Indian wrangler, Dick Campbell. You'll travel more comfortably and quickly on horses than on foot."

We started off in early morning, Joe singing and the horses's bells ringing. There were prospector's claims along the way where we stopped so that Joe could examine their showings and give technical advice. About eight that evening the horses needed a rest and feed

Madge and Joe at supper on trail from Quartz Creek to McDame Post.

and so did Joe, Dick and I. Supper was cooked over a campfire and we were drinking the last of the coffee brewed in a pot suspended over flames when we heard McDonald's plane taking off. The pilot had flown in during the morning and had sent a man along our trail to ask if we would be his passengers returning to McDame Post. Joe had answered in the negative. Three times we heard the plane try to lift itself off the small lake where we had landed three weeks before. The noise of the first attempt was moderate, the second a roar and the third a zoom ending in a deafening crash.

"Oh, sounds like she hit a mountain," said our wrangler.

"She certainly hit something," answered Joe.

Dick guided us to Dan Kean's cabin. We wanted to assist if anyone had been injured, Joe having some knowledge of first aid. The prospector was sure to know of a short cut to the lake. The take-off sounds, thunderous in wilderness silence, had warned prospector Dan of tragedy and he was getting ready to go to the fallen plane. He told us that all the prospectors around and the Geological Survey party would give help and this assurance turned us back to the McDame trail. At midnight we reached Centreville, a long deserted gold camp. I was so tired that Joe had to lift me off my horse and half carry me to an old government building of two rooms. One room with a large hole in the roof was not habitable and we welcomed the other which offered shelter from rain now heavily falling. I staggered into the crumbling cabin and was asleep as soon as I stretched out on a hard wooden bunk. Joe woke me to drink coffee and munch cheese-topped rye krisp and this gave me the energy to undress and crawl into a sleeping bag. Joe spread his sleeping bag on the floor and Dick took his thin blanket covering to a small back porch. Mice and mosquitoes shared the cabin with us but we were too exhausted to be kept awake by them.

Joe and I were finishing breakfast the next morning and Dick was rounding up our horses when we heard a loud knock. My husband opened the door and Lester Anderson, the young chap who worked for the Wings, hurried in. He was hysterical and could only stammer, "The - the plane - went down." Joe gently guided him to a stump chair and put a cup of coffee in his hand saying, "Yes, Lester, we know the plane crashed. Tell us about it."

Slightly calmed Lester began, "The plane - it hit them tall trees - at the end of the lake. That secondhand rattletrap was overloaded and underpowered, Dr. Hansen says. McDonald throwed out some of the ore samples and that didn't help none. Tail's all right, wings is broke -whole thing's a mess. Funny thing, nobody got killed but everyone on the plane is hurt. McDonald's hurt worst, stomach punched in and face cut just awful. His navigator partner got a broke leg. That man from Utah ain't hurt really, just cracked his ribs and only one complainin'. The Geological Survey party's first aid man says Lynch Callison has broke his collar bone and put his shoulder out of place. I'm sent out 'cause Constable Meek at McDame Post may be away. I can't receive on his radio but sure can pound out word to get a rescue plane from Whitehorse. Got to get along now. Picked up a horse from an Indian. He's so pesky slow, I'd do better to walk."

We gave Lester breakfast and then Joe followed him outside to say, "You must get to McDame Post as soon as possible. My horse can gallop, so up you go on Glass Eye. I'll either ride or lead your slowpoke."

We were passing a hill when the dunnage began to slip off the back of the horse carrying it. Joe saw an Indian encampment on a flat of the slope beside the trail and suggested I call on the Indians while he and Dick wrestled with the packing problem. I climbed to where tents were pitched and saw a very plump, middle-aged Indian woman in a bright purple dress sitting on the ground. The rest of the camp women were gathered around her with children of varying ages. All ran into their tents as I approached and peeped at me, except the centrally seated woman to whom I held out my hand. She seized it in a firm grip and looked me over from boots to hat before a smiling self-introduction.

"Me, Adele Captain."

I responded in kind. Me, Mrs. Mandy.

"You good woman. Me like." she said and continued talking in her own language. Adele indicated with a sweep of the arm that I should sit near her and soon the children came out of their tents to cluster around us. Adele and I carried on a conversation, each in our own tongue. Emphasis was on gestures, smiles and laughter and this combination brought the hiding women from concealment to watch and listen. Half an hour later Joe and Dick joined us to say we must now ride on. Joe told Adele, "My woman come." Adele pointed to him and commanded, "Mush." Then she looked at me and pantomimed cradling me in her arms and ordered, "Stay." My husband explained, with interpretation by Indian wrangler Dick, that he must take me away as we had a long trail ride ahead. She nodded in reluctant agreement and stood up to watch us walk down to where the horses waited. Her farewell wave spoke of friendship. I asked Joe, Why is she more interested in me than in you? He then gave me some information about the natives in that part of the Cassiar in the '30's.

"Here the Indians are nomads, living where the fishing is good in summer and the trapping is good in winter. Most speak no English. They see a few white men but a white woman is a rarity. I can understand Adele wanting to keep you. That was my instant wish when I met you!"

At McDame Post, Glennie asked us to have supper with him and Jack Meek. We were sitting down to eat when we heard a boat approaching. Glennie looked out the window and started for the door calling back, "Marion, Captain of the Hudson's Bay freighter, is out there on the boat with the Catholic Bishop from Prince Rupert. I knew Bishop Bunoz was coming to hold special meetings for the Indians along the Dease and Liard Rivers, but something's wrong. Father Allard of Telegraph Creek isn't with him. He was to come, too." Glennie came back directly with Marion supporting the tottering Bishop to the house. The elderly priest was obviously in shock but his voice was strong in telling us of tragedy and in directing the immediate action to be taken.

"A terrible thing has happened. Father Allard drowned yesterday on the way here. Constable Meek, I understand you have a broadcasting set. Will you please send some messages for me?"

Glennie placed a plate of moose mulligan before the Bishop but he couldn't eat. I shall never forget what he said or the controlled emotion behind his account.

"Father Allard and I were peacefully travelling down the river in his little boat until we came close to Cottonwood Rapids. There the Dease River, my rescuer Marion tells me, divides into two channels which eventually merge. We could have continued on comparatively safe water but, unfortunately, took the wrong channel and plunged into a swift current leading through the rapids. Nearing them, I saw a sweeper and put my head down until we passed it. While doing this, I heard a crashing sound and turned my head to see our piled luggage partly gone and Father Allard was gone also. I think he saw that projecting branch, leaned forward to protect our belongings and was swept overboard.

"I knew nothing about an engine and sat still. The boat glided around a bend and the motor stopped. Suddenly, as if the hand of God was guiding, the boat drifted to the river bank and lodged under a partially fallen tree. I latched on to the trunk with a rope lying beside me and made the boat fast, threw the remaining luggage on the bank and climbed to safety. I had a tent and food and found plenty of wood for fire. Dry matches were in a tin among supplies carried. A white handkerchief tied to a twig served as a signal for help. All through the night I prayed. My prayers were answered this morning when the Captain of the Hudson's Bay freighter, Marion, came. Yes, God does respond to prayer."

Glennie offered his bedroom to the Bishop for a night of resting and recuperation from his ordeal. The dedicated man refused this proposal saying, "Thank you, but I cannot accept your kind hospitality. I came to the Cassiar to conduct services for the Indians and worship is scheduled for this evening. There is a cabin for me across the river next the church and I hear voices of my parishoners who have come to row me over there. I thank you all for your sympathy. You have given me strength. God bless."

Shortly after the Bishop left, Marion hurried away to the scene of the disaster with Joe and I accompanying him. The river bank above the rapids was very high and must have been difficult for the Bishop to climb as he was a portly man with a broad frame. The bush he gripped to propel himself to safety didn't look strong enough to support my light weight but must have been tough and deeply rooted. Marion's freighter crew had camped at the site and were carving a living memorial for Father Allard with a hunting knife on the blaze of a tall tree overlooking Cottonwood Rapids. During these moments of tragic remembrance a bit of humour crept in through Marion's sincere wish to have a "right" inscription.

"You know," he reflected, "there ought to be letters at the top. Let's see. R - R - R -- O - M. That's it. R.O.M."

A young Catholic carver retorted, "Aw, Marion, ain't you never been to Sunday School? There should be three letters right enough. They're R.I.P. Means rest in peace."

Joe and I helped Marion and his men to carve and darken the letters with a lead pencil. Bush

Memorial for Father Allard above
Cottonwood Rapids on Dease River.

was cut and cleared away from the base of the tree so travellers could see the memorial from a distance upstream. The tribute read, R.I.P. IN MEMORY OF FATHER ALLARD JULY 13/35. We all bowed our heads in silent prayer for the priest who had devoted many years to better the lives of Indians in the Cassiar.

Marion and his men, after a campfire supper with Joe and me, were busy far into the evening. They had blown out some river snags and now blasted those remaining. We camped for the night and were off with Marion in the morning on his freight scow, fully exposed to the elements. At the start of rain, a tent was put up for Joe and me. It was constructed from a tarpaulin slung over a pole which was held up by crossbars nailed to the deck. We passed from Dease River into Dease Lake and stopped at Porter Landing. There, genial Billy Noel, "Pea Soup", invited us to lunch in his cabin. I complimented him on his fresh, fried fish and his bright, roomy cabin.

"Glad you like my home," he responded. "I like it, too. Lots of windows for light so's you don't stumble over yourself. When you folks finish grub, I want to show you a monument. It's for Warburton Pike. I knew him right well. He was behind the Thibert Mining Company. That goes way back to 1901 with a first clean-up in 1902. The company took out gold worth more than thirteen thousand dollars. That's big pay for them days. Come along and you'll see how pioneer Pike is remembered."

We walked a short distance on a well preserved trail and stopped in front of a large, artistically chiselled boulder on which was carved these words:

IN MEMORY OF
WARBURTON PIKE
AUTHOR SPORTSMAN EXPLORER
BORN SEPT 15 1861
DIED OCT 20 1916

"Pea Soup" laid his hand caressively on top of the monument. He was in a reminiscent mood and resumed his monologue.

"Quite a man Pike was. He believed in the Cassiar. Yes sir, he got good backing for Thibert Creek, third largest producer of gold in these parts. Know the big thing he done? Wangled a charter for a railway from Glenora on the Stikine River to Dease Lake. Had that gone through, the Cassiar would have boom times by now. My, he was plenty tough. Never carried blankets, sleeping bag or tent. Used to curl up under a tree to sleep."

The man was silent for a moment and then told us, "Mind you, Pike had peculiarities. Didn't think it was necessary to wash hisself or his clothes. Why, he'd only get new shirts when his old ones was a bunch of rags. He'd wear holey clothes till they was filthy enough to drop off. Underwear the same, I 'spose. When you asked someone if Pike was on the trail and he says yes, you'd ask if he'd seen Pike. If the answer was no, you'd ask how he's sure Pike is coming. Always the answer was, 'Didn't see him, smelled him.' In spite of them queer habits, Pike was respected. Died in his own country of England. His heart was broke because the army wouldn't take him in the World War. Guess he was too old, but he'd have been a devil in a fight. I has to say that Warburton Pike was a fine fellow, a great man."

Back at Dease Landing we were met by Red Latimer, the builder and owner of a new roadhouse erected across from the Hudson's Bay Post. The building was still under construction and the room we were given the only private one, Red's room. It was above the kitchen and heated by a stovepipe which was inserted through a floor opening and then continued upward and out through the roof. The rest of the second story was a dormitory where guests could throw sleeping bags on a cot or on the floor. On the side fronting the road, a door opened into a shop stocked with packaged and tinned food and gear for bush travellers. Another door led from the dining room into a large kitchen where Red had a broadcasting radio. This means of communication with the outside was rewarding as it informed Red of world happenings, developed friendships and enabled him to provide emergency assistance for illness or accidents in this isolated corner of the Cassiar.

Breakfast in the roadhouse was in a combined lounge-dining room which had very attractive walls of peeled logs. A blue-patterned oilcloth covered a table large enough to accommodate six diners. Shortly after the meal, Joe left with a guide and wrangler to investigate prospects in the Tanzilla River valley. Only three horses were available for the trip and that meant I must remain at Dease Lake Landing. The people I should meet there, other than Red Latimer, were the newly employed factor of the Hudson's Bay Post, four camping American men waiting for their promoter-guide to conduct them to a likely gold-bearing area and a lone Indian living in a nearby cabin. There were also several nomad Indians who wandered in and out to shop at the Post.

My husband entrusted me to Red's care and to insure privacy he pitched a tent for me at the side of the lake overlooking the roadhouse. It was reached by a tree bordered path. Red, so called because of his hair colour, provided for my comfort by bringing there a cot, mattress, small table for my typewriter and a wash basin. How thoughtful he was to also place a pail of hot water outside the tent each morning. Since I was the only guest at the roadhouse, Red had time to talk to me at length over his hearty meals which we ate in the comfortable kitchen. Our conversation covered a wide range of subjects and his vocabulary and sentence structure were generally good. I guessed he had acquired them from reading copies of Shakespeare's plays, The National Geographic Magazine, Time and Magazine Digest. Joe and I had seen this library in his bedroom. He satisfied my unspoken curiosity about him by relating a brief biography on my second morning as his guest.

"You probably wonder where I came from and how I happen to be at Dease Landing. You'll understand me a bit if I tell you. To begin, I was born in eastern Canada into a big and very poor family. Schooling wasn't considered necessary. I had enough to learn a smattering of reading, writing and arithmetic. My working days started at an early age. I was only fourteen when I ran away to San Francisco and took any job I could get. Then I started wandering, even went to live with a sister and her rich English husband who spent most of their time on a yacht sailing on the Mediterranean. They taught me to speak and behave properly, but I didn't like their stuffy formality. The dressing for dinner and carrying on old traditions was not for me. Canada was my country, not England. I came back and heard about the Cassiar in British Columbia where a man could live a life of freedom. I built myself a cabin on the bank of the Stikine River and just missed meeting you at Barrington's mining camp.

"Did Sid Barrington tell you about his cook? He needed one and I didn't want the job but did want the salary it paid, so I took it. Required to be on a schedule was bad enough but having one of the miners sleep in the cookhouse where I did was intolerable. One morning when the alarm clock went off, I got mad. The thing was destroying my freedom. I picked up a butcher knife and threw it at that beastly clock and just missed hitting my roommate. The poor chap was naturally scared. He ran out shouting, 'Help, I'm being murdered!' I didn't wait for wages, just grabbed my belongings and left. Knifing gave me a bad reputation and the title, Terrible Red. I went back to my cabin and — well, I guess you wouldn't associate with me if you knew what I did for awhile."

Red paused for so long that I finally asked, Do you want to tell me about that part of your life? You don't have to do it.

"I'm sure if I don't, someone else will. Somehow, I think you won't judge me too harshly. That was a shameful period. I was a bootlegger and felt degraded being one, but needing money kept at it. I shut my mind to the fact that the men who bought what I brewed had little cash. I went on with that filthy business until a fellow came from Telegraph Creek whose family didn't have enough to eat and his baby had no shoes. While looking at such a selfish creature, this thought came to me. I'm no better than a skunk and heading lower. That made me angry at myself and I pushed the weakling through the door. Then I threw all the hootch I had in the river. I've never sold any since.

"I believe I fought a battle with myself and won. Now don't praise me. I'm certainly no saint and never will be. I still bootleg for me, gamble and drink the liquor of men who come this way and I'm an equal with anyone in swearing. I can tell profanity is something you don't know anything about and I'm glad you don't. This may seem strange to you, considering the likes of me, to know I really think cursing is disgusting. I like good words properly spoken and rightly used. The grapevine says you've been to university and taught in college. That means you can help me. You've noticed my reading material from which I like to get words. Trouble is, I'm not sure of what many of them actually mean or how to pronounce them. While you're here, will you correct me every time I'm wrong, show me how to be right and to remember corrections?"

Red's request was startling and I stammered in answering, I - I'll have to think about what you ask. After all -- you're much older than I and -

Red cut me short. "I know what you're thinking. The man with the terrible temper might throw something at me. Honest, Mrs. Mandy, I won't do that. You're a lady I respect and I wouldn't do anything to hurt you. You've got the learning I wish I had and I beg you to help me. I can't pay you but I'll be grateful forever."

The man was so eager to learn that I gave in to his persuasion with the warning, If you ever show anger, the lessons stop. I asked Red to write down each word I heard him use incorrectly or mispronounce and, after that, to practice corrections daily when conversing with me. He kept his lamp burning far into the night poring over periodicals and books to acquire additional vocabulary. Very soon Red was following my instructions to discard written work for the development of memory. His steady progress was a delight and I could truly say he was one of the most responsive and achieving students I had ever taught. In appreciation of his co-operation and accomplishment I told him, I shall send you a dictionary to help you in acquiring vocabulary, definitions and correct pronunciation of words.

He rejected the gift. "No, don't do that. I wouldn't know how to use it and I'd be embarrassed asking help from anyone in this neck of the woods. People around here think of me as Terrible Red, an ignoramus to stay away from."

Joe returned two weeks later and called out as he dismounted from his horse, "Can you be ready to start down the lake in half an hour? We'll stay the night at Porter Landing and take the trail to Mosquito Creek tomorrow."

Prospector Homer Finklin guided us to his cabin at Porter Landing with a warm welcome. "Dr. and Mrs. Mandy, as guests you honour my home. Don't expect a palace, just a log cabin. You'll find it's snug and warm and suits me and Cassiar mice." He was a literate man as well as a seasoned prospector. His wit entertained us while we ate supper which he insisted on preparing and cooking on a rusted stove.

"I'm going to tell you Mandys," he began, "about prospecting men. We're a queer lot. A prospector is like a dog chasing a porcupine and like a perpetual drunkard. The dog comes with his mouth full of quills after he's tackled a porcupine. He's suffering terrible pain, his howl and moans mean he won't chase a porcupine again. He expects you to take out the quills and you do. But let a porcupine come along and the chase starts all over. The drunkard gets sick and while he's taking pickles, alkacelsor and what not, he swears he'll never drink any more. But rattle a bottle and he's good for another stew. A prospector is just the same. He goes on a stampede, gets skunked and says, 'Never again.' But the first whisper in his ear, 'I'm telling you about this find — better get in on the ground floor,' and off he goes."

"You'll always be a prospector," said Joe.

Homer agreed. "Reckon so. Prospecting gets into a man's veins like nuggets in a creek. Guess I'll keep on looking for gold till I either climb up the golden stairs to Heaven above or get pitched down into Satan's fiery pit of Hell."

I had a question for Homer. Could you tell me the name of the birds I've seen near your cabin? They're around every camp.

Homer chuckled in replying. "We call them camp robbers. Don't know their fancy book name. These birds are very smart and don't migrate. They stay here all the time and follow a fellow hunting. Soon as a moose is shot and skinned, they're ready to eat. They've followed me so much that I understand their lingo. This can be a great help.

Sometimes I've been trying to track game and couldn't find any. Ready to quit I look up and see a camp robber sitting in a tree ahead of me, singing his little ditty. It goes like this, 'I know where the game is. Come close and I'll tell you.' Sure enough, I go where he tells me and find a moose."

Joe was trying to hide his exhaustion but Homer knew the signs of trail fatigue and declared, "Don't often have an audience for my tales. When I do, I want to talk all night. I won't keep on now because early in the morning we head for Mosquito Creek so — bunk time. You folks bed down in the cabin and I'll do the same in a tent. Oh, before I go, I'll lock up the food in a tin box. There it'll be as safe as in God's pocket — that is, from mice."

I was wakened in the morning by Homer's whistling and Joe's cheery, "Good morning, my dear. Time to get up and hit the trail." Homer made a crackling fire in the stove and breakfast was soon ready. Thick porridge, bacon and sourdough flapjacks smothered in syrup provided a sustaining start for the day.

"Sure you can eat as big a stack of flapjacks as I give you," insisted Homer. "You need fuel and three cups of coffee to keep you awake. We've got climbing miles ahead. Dr. Mandy, I've only got two horses and one of them is for packing. Not riding doesn't bother me. How about you two?"

"Mrs. Mandy rides," said Joe. "There's no question about that."

How I tried to persuade him that walking was what I needed for it would help remove excess weight I'd put on during the summer. Finally, we compromised in agreeing to take turns riding. I wasn't sure, though, of keeping my promise to hang on to the horse's tail when on foot. As we started I was mounted, Joe was hiking close behind and Homer brought up the rear leading the packhorse. After a time, my feet were on the steep trail and my boots seemed frozen to it. I needed help to climb and yet I was afraid to get it from the horse as Joe said I must. Homer encouraged me to action by blunt direction.

"Mrs. Mandy, little you are like a flea to that people's friend. The horse won't feel your puny pull. Grab his tail. Now, now, a few horse hairs won't get you anywhere. Take the whole tail, hold on tight and let yourself be pulled. That's the girl. Fun, don't you think?"

I had engaged in activities I thought were more fun. Somehow, I managed to hang on to the horse's tail and, with intervals of riding, keep up a steady pace to Mosquito Creek. J. R. Gibson of Seattle was in charge of a small crew working in the creek's canyon where there had been a sizeable yield of gold in the '70's. Gibson Hydraulic Association, formed by a group of men trying to combat the Depression, was spurred on by the optimistic Gibson. He told his fellow workers, "If we don't strike pay this year we will the next." He wanted all working examined, comment and criticism on what had been done and advice for the future. The tireless man walked us miles while Joe inspected, recorded notes, mapped and took samples.

In early evening we were shown to the best accommodation in the camp, the cook's quarters beside the kitchen storeroom which held two cots. The cook relinquished his bush bedroom for the night,

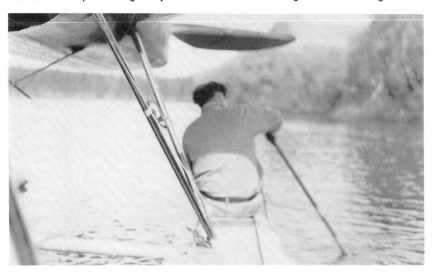

Barr's plane on Lake Atlin and, below, drifting down the Dease River. Frank Barr is rowing, while on the other side Joe Mandy is paddling with an axe handle and Madge is in the cockpit steering. They were seven hours reaching McDame Trading Post.

Gibson whispered, "Only because a lady is in the picture." One cot in the room had a mosquito net tent draped above it. Joe noticed this and said, "Swarms of mosquitoes are in this place. I'm bigger and stronger than you and therefore better able to fight off these invaders. You'll sleep under the net." Though I protested, he tucked me into a sleeping bag with the tent above and around me, adequately shielded from disturbing stings. Drifting off to peaceful sleep I murmured thanks, as I had done so many times, for a considerate husband like my Joe.

Two mornings later, Homer guided us up a gentle mountain slope to the location of his mineral showings. I rode his packhorse and he and Joe walked slowly ahead, discussing Homer's findings. Halfway up we stopped, tethered the horse and then I watched as an examination of claims proceeded. The men were so absorbed in their task that it was nearly three o'clock before they turned from mining discussion to the lunch we carried. This welcome pause for eating was delayed by a request from Homer.

"Mrs. Mandy, could you do a little thing for me? My daughter down in the States is forever writing to ask, 'Why don't you get married again? It isn't good for you to be alone.' She always puts in, 'Now, father, get yourself a wife your own age. Don't you marry a giddy young girl.' Mrs. Mandy, I'm more than old enough to be your father, so if Dr. Mandy takes a picture of you and me together I can send it to her. Surely it will make her think I've married a cute, little flapper. Won't that be a good joke?"

Joe and I cooperated to produce a romantic scene. Homer panned for gold and I posed beside him. Then the prospector had an idea for another snapshot, he and I standing beside the nearby grazing horse. I grasped the horse's rein with my right hand and Homer took his position at my left, handing me a walking stick to hold while he held my arm. At that instant the horse leaped into the air, giving me a kick in the side which knocked me to the ground. I did not black out but instinctively closed my eyes in alarm. The men picked me up and carried me to a bunk in Homer's tent. A few minutes later I opened my eyes to see Joe's anxious face and Homer pacing up and down, his hands clenched behind his back. Both, seeing I was conscious, exclaimed as one, "Thank God!"

"Are you --- all right?" asked Homer.

I said weakly, Yes - I am. I just feel a bit dizzy. Homer's reaction was, "Hot tea will help you." He hurried off to gather wood for a fire in the tent's stove. Joe quickly examined my side and found the hoof had lightly grazed it. No skin was broken but the blow left a bruised spot which did hurt and would undoubtedly be discoloured and sore for awhile. How fortunate I was! A strong, flat blow from the horse's hoof could have killed me. Food and stimulating, hot tea helped relieve the shock of the accident and Joe promised aspirin to soften pain when he could open his first aid kit at Gibson's camp.

Homer shouted on hearing I was not seriously injured, "Glory be! I'd never forgive myself if you was hurt permanent just to please a silly old man. That kicking horse is as gentle as a lamb. The reason he hit out is this. The walking stick I gave you reminded him of an owner who used to beat him with one like it. I should have remembered that. The horse has nothing personal against you, Mrs. Mandy. You needn't be afraid to ride him down the mountain."

Our home in Prince Rupert was so restful after the excitement of dramatic days in the Cassiar. At leisure I reviewed highlights there: a forced landing which permitted me to pilot a plane on a dangerous river, barely escaping an accident when McDonald's plane brushed tall trees while landing on a small lake, missing the crash of the plane because Joe and I refused to fly back from the tree bordered lake with McDonald, safely crossing a perilously inclined, swinging pole bridge and my almost serious injury when kicked by a horse on a mountainside. Remembered also was the sad drowning of a good and dedicated priest in the Dease River and my teaching of vocabulary acquisition and useage to an appreciative pioneer. Certainly, high adventure was a companion to the Mandy's trail in the Cassiar.

# STEWART, TOWN OF MINERAL FAME

"The northern mining town of Stewart with its awesome mountain setting is fascinating," remarked Joe, "and field work there is always dangerous. Here is some data to digest in preparation for your going to Stewart with me. You should have unforgettable experiences in that part of my district."

I read the report given to me with interest and mentally compiled these facts from it. Stewart is situated at the mouth of the Bear River and at the head of a long canal. The town is shut in by very high mountains whose dangerous accessibility presents a challenge. Discovery of the site dates back to 1898 when rumours of gold in the rugged surroundings brought many prospectors. Their numbers grew and when the Stewart brothers, Robert and John, staked claims in the vicinity during 1903 a town began to develop. The name chosen for it honoured Robert Stewart, the first postmaster of the community. The lure of a possible fortune in gold quickly led to settlers with families and to the establishment of homes, hospital, school, shops and essential services.

There was good reason for the Stewart pioneers to be optimistic. The potential mineral wealth for growth was enhanced by the prospect of a profitable shipping port. There was also a proposed railway connection with the Groundhog Coal Fields and the Peace River agricultural belt of the interior. The construction of a railroad to link Stewart with these inner areas actually started in 1910 and plans called for an extension to Edmonton, Alberta. Regrettably, only fourteen miles of track were laid before the World War began in 1914 and financing for the project stopped. At that time, too, the town was almost depopulated when residents left to join the fighting forces. Happily, Stewart boomed, post war, with the advent of Premier Mine, high in the mountains behind it. This mine, a major producer of gold in British Columbia, helped restore prosperity in Stewart as a large percentage of its payroll was spent in the town. Small mining companies and prospectors also contributed to this restoration of affluence. The data indicated no worry about Stewart's future. It had survived becoming a traditional ghost town and from this I could predict, The pioneer spirit of Stewart will never let it die.

Stewart, one hundred and twenty miles north of Prince Rupert, had an entrance of a sixty mile long and mile wide inlet. While sailing there, I read a travel brochure which described the scene through which we were passing as, "A land of towering mountains and hanging glaciers, scenic wonderland of British Columbia." The inlet was called Portland Canal and formed a dividing line between British Columbia and Alaska, and the international boundary ran straight through the centre. The sight of enclosing majestic mountains brought Robert Service's description of such snow-capped heights to mind and I murmured, He was right. They are indeed a part here of "naked grandeur where there's nothing else to gaze on." Joe spoke about these mountains realistically rather than poetically.

"The trails in this terrain are so dangerous I can't let you take many of them. They're steep and exhausting, even for a bush man like me.

On one trip here with a surveyor, we walked our boots off. There were so many rocks, boulders and stony cliffs to cut into them. By the time we got back to Stewart, our high boots were in shreds and the soles completely gone."

Joe's story sounded far-fetched, but I found it was true when I met Eardley Wilmot, the man who was with him when both had their boots demolished on their feet. Wilmot had lasting, painful recollections of that episode and spoke feelingly about it.

"Dr. Mandy, remember that tough trip we took in the mountains around Stewart? We can laugh now about walking our boots off and feel annoyed when some people don't believe our story. It was no laughing matter. At the time, all I could think of was my literally bloody, sore feet. I really thought I'd be lame for life."

"We have to go two miles from the dock to get to the town of Stewart," Joe said as we left the steamer. He hailed a taxi driver who drove us to Fifth, the main and only business street. Buildings on either side, fronted by board walks, rose starkly in varying heights to resemble a typical frontier town of western films. The Welsh proprietors of the Bayview Hotel, Mr. and Mrs. John Hutchings, registered us and "Honest John," so called locally, stated how they maintained a safe and respectable hotel with strict regulations which were rigidly enforced.

"You don't have to be afraid staying at the Bayview. I don't tolerate parties or other goings-on. Anyone who tries to break the rules gets thrown out."

The hotel was sandwiched between a grocery and a barber shop. Its lounge-dining room entered from the boardwalk was crowded by a piano, a buffet, a round dining table with chairs around it and was backed by a dark, poky kitchen. A door on the side wall near the front of the room led into the entry for a steep, narrow stairway which took us to five bedrooms and a shared bathroom. Joe and I were the only guests that day and we soon discovered the hotel's cash intake was so small that dining provisions were bought daily according to guest occupancy and the needs of the four local men who were permanent boarders.

I had heard of Stewart's active Board of Trade and a member of the organization knocked on our door about fifteen minutes after we checked in at the hotel. I recognized Bill Tooth from Joe's description of the people I would meet in Stewart. Bill was a Mormon from Salt Lake City who had been in the gold rushes to Fairbanks and Nome in Alaska, working there as a cook in camps and restaurants. Hearing of good gold prospects in British Columbia, he drifted down to Stewart where he dabbled in mining, acquired choice real estate, established a home, became a Canadian citizen and a dominant leader in community activities. He was known as the unofficial mayor of the town and wasted no time in stating the purpose of his call.

"I'm here to say we in Stewart are glad you're in port again, Dr. Mandy. We congratulate you on finding a wife to take the trail with you in our wonderful north. It's a pleasure to meet you, Mrs. Mandy, and I hope you'll enjoy being here. The Stewart Board of Trade has read of your speeches in Prince Rupert, reported by the press, and has sent me to ask you to give a talk at our next luncheon meeting.

It's at the King Edward Hotel a week from today. How about it?"
Joe's expressive face told me he wanted me to say yes and I did. Of
course, I had to ask, What do you want me to talk about? His answer
surprised me.

"Tell us about your experiences with your husband on the trail and
what you think about our great Northwest."

Bill then turned to Joe to say, "As arranged by letter, you'll be off
with me in the morning to climb halfway up a mountain where I have
claims for you to examine. Mind you, Dr., be ready to start at the
crack of dawn. You'll need a full day to do all you should."

Joe left before I was awake and his note propped up on a bedside
table read, "Dearie, I'll be back to eat supper with you." I kept myself
busy by outlining a speech for the Board of Trade and entertaining
some friendly local women, who wanted to get acquainted with the
bride of the well known Dr. Mandy, at afternoon tea in the dining
room. Joe did not appear for the evening meal. I became worried and
paced up and down on the board walk outside the hotel. Then I
restlessly read a magazine in my room upstairs. Kind Mrs. Hutchings
came up with a cup of tea, a plate of tarts and the comforting words,
"Don't you fret. Dr. Mandy'll come any minute now. Know why he's
late? Men don't pay any mind to time when they look for gold." The
motherly woman was so soothing that I relaxed and was able to greet
Joe with a smile when he came in at ten dragging his feet. I
remembered his story of worn boots when exploring in the mountains
around Stewart and inspected those he was wearing to see if they
were in shreds.

"No," said Joe wearily, "I didn't walk my boots off but I did
something stupid to slow me down. Bill and I rode horses up the
mountain and he wanted to tether or hobble them when we reached
his claims. A wide, grassy flat offered feed for the horses and I
thought they'd stay put and eat. So, I suggested we let them roam
about the meadow until we were ready to leave. Bill reluctantly
agreed. They certainly roamed, not on the feeding ground but
straight back home to Stewart. Bill and I had to carry their saddles on
our backs. It was a long tramp down the mountain and into town. I'm
still fond of horses but won't give them another chance to desert me.
My back is not as strong and broad as that of a horse and doesn't
take kindly to a saddle."

There were many "might have been" big mines in the Stewart area
and some were productive at intervals. Among them was the Dunwell
Mine which in 1934 was engaged in a small-scale hand operation,
obtaining enough gold, silver, copper and lead to produce a small
income. The company's accountant and manager, L. S. Davidson,
who was also a salesman for mining equipment, proved to be an asset
in keeping the company alive. Access to the property was
comparatively easy by truck along the Bear River road and up the
side of a mountain by a bumpy road. I went to the Dunwell with
Davidson and Joe and listened while they discussed reports in a
spacious office, after which I was handed some magazines to read
while they were underground. Davidson was embarrassed in explain-
ing the type of reading material on hand.

"I haven't much to entertain a lady here but you may find this stuff to your liking. You'll wonder why women's magazines are found in a mining camp. Well, this is how it happened. Four young women came to Stewart a few weeks ago. They split into pairs and went to wherever they learned men were mining or prospecting in the vicinity of Stewart. They came to the Dunwell when I was in town and the boys fell for their sales pitch. They said they were selling magazine subscriptions to earn money for an aviation course. They even had the fellows believing they'd be flying their own planes in a short time and would come back to pilot them as preferred passengers. I'm a salesman myself and should have recognized their promise as a sales gimmick. Can you imagine the miners reading this nonsense? My men need boots, socks and longjohns, not these female periodicals."

Joe interjected, "At least they're preferable to what some girls left in logging camps. There they sold subscriptions for a mother's magazine with the focus on the care of a baby."

Clay Porter wanted Joe to examine a syndicate property located on the north slope of a mountain overlooking the Marmot River. It was about three miles from tidewater and easily reached by a packhorse two-thirds of the way and then by a very steep foot trail. Four of us climbed to the site one morning — Clay, a wrangler, Joe and myself. Upon reaching camp, Clay and Joe immediately went into the old mine with picks and sample sacks. The wrangler hobbled the horses and unloaded the food he'd brought for lunch. The building in which we were to eat was a well preserved reminder of a once prosperous mine and held a huge range, long table, benches and a few delapidated chairs. The young wrangler and I conversed until time for him to prepare the lunch of tinned vegetables, bread and butter, fruit and a special treat of juicy steaks. He quickly dumped the vegetables into a pot and heated a skillet when hearing Clay and Joe approaching. The men came inside and Clay anticipating a good lunch remarked, "I'm as hungry as two wolves. Got them steaks ready?"

Food was placed on the table sizzling hot, with steaming cups of coffee to wash it down. The cook waited for compliments. Instead, there was a bellow from Clay.

"Where's the spuds, boy?"

"I never brung none. Ain't necessary to lug potatoes for lunch."

Clay exploded. "If that don't beat all! What's a meal without spuds? Get some old ones out of that bag by the door. Cut 'em small. They'll cook quick."

The disgruntled wrangler began slicing some sad looking, sprouting potatoes. His compliance moved Joe to remonstrate.

"This is a good lunch, Clay. Surely you could survive one meal without spuds."

Clay retorted, "Sure I could. But this chechako must learn spuds are a must in the Northwest."

Joe had to start on a five day reconnaisance the very day I was scheduled to address the Board of Trade. He encouraged me in saying, "You'll enjoy meeting some honest-to-goodness pioneer men and they'll enjoy listening to you." I felt apprehensive speaking to northerners about the north but Joe reminded me I had firsthand experience in wilderness parts in which this group had not travelled. The organization's members, all many years older than I, were so friendly and responsive that I soon lost my fear of pleasing them. They could relate their transportation problems to those of isolated Squaw Creek, remote Atlin and the expansive wilds of the Cassiar. My amusing trail incidents were compared with their own and my character sketches drew interjections of "We've got some like that in Stewart." The discussion following my talk clearly revealed the secret of Stewart's continued existence. These men had courage which was developed and strengthened by hardships. Furthermore, they possessed boundless belief in the discovery of many more gold deposits in the local mountains. Their optimism brought to mind the truism poetically expressed by Douglas Malloch which was certainly applicable to them:

Ah, that's the reason a bird can sing -
In his darkest days he believes in Spring.

I was in my hotel room the next day when I heard a commotion and rushed to the window to look out and see what was happening. Several people were shouting as they ran toward the dock and curiosity led me to join them. A teen-ager in the crowd didn't lessen his speed but yelled as we were jostled, "Some fun we'll be having. Tommy McKay, he's from Premier Mine, and Bill Crawford are going to put theirselves and a horse in a little plane. They're off to the Unuk River country, miles and miles north. How'd you folks like to fly with a horse?"

I watched the attempt to load the trembling horse, Tony, into a small airplane. Finally, with the help of several men hobbling and pushing him up a ramp, Tony became a passenger. He had been turned lengthwise and Tommy sat on his rump, while Crawford was seated near his head. Someone said as the plane took off, "My gosh, they have to fly over mountains seven to ten thousand feet high and all laid over with ice and snow. What happens if they have a forced landing on a glacier?" That question was uppermost in my thoughts when Joe and I flew over the same icecap the following year.

Joe's itinerary included consultation at the Big Missouri Mine on the Missouri Ridge twenty-one miles from Stewart's dock. My husband tucked me and himself into the rear seat of a local taxi and prepared me for the winding, mountain road the car must climb, the first eleven miles being in Alaskan Territory, to reach the mine.

"Madge, you've not been on such a road as this and I must admit it is scary. You needn't fear. Our driver knows every twist and turn and cut-out of the narrow road where when two cars meet one must wait while the other goes on. There's no passing and little traffic. Isn't it beautiful here in the mountains? Feast your eyes on the perfect, natural picture they present and listen to a few facts about the Big Missouri. The original group of its claims was among the oldest mineral locations in the Portland Canal area, having been discovered in 1903. Individuals and partners have worked the claims on a small scale ever since. Now, in the '30's, Consolidated Mining and Smelting Company of Canada is vigorously developing them with a crew of sixty miners under the supervision of Doug Campbell. He's a fine chap. You'll like him."

Doug provided a room for us in his comfortable company house. His wife and children were away on holiday as was the wife of another staff member. Consequently, I was the only woman in camp and it was up to me to entertain myself. My husband and Doug were busy all day and far into the night with examinations and discussions. I spent the time happily reading books selected from many in the house and in hiking on contiguous trails. After three days in the Big Missouri tunnels, Joe turned his attention to an old prospector who had walked several miles to meet him. The man spoke loudly and emphatically.

"I'm come to say, I wants to show you what I got. Talkin' ain't enough. Will youse take off with me tomorrow?"

Joe agreed to go with the man, and he was housed overnight at the camp. The two started early in the morning, my husband assuring me he'd be back in time for supper. He did not arrive for the evening meal. When nine o'clock came, I began to worry and sat down on the front doorstep of Doug's house to watch for him. I was soon joined by a grumpy looking elderly man in well worn bush clothes. Doug had told me about a prospector who had come to the camp around noon inquiring about the engineer, Dr. Mandy, and I inferred he was that person. Doug also reported, "The chap was quite put out to hear Dr. Mandy had gone off early with another prospector instead of being available for a trip to his showing." The disappointed man must have learned of my presence in camp, I thought, and had come to chat with me in the friendly way of the north.

"Waitin' fer the Dr., ain't you?"

Yes, I am, I answered. I expected him to be here for supper.

"Don't youse expect him back. I been to where he went. Trail to there's turrible dangerous. 'Spect he's dead. The mountain's got him."

I cried out, and there were tears running down my face. Don't you dare to say that again. Of course he's coming back.

"No, he ain't. I got the gift of prophecy. His number's been called. He's plumb gone. Well, we all got to go some time."

One of the miners, walking by while the prospector was pouring out his dreadful prediction, informed Doug at the cookhouse of what he'd heard. Doug immediately came running, helped me to my feet and spoke positively.

"Don't pay attention to what's been said. This skunk doesn't know what he's talking about. Dr. Mandy will be back. Just go in the house and I'll be with you soon. As for you — you disgrace to prospectors, come with me."

Doug yanked the man up and practically dragged him to the cookhouse. He sent a maintenance worker to fire a wood burning stove in his house to warm me, having noticed I was shivering. The stoker advised me of what was taking place between Doug and the troublesome prospector.

"Doug's givin' that old so-and-so a real dressin' down. Bet he don't do nothin' again like he's done to you."

Doug came to the house shortly, opened a tin of chicken a la king, heated the contents and spread a portion over toast. "There now," he encouraged, "a little food will make you feel better."

I picked at the appetizing dish, drank extremely strong coffee and tried to listen to Doug's humorous anecdotes and analysis of current events. How hard Doug tried by food and talk to keep me from being overwhelmed by fear! At eleven o'clock he asked if I didn't want to lie down for awhile. Nervous tension would not allow me to do that, so Doug carried on a cheery monologue and I drank a sixth cup of coffee. Half an hour later we heard footsteps and Doug hurried to open the door. My husband stumbled in looking worn-out and his speech, at first, was hesitant.

"Sorry to be - so late. Something -- happened on the trail -- to remember always. I -- came nearer - death today than I've ever been before. The prospector, whose claims I examined, was so pleased to have company that he wanted me to stay over night with him. The poor chap delayed me as much as he could. Finally, I was well on my way back when the unexpected occurred. A minor slide started while I was skirting a mountain, pelting me with stones. I threw myself on the ground face down just before a big boulder whizzed by, grazing the packsack on my back. After that, I lay still for quite awhile in a state of shock and then walked more slowly than my usual pace. How about a cup of coffee?"

Doug decided to tell Joe about the prospector's conversation with me before someone else did. Tired though he was, my protective husband jumped to his feet and shouted, "Where's that man? I'll fix him." He calmed down after Doug told of the measures already taken for punishment.

"I said to that old coot, in language he understood, what I thought of him and that he'd better get going right away. Some of the boys gave him a rough push-off. It seems he wanted you to go to his prospect today. When he came, after you'd left this morning, the chap worked himself into a fit of madness. That's why he said such a dreadful thing to Mrs. Mandy. I think he's 'touched' or, as we say up here, has missed too many boats. One thing is sure. Every man in the camp will take good care of Mrs. Mandy. We have some men in camp who'd give a certain kind of woman what she's asking for, but all would lay down their lives, if need be, for a lady and your wife is indeed a lady."

Back at the Bayview Hotel we sat down to dinner with Dalby Morkill, a surveyor who had just come to Stewart. He had met Joe several times in the Portland Canal area and was not only interested but critical when Joe told him we would be riding up to the United Empire Mine the next day.

"Why, Dr. Mandy," he exclaimed, "you don't want Mrs. Mandy to have a last ride, do you? Surely you won't let your wife cross high above the Bear River and climb a steep mountainside in an ore bucket! The cables carrying those buckets were used years ago by a company in southern British Columbia, and they've been rusting for over twenty years since that operation closed. They're bound to be weak and could break, or the mechanism controlling the cables might fail. A strong wind is capable of stopping and rocking the bucket and stranding it high over the Bear River and -. Need I say more?"

Joe answered his warning by acknowledging, "I know of the dangers you mention and I thank you for your concern. However, there's no other way to get to the United Empire Mine except by trail. That particular trail is so rough and steep that packhorses are

Aerial tramway to the United Empire Mine.

reported to have leaped over the cliff rather than keep on climbing. I think it best to take a chance on the buckets."

Some data about the United Empire Mine was given to me to read in preparation for taking the "air trail" to it. I learned from the report that the mine's lower aerial terminal was located beside the Bear River at an elevation of one hundred and eighty feet and across the river rose to an elevation of four thousand feet at the upper terminal. A summary of the bucket transportation was this candid statement, "The trail route to the United Empire involves two hours of difficult climbing and the ride in the aerial tramway involves eight minutes of suspense." I knew from this conclusion that Joe's choice of routes would be thrilling and dangerous and braced myself to face up to it. The ride would be another challenge in sharing perils with my husband and an unusual conversational story for the rest of my life.

Fortunately, the next morning was sunny and bright, an auspicious start for an adventuresome day. Joe and I were driven along the Bear River road to the office of the United Empire Company. Breezy, cocky mine manager, Billy Dann, met us there with boisterous enthusiasm and a promotional prediction about "an enormous and very rich mine in the offing."

"Dr. Mandy," Dann palavered, "You have a great treat ahead when you examine the United Empire. She holds a fortune in gold and silver. Rich, I tell you. She's rich! Mrs. Mandy, it's certainly a pleasure to meet you. What a wonderful wife you are to trail around the north with your husband in the fascinating field of mining! Now, here are my living quarters, as well as an office, with all the comforts to which you are used to at home. They're yours while Dr. Mandy and I are across the river in the mine and a well stocked freezer will provide your lunch."

I've planned on going to your mine, too, I said.

Dann seemed surprised and asked, "Little lady, are you sure you want a ride on the tramway?"

Yes, I am, I answered with assumed assurance. It'll be different from any ride I've ever had.

"Well," and he sounded doubtful, "you can take the ride if you want. You can go up but I don't allow any woman underground. Now — before starting, there's a little formality to attend to. A company rule requires each of you to sign a document absolving the company from all blame in case of an accident."

I must say, signing that form was such a dampener that my signature turned into a scrawl. Something equally startling confronted me when I saw the waiting ore bucket. It had room for only one rider! I had expected Joe to hold me in a tight embrace and talk or sing to me as we ascended together and I'm sure he had expected this too. The situation demanded immediate action and my husband instilled some bravery into me by jumping in the carrier to ride up first. He called back, "A perfect day for an aerial trail! See you at the top in a few minutes, dearie."

I watched until Joe became a speck in the distance and asked Dann, Do you ride in the ore buckets? His response was hardly comforting.

"Gosh, yes. I go up and down on the tramway every day. The thing sways, but that's nothing to worry about. Makes you think of a rocking chair. Hasn't killed anyone yet, though there could be such a problem. If it gets hung up and stops before you reach the top, don't yell and don't move. You could be rescued in a few hours, maybe. You're a lucky girl to have a ride on the longest single span tramway in the world. Get ready. Here comes an empty. Let me help you in and away you go. Enjoy yourself!"

I swung out from the terminal sitting upright in the ore bucket as my husband had done. The view of surrounding mountains from my elevated perch was magnificent, but how cold I was in spite of layers of woolen clothing and high leather boots encasing woolen socks. I leaned forward and looked down over the bucket's rim to see the river rushing toward the sea and became dizzy. This feeling alarmed me and I hurriedly sat upright again. Then a sickening thought came to me. I was completely cut off from mankind, so isolated that I began to feel like the Ancient Mariner of Samuel Taylor Coleridge's poetic tale:

Alone, alone, all, all alone,
Alone on a wide, wide sea.

Yes, I was indeed all alone but unlike the Ancient Mariner I was suspended high on a wide sea of space. There was nothing as substantial as the sea directly beneath where a swim to safely might be possible. Practical common sense came to my aid in that moment of distressing loneliness which directed me to give myself a sensible command in a loud voice. Consequently, I shouted, Look up at the sky! Think how very lucky you are. Your husband is a big man and had no choice but to sit up in this cramped bucket. You're small enough to lie down. Do that.

From a reclining position I surveyed the sky of soothing blue and calming white clouds. The serenity above helped control my anxiety until I felt a definite tilt and remembered that the tramway started at an elevation of one hundred and eighty feet and rose to an elevation of four thousand feet. The bucket and I were now climbing up the mountainside nearing the upper terminal and, as the angle tipped us precariously, I became fearful of falling out. There was nothing to which I might cling. I felt much safer after my arms and legs instinctively cooperated to form me into the semblance of a ball in the middle of the carrier.

Suddenly, a fog hugging the cliff enveloped me and I lay in a shroudlike vapour of gray. Moisture dripped on my face and I pulled my wide-brimmed hat down over my eyes to shut out the sight of the menacing mist. I lay motionless for what seemed hours. At last, movement slowed and I peeked from the side of my hat. I had finally passed though the fog into sunlight and was stopping at the upper terminal. There on solid ground stood Joe beside the cable operator. He cried out, "My wife. She's gone!" He couldn't see me because my legs and arms had been temporarily immobilized and I had trouble sitting up. When my head became visible, Joe shouted, "Thank God. You're safe!"

I tried to relieve the agitation of my dearly loved and loving husband as he lifted me out of the bucket by quipping, What speedy and exciting transportation! Taking the trail with you can never be dull. Joe gave me a bearlike hug and his voice was husky with emotion when he could speak rationally.

"Madge, my dear little wife, you'll never know how much I suffered when I thought I'd lost you. Your progress was followed by binoculars until you faded into the fog. Then you didn't appear to be in the bucket when it stopped here. What a terrible moment! I'll never subject you to such danger again or myself to such agony as thinking you had fallen and been carried away by the Bear River."

The operator of the tramway was standing beside Joe. He scratched his chin and looked regretful before admitting, "Ma'am, I didn't help your husband none. I kept wonderin' why he was all steamed up and says to him, You acts as if you're expectin' someone special. He says, 'I am.' Who, I asks. 'My wife,' says he. I says, My God man, what have you got against her? Why, ridin' this thing is plenty dangerous. I'd not do it for all the money in the world. Gee, Mrs. Mandy, there's a chance of gettin' stopped and stuck when crossin'. Guess you could die from bein' scared or go plumb loco if you had to hang up there alone in the air for a spell. If one of the cables had broke, you'd have been dumped out and dead for sure. By golly, it's good you made it!"

Joe held my hand in a viselike grip as we walked a few feet to the upper terminal office. He needed assurance that I was beside him and not in the river. Dann arrived in the bucket following mine and wasted no time in telling Joe of procedure for the day.

"We start now, Dr. Mandy, for hours of examination and sampling. I've got so much for you to see and report on in our fabulous showings. A woman couldn't stand up to our pace, Mrs. Mandy. You'll be fine here in the office. Let's go, Dr. Mandy."

The men were off after Joe checked the safety of the small office and told me not to worry about the length of time he'd be in the depths of the mine. I ventured outside and came right back because a walk on this site was impossible. There was a lovely view from a large window of mighty mountains which shut out all the rest of the world to remind me I was "behind the beyond" where stillness prevailed. I sat down to re-live the climb to this quiet place, so unprepared for a knock at the door that I jumped up and backed myself into the farthest corner of the room. My caller was a shy young man whose timidity made him stutter.

"I, uh - Mr. Dann he - uh - sent me. I'm to - uh - ask - if - you want anything."

I thanked him for coming and said I would like some paper and a pen or pencil. The nervous youth drew from a desk drawer a pen, two pencils and a box filled with typing paper. He also handed me a magazine with a doubtful, "You - uh - would - maybe like - to read this?" The periodical was Esquire, a man's magazine I hadn't seen. My caller turned to leave and saw a paper bag on top of a filing cabinet. He picked it up and laid it on the desk. While hurrying to the door his words floated back. "You - would like - the candies in - uh -the bag? You can - uh - eat them all." The shy visitor didn't linger for he was obviously not a lady's man.

I read articles in Esquire and wrote letters until noon, stopping then to eat sandwiches and cookies Mrs. Hutchings had prepared to fit into my jacket pockets. The candies provided energy in the afternoon while I was writing or walking a bit around the little office for exercise. It was early evening when Dann and Joe returned to escort me to the tramway terminal. Dann was still talking of the vast deposit of gold and silver in "his mountain." The descent down the mountain and across the Bear River was less frightening at night than swinging along in the brightness of a sunny morning. I lay on my back with knees bent upward and gazed at the beauty of the full moon above me. The stars were equally enchanting and confirmed Henry Wadsworth Longfellow's description of them:

Silently one by one, in the infinite meadows of heaven
Blossomed the lovely stars, the forget-me-nots of the angels.

There was a spiritual quality in the moon and stars, inducing such serenity that my eyes began to close. They were still shut when the ore bucket halted at the lower terminal. I was just beginning to waken, drowsily aware of being lifted out of the carrier and hearing Dann's exclamation.

"Great Scot, Dr. Mandy! Can you believe it? Your wife's asleep!"

The next morning Dalby Morkill was seated at the breakfast table when Joe and I came into the dining room. He looked at us as if we had come back from the dead and his voice was filled with relief.

"You're alive! I worried about you two all yesterday. Am I ever glad to see you!"

I couldn't resist asking, Will you ride up to the United Empire as we did?

"Absolutely no. I wouldn't do that for anything or anybody."

Two weeks later, the government assessor in Prince Rupert was sent to the United Empire Mine on official business. I met him on the street when he returned and was surprised at his shaking a fist at me and saying angrily, "Mrs. Mandy, am I ever mad at you!"

I hardly knew the tall, broad, overweight man. I was surprised by his rage and inquired, What have I done to make you so angry, Mr. Cripps?

"You went to the United Empire Mine in that little ore bucket. I intended to take the trail to it but the whole town of Stewart questioned that. 'Aren't you going up on the tramway? Mrs. Mandy did.' That forced me to do the same."

You didn't have to do what I did, I argued.

"Oh yes, I did. Stewartites would have branded me a coward if I hadn't."

Well, having gone up on the tramway, did you like the ride?

"Like it? I was almost scared to death, the most terrible thing I've ever, ever done. To make matters worse, when I came home and told my wife about it she asked, 'Did you think of me when you were in such danger?' I told her the truth. All I could think about was that I wouldn't have to keep a date with the dentist next month. She's hardly spoken to me since."

The angry man and Joe and I must have had a guardian angel protecting us on the perilous tramway, considering what happened a few days after we three were passengers. An ore bucket stopped halfway to the upper terminal and in it crouched a chap from Stewart en route on business to the United Empire Mine. He and his metal carrier hung high in space above the Bear River for two hours before a raging wind subsided, operating mechanism was righted and he was pulled up the mountain. On hearing of the man's ordeal I cried, knowing that the same frightening experience could have happened to Mr. Cripps, Joe or me. The press reported the rescued man admitting, "I was most scared out of my wits. I couldn't move, had to stay still and keep my mind active. I'm not overly religious but I prayed and kept saying, I'll get out of this and I did." I asked myself how I should have reacted had I been trapped in the very same way. Could I have been so courageous? I'll never know and certainly wouldn't want to try to find out what my reaction would be.

The next year Joe and I went again to Stewart. After his examination of promising properties, during which time I remained in the hospitable town, my husband took me to the adjacent Premier Mine. On the Sunday before visiting Premier, Joe and I joined Bill Kergin, the doctor for the mine, and his wife Helen for a ramble on Chickamin Glacier. It was reached by the road which led for fifteen miles to the mine, eleven of these miles being in Alaska. The expansive field of ice had many crevasses and long-legged Bill leaped like a mountain goat over the small ones. I shivered when Joe snapped a picture of me backed into a fissure and tried unsuccessfully not to look scared.

Helen guessed from my reaction to glacier danger that the winding, hair-raising mountain road to the Premier Mine would be alarming to me. She kindly offered relief from this tension by asking me to have lunch with her in the Kergin apartment while my husband was conferring on mine matters. I accepted the invitation and our walk in the afternoon let me see the general layout of the community. There were buildings with accommodations for single and married men, attractive homes with colourful flower gardens, tennis courts, a hospital, a school, recreation hall and a few shops. Helen told me that the mine was equipped with a concentrator of about five hundred tons daily capacity and power was supplied by its own plant. Concentrates were carried eleven and one half miles by aerial tramway to the Stewart dock for shipment. I saw four appealing aspects of living at the Premier Mine site: the Alpine setting was unusually beautiful, snow on the mountains provided first-class skiing and the close proximity of Stewart and Prince Rupert offered shopping opportunities and social activities. Added to these assets was the neighbourly spirit of the Northwest.

In the late afternoon, Joe came to tell me he was expected to spend the next two days at the United Empire Mine. That meant staying overnight there. He said he would go to the property by the worst trail imaginable and he thought it best for me not to climb it.

"Wait for me at the Bayview Hotel, little pal. I'll be there with you in the evening of the second day from now," he promised.

Bill Kergin had come home in time to hear Joe's scheduled trip and suggested, "Why don't you stay with Helen and me, Mrs. Mandy, until the day when Dr. Mandy gets back to Stewart?"

Joe approved of this proposal and I remained with the Kergins. I hoped their moral support would lessen my anxiety about Joe being alone on such a hazardous trail. My peace of mind was shattered at dinner that evening by an ominous prediction from Bill.

"Mrs. Mandy, I don't like to frighten you, but it is dangerous in more ways than one for Dr. Mandy to go the United Empire Mine."

The thought of more than trail danger for my husband terrified me and I demanded, Just what do you mean, Bill?"

"Dr. Mandy's report, after his examination of the mine last year, indicated it was still a prospect. He concluded that a profitable operation could not be assured until proven by more exploratory work. That evaluation implied a speculative venture which was not written into the publicity brochures of the company. His report practically stopped financing. One man connected with the mining company was furious over this adverse effect. When in his cups at a Stewart beer parlour, the fellow damned the report and shouted, 'I'm going to get Dr. Mandy!' Of course that was the threat of an infuriated bully but should be seriously considered. I'm worried because that chap who made the threat will be conducting Dr. Mandy around the mine where the tunnels are long and dark."

I was very upset and angrily asked, Why didn't you tell my husband of this?

"Because Dr. Mandy is a conscientious and courageous man. It is his job to go up to that mine to check on what has been done since he was there. An up to date progress report is required. He wouldn't allow any warning to keep him away."

Why are you telling me this? I tearfully queried. Can anything be done to stop a tragedy?

"Yes, I think so. You must tell your husband what I've told you and advise him to be very careful. Here's the telephone. Talk to him."

My quavering voice retold Bill's story and I begged Joe not to go to the mine. His response was what Bill had anticipated.

"My dear, I must go. The Department Of Mines needs another assessment and report. I shall be cautious, though, walk behind my guide at all times and bed down at night with the cook as a room-mate. Try not to worry and remember my promise — I'll be with you in the evening of the second day from now."

That night was far from peaceful as I dreamed of a man pushed over a cliff and of another fatally stabbed and buried under fallen rock in an induced mine cave-in at the end of a long, black tunnel. How anxious I was during the two day waiting period. The Kergins did their best to entertain me but I have no recollection of what they did. Back at the hotel, Mrs. Hutchings tried to calm my nerves with tea and cake. However, it was impossible to end my anxiety until Joe came slowly in, tired and dirty, but alive. He smiled and patted me on the shoulder saying, "I told you I would meet you here at this time. I always keep a promise."

It was soon time for Joe and I to return to the haven of home in Prince Rupert. We had so much to remember from our experiences in the highly mineralized Portland Canal area where Stewart was the hub. Prospectors and mining companies had developed the all important centre and their invincible spirit and optimism had been carried on by the following settlers to prevent the ghost fate of mining communities. Now, in the '80's, prospecting for gold and the opening of new and reopening of old, abandoned gold mines in the vicinity should lead to a new era of prosperity for the town of mineral fame which my husband always called, "Stalwart Stewart".

## THE ISOLATED UNUK RIVER REGION

"Flying into and seeing the isolated and uninhabited Unuk River Region should be memorable for you," said Joe as we climbed into a plane at Stewart's dock.

In my memory was a picture of the horse I had seen the year before, a reluctant passenger in this plane, his destination the same as ours. He'd made it and this was reassurance for the flight in spite of Mrs. Hutching's warning.

"You oughtn't to go. It's dangerous up over all them miles of glaciers."

I answered, Flying over a ninety mile icecap can't be more dangerous than travelling on the United Empire Company's aerial tramway. You'll remember I survived that air trail.

We had some anxious moments on take-off as our airship taxied around the harbour near the dock. Not a breath of wind helped or hindered but the plane did not respond to mechanism. Although a heavy box was thrown out to lighten the freight cargo, further circling kept us on the water. We felt a fluttering on the third attempt and Joe and I were bumped hard against each other as the man-made bird began to soar. Gradually the perspiring pilot relaxed and so did Joe and I. Our plane flew swiftly across the vast, dazzling white and forbidding icefield that capped the coast range. We looked down on the Salmon River and saw the road climbing through Alaskan Territory and crossing into British Columbia to the Big Missouri and Premier Mines. The Premier looked like a tiny jewel in a setting of forest fringed mountain. I asked, Why are so many mineral deposits in such inaccessible places?

Joe recalled many arduous climbs burdened with heavy mineral samples taking a toll of his back and replied with a sigh, "I wish they weren't. Geology will give you an explanation, but sometimes I think the Devil played a part in their locations."

On we flew and these thoughts were with me all the way. If we have to land on this massive expanse of crevasse-indented ice, it will be a long way to walk back to Stewart, that is, if we can walk back. Probably we'd be caught in a crevasse and held frozen there forever. Oh well, I rationalized, if there is such a disaster, I'm sure freezing will be preferable to burning to death. No matter what happens, there's always some compensation. Finally, we were beyond glaciers and sighting something spectacular I voiced the discovery to Joe.

Look. A red cliff! Isn't it a striking contrast to the white icecap?

Joe turned from snapping a picture to say, "That's an oxidized knob and its colour is a welcome contrast to the whiteness of the glaciers."

A few minutes later I whispered to Joe, The pilot's getting ready to come down. I hope we land on the right lake. There's so many and they're so small. I held my breath when a downward dive almost stood me on my head before a perfect landing on the water was achieved. The pilot began unloading freight while telling us, "Camp's only three miles away. Dr. Mandy, you and I will each take a pack and some of the men I freight for will pick up the rest." I insisted on carrying my little packsack and followed the men on a marked trail. Just beyond the landing lake we tramped through snow and then up and down slopes into flowering flats. Before long, the figure of a man appeared on the skyline. Coming close, I saw his thin face, curly hair and shirt were wet with perspiration from his hasty hike. When he spoke his voice rang out with a cordial greeting.

"Hello Mandys! I'm Bill Prout. Radio said you'd be here about now. Saw the plane coming and I'm here to welcome you to our Unuk River camp. You go right on. I'll load my back and catch up."

We hiked to the camp of a syndicate formed in 1930 by Tommy Mackay, Harry Melville, Sam Coulter and Bill Prout. These men from the Premier Mine persuaded a few friends to join them in their venture of prospecting for gold in the Unuk River Mining Division of the Portland Canal. Two camps had been established for exploration during some short summer periods and now in 1934 a request had come to my husband for an examination of and report on staked claims. The men were lured into their exploration by the hearsay tales of old-timers and by a 1929 report of the British Columbia Department Of Mines relating to the isolated region. Some mineral development in the area dated back from 1901 - 1903. At that time the only entry was from Ketchikan, Alaska, to the mouth of the Unuk (still in Alaska), then on by a specially constructed boat. The turbulent river was navigable just a short distance before trail travel on foot led into the province of British Columbia. There had been practically no mining development in the region since the turn of the century because of transportation difficulties. A plane in the '30's offered quick, though hazardous, access.

The syndicate's lower camp was ideally situated on a slight rise above a meadow dotted with a variety of wild flowers. It was bordered by a little lake, patches of hemlock and spruce, a naturally coloured rocky knoll and an enchanting view of highly stretching, snow and glacier-topped mountains. The pilot nodded toward a chunky, red-faced man coming out of a log cabin and introduced him with a chuckle.

"This fellow is Sam Coulter. He's the assayer and has a substantial building here for testing. It's so hot inside that nobody goes into it but him. Sam, this is Dr. and Mrs. Mandy."

Sam's voice was as warm as his face. "Glad you came Dr. and Mrs. Mandy," he said with a smile. "It's good to have guests and especially nice to have one of them a little lady. You'll bring some refinement to us roughnecks here, Mrs. Mandy. We haven't much luxury to offer you. In fact, none at all. But everything we have in a civilized way is yours. Say, what's this?"

Sam picked up a parcel from the mail and handed it to me saying, "I present to you, Mrs. Mandy, the book of the month to read while you're in camp. Didn't think you'd find a lending library in this unpopulated spot, did you? Sniff, sniff, I smell something burning. That'll be Bill's cake. Guess he forgot about his baking in running to see what the plane brought. You in there, Harry, what's wrong with your smeller? Rescue the cake and then hurry out and meet the Mandys. I've got to get back to my fiery assay furnace."

Harry shouted, "Be with you Mandys soon as the cake's out of the oven."

Seconds later Harry was with us, a slightly stooped, tall man who moved leisurely and awkwardly. His informality and candid humour were delightful and made the camp a homey place.

"Hello folks. My whole name's Harry Melville. Good thing I'm here to show you the ropes. That Sam never stops except for a few minutes to feed his face. Works from sunrise to sunset and gets fat doing it. Fellows at the upper camp are like him. They say they work almost day and night. As for me, I'm a lazy lout but I've got enough energy today to show you our camp layout. Then I'll scare up some grub for lunch before I amble around to get supper. Right here's our bunking and cookhouse."

The combined living-dining and sleeping quarters and the tool shed nearby had substantial walls of logs and colourful green canvas roofs. The cabin contained a table, a stove, two benches and two stump chairs. It also had lower and upper bunks along one wall and a single bunk at each end of them, all with mattresses of hemlock boughs. A guest bunk, where Joe and I would spend our nights, was fitted into the rear wall of an adjoining utility cabin and reached through a narrow aisle between boxes and bags of varied supplies. What a different bedroom from any I'd known, but adequate for sleeping.

Bill helped Harry to prepare a lunch of cheese sandwiches, tomatoes, canned green beans and stewed dried apricots with burned cake for dessert. Burly Ed Edwardson, down from an upper camp, was asked by Harry to "Sup with us. Mind you're polite and let our guests have their fill in case there's not seconds for everybody." Ed had some outcroppings he wanted Joe to see and asked me to go with them for an examination. We were soon off on a hiking survey and upon returning for supper Joe's appetite and mine compared equally with the appetites of Harry, Bill, Sam and Ed who had guided us back. Joe patiently answered the geological questions asked in after supper conversation. Even Sam took time off from assaying to join in. The night was cold and I was content to sit near the stove and listen. I was cheered, in this cabin lit by a candle and miner's lamps, by the intense interest of the men.

Ambitious Bill Prout wanted to glean as much information as possible from Joe during his limited stay. At midnight he babbled, "We've got so much to show you, Dr. Mandy. Wish we could start out right now and ·,"

Sam interrupted, "Say, give the man a chance to bed down. He's got to have some sleep. We all need to snooze and ·. Look at Mrs. Mandy! She's trying not to fall asleep, so tired she should be carried to her bunk. Goodnight all."

Joe and I found getting to bed in this camp was not an easy thing for us to do. I could slip through the narrow passage of the utility cabin to the bunk at the far end but Joe had to maneuver himself sideways to get to it. There followed a laughable manipulation of undressing and hoisting ourselves up into sleeping bags laid on the fragrant boughs piled high on a wooden frame. When we were finally recumbent, trail tiredness put us to sleep in seconds. We were wakened in the chill of an early morning by the pleasing aroma of bacon and coffee calling us to the adjoining cookhouse. Harry had learned from old-timers how to make good flapjacks, a staple of northern camps, and his were a supporting start for the day. Breakfast over, Joe and I followed Bill who told us the trail we'd take would involve much climbing. Suddenly I stopped, startled. Someone in this isolated spot was whistling at me! Bill and Joe paid no attention to the sound piercing the stillness. I hurried to them and whispered, Somebody is whistling at me. Who can it be? Bill laughed and pointed. "Look over there. See that little fellow? He'll hop into his hole if he thinks we're going after him. That's the marmot, commonly known as the whistler. Sounds like a man, doesn't he? Of course you've got to be afraid of whistlers in the city, Mrs. Mandy, but not of gentle, whistling marmots in the wilds. He's harmless, real cute and pretty, too."

The air had been frosty but the combined sun and hiking soon warmed us. There were frequent and prolonged stops while Joe and Bill went into a huddle over mineralization along the trail. Open cuts of the previous season demanded close examination and samples were chipped and collected in sacks. Eventually, we came upon the crew of the upper camp diamond drilling an oxidized knob and, as always, I was impressed by the use of diamonds to penetrate hard rock. At one o'clock, lunch was ready in the cook house a few strides away. The men laid down their tools and led us to the same type of structure as that at the lower camp, log walls and canvas roof.

Ed Edwardson was cook for the day. He offered the miners a basin of hot water for a refreshing cleanser of sweaty, sun-scorched faces and grimy hands before serving them lunch. Joe and I were welcome guests and sat down to eat with the men. Invading mosquitoes constantly attacked all of us as we ate with difficulty, one hand feeding the mouth and the other brushing off irritating insects. There was lingering for technical discussion to which I was too drowsy to listen, so I went outside to throw myself on the ground beside a big boulder which provided some shelter from the sun. Here rest was impossible with scores of mosquitoes attacking my face and hands until big Ed thoughtfully draped several yards of mosquito netting over me. Oh thank you, I murmured and fell asleep under the protective covering, knowing I should never forget his kindness. I was roused after this needed nap by the voice of tireless Bill.

"Mrs. Mandy, wake up. There's much to see and do. We must go on."

Progress was slow, as Joe scanned the near and distant scene and Bill hurled innumerable questions at him. My knowledge of geology was limited and when my husband referred to a tuff I chose to apply the term, spelled tough, to the uninhabited Unuk River Region, a vast and forbidding wilderness of natural grandeur to explore. I had managed to keep up with Joe and Bill in spite of my legs being much shorter than theirs. However, I was beginning to tire after a bit of speeding on their part and was glad when Bill paused to point at a high, rounded ridge in front of us.

"That's what we fellows call Battleship Dome," he said enthusiastically. "You're going to the top with me. From up there you'll see the most magnificent mountain panorama in the world."

The Dome looked terribly steep to me with no horse's tail to help pull me up. Bill and Joe demonstrated the best climbing technique

Joe and Madge on Battleship Dome in Unuk River region.

for the slope and with the walking stick Joe provided I worked my way up trailing behind them. The view from the summit was, as Bill had asserted, magnificent. Below and around us in nature's blending colours was a succession of hills, valleys, creeks and lakes of varying size and in the distance towered rocky, snow and glacier-crowned mountains of indescribable beauty. We stood in silent awe for a few moments and fed our souls on this sublime scroll of a Mighty Maker, as yet uncontaminated by mankind. I wished we could stay there for hours exalted by a pervading spirituality. Bill could not tolerate a delay which did not concern mining and soon shattered our unwordly mood by a brusque, "Time to go." Bill demonstrated how Battleship Dome was easily descended by sitting down and grasping a spray of heather on either side, shifting those flowering brakes to maintain balance and speed. Never could I have imagined a heather slide and had there been time I would have gladly climbed up the Dome again for the fun of coming down in that way.

The afternoon had lengthened when Bill said, "We'd better turn back to the upper camp for supper and go below later. Say, wait a minute. See that ledge above the side of the lake ahead, Dr. Mandy? It'll only take minutes to look at it."

A good half hour passed before the men completed their investigation. At last we started campward and were startled by a shout. A long figure appeared to rise out of a hillock and rush by with a wave of a long arm. I laughed and said jestingly, He must be a ghost who lives in the red cliff I saw when flying here. Probably he has certain hours for wandering! I was corrected by factual minded Bill.

"That's Harry Melville. He's a camera nut and is photographing today. His pictures help get more financing for our syndicate. They're really professional."

We tucked heartily into Ed's supper at the upper camp and the crew relaxed after a hard day's work. Questions and discussion lasted for three hours and might have continued longer had not my husband noticed me blinking my eyes furiously in order to stay awake. Then Joe suggested, "Rest and sleep will benefit everyone around the table," and all agreed. Fatigue made the trail downward steeper, rockier and longer than when I climbed it in the morning. The cookhouse was a pleasing sight when tired and hot, in spite of the chilly night, we stumbled into it. There we were refreshed by strong tea and a remnant of Bill's burned cake before literally falling into our bunks.

In the morning Bill and Joe announced their intention of roaming miles that day and thought it advisable for me to rest at the camp. They left me crowding down more flapjacks. When Harry poured my second cup of coffee I asked him, Do you think I could do something special? I'd like to explore a bit on my own, close to camp of course. He did not think it advisable but yielded to my persuasion and packed a lunch of two cheese sandwiches, a small package of raisins, an apple and a chocolate bar for me to carry in my small kit bag. He also gave me guidance and restrictions.

"Do you know I'm responsible for looking after you today? Well, I am and I don't think you should be traipsin' by your lonesome in this land behind the beyond. Should anything happen to you, off with my head. I'll let you go if you will follow my instructions. Here they are. Mark a trail with little piles of stones so's you can't get lost. Don't go far. Watch your step when climbing so's you won't have a fall and break a leg. Get back early, and that's important. Wouldn't want your Uncle Harry to worry, would you? So long, and mind what I've been telling you."

An almost obliterated trail led me to the deserted camp of a prospecting group with its name and mining results printed in pencil on a blazed tree:

Unuk Syndicate
Here in '31
Back in '34
And find
We have lost the ore

Evidently the men in that exploration had been encouraged to prospect in the area by reports which I had skimmed in Stewart about H. W. Ketchum. The prospector had staked claims with high gold content in this remote wilderness in 1890. He then sold them in 1900 to a company which started development by constructing a wagon road from the mouth of the Unuk River at Burroughs Bay, in Alaska, to claims on a mountain approximately 7500 feet high in British Columbia. Unfortunately, the transportation of machinery to the property was a failure and the operation ended. The exploring men my husband now advised must, I concluded, have the same golden dreams as prospector Ketchum had and I hoped theirs would be fully realized.

Peaceful solitude in a setting of sublime beauty on a grand scale wrapped itself around me. I walked slowly, feeling as alone as when in the ore bucket suspended high above the Bear River en route to the United Empire Mine. At noon I sat down to eat lunch and to ask myself a question. Why did men risk their lives to get here and then cheerily endure backbreaking work and the privations of isolation? Reflection told me there were two compelling reasons, the possibility of acquiring wealth from discovering gold and the joy of adventure — each the secret dream of many a man. How privileged I was to share those dreams and to combine mine with romance!

After a time I was serenaded by whistling marmots. The wary rodents now accepted me as part of the environment. They made me feel I was no longer alone and I wished they were tame enough to pet. I had let my mind wander from the outside world of people and now turned to their problems in the book of the month which Sam had loaned me. I became so absorbed in reading the novel that I only stopped when my back began to pain from leaning against a hard boulder for support. A glance at my watch reminded me that the trail back to camp was a long walk and I'd better hike there quickly. Harry voiced approval as I entered the cookhouse.

"So, you did what Uncle Harry asked, got back early. I hoped you'd have sense enough to do that. Good girl. Gee, your face is red. Some sunburn you've got and you look tuckered out. Sit down and have a dish of tea. I don't go for the afternoon tea bit but having tea with Doc Mandy's wife, who goes on dangerous trails with her husband, makes it all right. I'm getting up a dandy supper — roast mountain goat, baked potato, canned tomatoes, dessicated vegetables and the best rice pudding black with raisins you ever ate. Sounds yummy, don't it? Say, did you feel scared flying over the long icecap? I sure did. But what's a scare to maybe finding gold? We syndicate fellows are spending our vacation and hard earned money prospecting in this hard to get to place and -"

"Don't let him give you a sob story," interrupted Sam who had come in to get a drink of cold water. "He thinks it a lark to be in this Unuk wilderness. You know, Harry, if we weren't here we'd be throwing holiday money away without having anything to show for it. Who knows what we may discover? Mrs. Mandy, wouldn't you like to see some assaying? Pretty warm in my set-up but come along and stay as long as you can stand it."

"Don't go in there," advised Harry. "The assay office is hotter than Hell."

Sam opened the door and a blast of very hot air almost knocked me down. I just knew I dared not enter or Sam would be picking me up off the floor. Sorry, I gasped. I - don't have what it takes to stand up to the heat an assayer does. I've learned something, though, from only a whiff. When reading mining reports in the future with their tabulated results of so many ounces to the ton of gold, silver, copper, etc., I'll know the information comes from those with stamina like yours. Please excuse my weakness.

It was far into the night when Bill and Joe returned and early in the morning they were off again. I told Harry before he started a day of photography that I would prepare Sam's lunch and he replied, "Fine. Why not help me prepare supper too?" Harry left a package of spaghetti, a tin of meat, a loaf of bread, tomatoes, cheese and a can of sliced pineapple on the table for the noon meal and directed me to add water and more coffee to what was left in the pot "so's you'll have a really strong, stimulating drink." The heat and problems associated with the camp cookstove were forgotten when I saw the smile on Sam's face as he looked at his filled lunch plate.

"This is great," he declared, "nothing I like better than spaghetti! I can eat at least three helpings. When I rnake my fortune from the development of our Mackay Syndicate claims, I'm going to Italy and live on spaghetti and cheese for at least six months!"

On our last night in camp, Harry pulled a letter from a file and asked, "You Mandys want to hear about a prospector who's not like any you've known? He lives in Switzerland and says he's been mining for years. Does it the cushy way, from an armchair. Lately, in the same country and from the same armchair, maps and reports have taken him prospecting in Canada. I'll read you what he's written.

Joe and I were made speechless by the preposterous contents of the letter and Harry commented with a grin, "Must be a smart guy to study the map of British Columbia, prospect on it and stake on the map at the exact spot of our location before we staked. He doesn't ask for but demands partnership in our syndicate. He forgot to enclose money to pay expenses for proving and developing the property. How he ever heard of us, I'll never know. What do you think, Doc? Should we divvy up?"

My husband laughed so hard he almost fell off his stump chair. "Boys," he said, "I've heard some ridiculous pretensions to prior staking and rights, but this one tops them all."

"Well," replied Harry, "when we fellows get over-tired and cranky, all we have to do is read this letter and howl ourselves into feeling bright enough not to be taken over by such nonsense. I've filed it away for those times when we need to laugh."

That same evening Joe spread out on the table a map he had sketched of the area and we all studied it. He had affixed names where none had existed and they were those of the men present and their co-partners. The syndicate associates whooped excitedly at finding themselves so justly and lastingly honoured. Each proudly pointed to his name on the map: Prout Plateau, Sam Coulter Creek, Harrymel Creek and Melville Glacier. Then Harry clapped Joe on the shoulder, his smile changing to a frown.

"Look here, Doc, you haven't put yourself in."

"Of course not," Joe responded. "That would be a conceited thing to do. If you all think I should be represented, why not name a mountain for my wife? Mount Madge sounds melodious, doesn't it?"

"Great," chorused the men. "She deserves a mountain. She's as much a trail blazer as we are. Throw in a lake for her, too. There's lots of them around."

Joe penned the names Mount Madge and Madge Lake on the map, mentioning an elevation of approximately 7,500 feet for my mountain. However, Harry was not to be silenced and after conferring with the other men spoke for all.

"You must be in on this, too, Dr. Mandy. We won't let you go to bed till your John Henry is on that map."

Reluctantly, my husband penned the name of Joe Mandy to a creek and emotionally stated the reason for his choice of that particular one. "This creek is at the foot of Mount Madge. There, symbolically, I shall be on my knees for all time in adoration of my dear wife Madge."

The only fast way of communicating with the outside world from the Cassiar-Stikine was the single wire of the Yukon Telegraph Line which extended some 1,900 miles from Vancouver to Dawson City via Telegraph Creek and Atlin.
The line was maintained by men such as Fred Appleyard. In June 1935 with his pack dogs he leaves on a lonely patrol from Echo Lake, some 110 miles from Telegraph Creek.

"Right on, Doc," approved Harry. "Bill and Sam, three cheers for the romantic Mandys!"

The men raised their voices in a traditional salute and my response to Joe's heartfelt sentiment was moist eyes and a fervent clasp of his hand. That was a precious moment to remember and I relive it every time I look at a copy of Joe's Unuk River Region map on a wall in the Mandy home.

It was necessary for Joe to return to the Unuk River area the following year, entering from the Alaskan side where the river originated. Joe sadly told me, "I haven't been on the Unuk, but from what I read about it the Tatshenshini, Stikine and Dease Rivers are very safe by comparison. It can only be navigated a short distance and is chock-full of dangers. I shouldn't let you risk your life there. You'd better stay in Prince Rupert."

I protested, reminding him of my survival on the hazardous rivers he mentioned. A compromise came to mind and I asked, Why shouldn't I go as far as the mouth of the Unuk with you and wait for your return at that point? There's bound to be a settler nearby who would welcome someone from the outside for a little while. Joe thought for a moment before replying.

"What you say sounds logical and you know I don't want to go without you. I'll book a sailing north for two."

Leaving a coastal steamer at Ketchikan, Alaska, we flew into the interior. The plane carried, besides the Mandys, Walter Blanton and George King of Ketchikan who were interested in mining prospects. The weather cooperated to give us a clear view of the scenic seventy-five miles to the mouth of the Unuk at Burroughs Bay in Alaskan Territory. Joe asked the pilot if we could fly twenty-five miles farther to look at the river and the wilderness he would be entering by foot trail into British Columbia. Bob Ellis agreed to do this and the additional miles let me look down on a river more turbulent than any I had seen before. No wonder Joe thought I should not attempt bucking that raging water. Circling back to Burroughs Bay, Blanton pointed to a little branch of the Unuk leading to a desirable waiting place for me.

"There, Dr. Mandy," he said, "is the Matney ranch on an Alaskan island. I'm sure the Matneys will be tickled pink to have your wife as a paying guest. Their price should be reasonable. Mighty fine people, I'm told."

The pilot came down in wide Burroughs Bay and we waited until Len King rowed out from the scowhouse headquarters of some Ketchikan prospectors which was anchored in a small tributary of the Unuk River. Then Joe and I were rowed by Len to Matney's island which was surrounded by sloughs. The family there had been watching our approach and stood on the river bank to help us scramble up. Len introduced us.

"Halloo Matneys! Meet some folks whose name is almost like yours, Dr. and Mrs. Mandy. You Mandys meet Harvey, his wife Josephine and their two children, Arthur and Olive. How old are you kids? Fourteen, Arthur, and you're taller than Mrs. Mandy! Olive, you say you're ten? Quite a young lady you are. The Mandys come from Prince Rupert in Canada. They want to know if Mrs. Mandy can stay with you till her husband gets back from up river."

Joe quickly completed arrangements for my lodging and meals, took time to become briefly acquainted with the Matneys and voiced his relief in an aside to me. "You'll be well taken care of here, my dear. Life on an Alaskan ranch should be a unique experience. Have yourself happy days and tell me about them on our way home."

Arthur, Olive and I watched Joe help George, his brother Len and a waiting prospector load a river boat which was shovel-nosed at each end and had a slightly curved bottom, so constructed for handling in swift water. The river was such a torrent of noisy violence that I was content to remain on land and looked forward to being part of a wilderness family for a little while. The children led me to a white painted frame house, instead of the log cabin I'd expected to see. They were anxious to show me around the house as soon as we entered their home, Olive speaking like an enthusiastic tour guide.

"Here's the living room, with lots of windows. Ain't it nice? Over there is papa's and mamma's room. Come on, let's walk though it. Open the door in the side wall and look. You see a really, truly bathroom. Papa says other people living in a place like we do don't have a bathroom. Let's go to the dining room. We eat here at this long table and next is the kitchen. Mamma's got a big stove, hasn't she? And, she cooks good on it. Come on back to the living room. See the stairway at the end? That goes up to where me and Arthur sleeps. Our house, it wasn't built here. Papa bought it off a town lot and floated it up from Ketchikan. Now, you must see papa's halibut boat."

The children took me to a vessel which served as the Matney home when Harvey was a fisherman on the Alaskan coast. On dry land it was invaluable for storing sundry household supplies and farm, hunting, fishing and trapping equipment and as well provided space for laundry and churning. I was amazed at the variety of odds and ends it held. Obviously, nothing was thrown away on this ranch and everything saved was neatly arranged and reserved for use in the future. It wasn't long before Mrs. Matney came in with a hamper of clothes and told me of the family's life at sea on this boat.

"Every day was exciting. I had to tie Arthur and Olive on deck when they was little. I couldn't take a chance on them falling overboard. How many times I dragged them in quick when rain and wind come up sudden. My washing was hung on deck and, goodness me, I had to run to get it in before a storm started. It was sort of a battle to live with fish, a husband and kids on a halibut boat. Somehow I managed. I'm glad we come to this island, away from people. It's good for the children here. They can't get into mischief on the island. Arthur and Olive, bring Mrs. Mandy to lunch in a few minutes. It's almost ready."

I was charmed by the children, so unsophisticated and well-mannered. They had evidently been kindly treated and properly disciplined by their parents. Olive was talkative and said honestly whatever came into her mind. Her brother was shy and timidly made a request.

"Mrs. Mandy, will you come to my workshop with me and Olive? I want to show it to you."

I was totally unprepared for the contents of his large, one room log cabin workshop. It was a laboratory filled with shelves and cubby holes holding yards of wire, magnets, small motors, a few books, pencils and pads, etc. and a long worktable. Most of his paraphernalia I could not identify except by guess as associated with electrical matters. I concluded the boy might be a budding Thomas Edison and inquired, How did you learn about such things and where did you get all this apparatus?

"Oh," he said, "papa looked in the mail order catalogue and sent off for this stuff and books about it. I read about how to do things. Papa's good at this and helps me a lot. He's smart."

"Arthur's smart, too. He makes all kinds of things not in books. Papa says he's an inventor," added admiring sister Olive.

It seemed to me Arthur should be given guidance and training to develop his natural talent in a technical school and I discussed my opinion with his father at lunch. Mr. Matney frowned and confided a belief quite different from mine.

"Mrs. Mandy, you're young and don't know the world. I finds out firsthand it's a wicked place. Me and the wife is from a western American state and when too many of them cities starts springin' up with all sorts of evil crowdin' in, we up and left. Same thing happens when we moves to the state of Washington. By now we has two children and we wants to get away from sin. Heard tell of Alaska and we heads north to log and finds not many loggers is God fearin' men. I tried halibut fishin' but them fishermen round about us didn't respect the Lord as we done. Next, I gets me this island and me and my family live in the wilderness like pioneers afore us and worship God as we ought. We're alone and we likes bein' alone. Prospectors, trappers and some Indians goes by oncet in awhile mindin' their own business and mebbe stoppin' a few minutes to pass the time of day. I farm and trap and we Matneys live natural.

"My children has never went to school and I say they never will. There they'd get wrong ideas from teachers and other boys and girls. Anyways, they don't need learnin' in a school. I get on and I ain't had much schoolin'. Me and the wife, she's got through grade eight and knows a lot, can learn them. All they needs to know is a little 'rithmetic so's they can handle money and how to read and write a bit. We helps them with a few books we picks out from Sears Roebuck catalogues. Then our little radio has some programs for teachin' that's not sinful. I'm protectin' my family from what is and what is to be. I studies the Bible and scripture prophesies another war. We'll be better off on our island than anywheres else when that happens."

I hauled out all the arguments I could think of in favour of sending both the children to school and ended with, They live in the world and must tangle with its problems. How, I argued, can they do this if they know nothing but life on this isolated island? Lunch was prolonged while Harvey and I debated, with neither yielding an inch of our convictions. Mrs. Matney and the children ate in silence, shocked that anyone would contest the views held by the head of the house. At last, Harvey left to attend chores and Mrs. Matney disregarded the controversial conversation to tell me of an arrangement for my comfort and privacy in the Matney home.

"It's good to have another woman here. I'll do all I can to make your stay nice. I must tell you we don't have an extra bedroom but we can make do. I'll put a cot in a corner of the living room and hang a sheet, with a drawstring through the hem, in front of it. Daytime you can pull the sheet to one side and stretch it across at night."

Preparations for the makeshift bedroom started at once. Arthur hammered a nail into the wall on each side of the room and attached a cord to the nail on one side with a firm knot. Olive was sent off to get a sheet through which the cord was threaded and fastened on the other side. Arthur tested the curtain to see if it would pull easily and the children laughed uproariously when he lost his balance and collapsed in a sprawl on the cot. They were as genuinely amused as outside children would be by viewing slapstick comedy in a movie. I laughed with them and their mother smiled broadly.

A small table, from which a medium sized, highly coloured globe of the world was removed, held my typewriter. I asked if the globe was used to study geography and Olive queried, "What's geography?"

I gave her a sketchy, simple definition and then elaborated. Geography, Olive, is a study of the earth and everything in it — mountains, lakes, rivers, oceans, islands, countries, animal and plant life and people. It tells you where men, women and children live and what they do, like — building houses, towns and cities and how they make thousands of things to help mankind such as furniture, clothes, shoes, dishes, stoves and equipment for workshops, Arthur. Geography lets you find out about so many places and they're all different. Why, with geography you can travel all around this great, big earth of ours. What could be nicer? I'll show you on the globe where you live in Alaska, where I live in Canada and where I grew up in far off Indiana. Olive's response was, "This is fun!"

I woke early in the morning to hear whispering. Pulling back my curtain wall, I saw Arthur and Olive seated close by with the globe of the world between them. They wished me a good morning and I hurried to wash and dress in the bathroom. On returning to the living room I was greeted by a request.

"Mrs. Mandy, can we play the game now?" the children asked.

I didn't know to what they referred and had to ask, What game?

"Why, the geography game," Olive answered. "I told you yesterday it's so much fun!"

I thought how pleased teachers would be if all their students regarded this subject so eagerly. I had never considered teaching geography but such interested pupils deserved an attempt. From then on the game was played each day. History was introduced after I mentioned George Washington and Olive inquired, "What radio station is he on?" Both Arthur and Olive liked the incident of how George Washington cut down his father's cherry tree and refused to lie about his wrongdoing. They lacked the background to appreciate his adult leadership as General and first president of the United States but agreed, "We'd like to have known a man like him."

Breakfast was considered important in the Matney household, as it provided energy for a busy morning. Porridge, eggs, bacon, fruit and waffles baked on an iron griddle were served. I was encouraged to eat four to six waffles and I crammed those waffles down to please Mrs. Matney who prided herself on their goodness. Lunch and supper were substantial meals also, with rich desserts made especially for me. I expanded all over as a result. Large pitchers of milk stood on the dining table and all around the board were expected to drink two or three glasses of milk at each meal. We were forced into doing so by Mr. Matney's refrain.

"Milk is good for you. The cow on this ranch gives us aplenty. Not to use it is a sin. Drink up everybody."

On my second day at the farm, I told the children I must type some letters. They sat down opposite me, watching every move as I typed. When I stopped an hour later, they were still sitting quietly in the same position and now Olive could question me.

"How do you know which keys to hit? You don't look at them."

I told her about the touch method I had learned. She immediately ran off and returned shortly, lugging an old Oliver typewriter, to ask a favour.

"Will you please teach me to touch?"

I hadn't taught typing, but Olive's wish to be "fast like you" transformed me into a typing instructor. I prayed silently for success in this new role and listed our requirements: a large, heavy sheet of blank paper (this was supplied by the reverse side of an old pictorial calendar), a yardstick, a pen, dark crayon, adhesive tape and scissors. Squares were outlined on the blank page and letters and punctuation marks to match a typewriter keyboard were printed therein and darkened by crayon. Arthur hung this chart on the wall directly opposite where Olive would sit to type. I directed her in placing and moving her fingers on the keys. After this study of finger placement, the children enjoyed cutting circles of adhesive tape and sticking them on the typewriter keys so that Olive could memorize what was on them by looking at the chart. In this way she might soon develop touch typing I thought.

I devised for practice a series of copy pages beginning with letters and evolving into combinations of letters, words, sentences and liberally punctuated paragraphs and poetry requiring indentation. Olive was determined to become proficient in typing and set aside daily periods for practice. Harvey approved of the instruction because the developing skill meant Olive could quickly write business letters for him and keep his ranch records in better form. Arthur was supportive of Olive's project and took over some of her chores to give her time to practice typing. Her mother helped by commenting, "The touch way sounds better than the jerky stop and go pounding you did." The girl was an apt pupil and became fairly speedy and accurate before I left the island.

Mrs. Matney was a busy woman with home and farm work to do. In spite of this, she kindly planned some entertainment for me every day, usually a short excursion in a small row boat around her island and occasionally on a little creek that flowed into Unuk River's main stream. Arthur and Olive accompanied us and taught me how to fish. They were as excited as I when I caught two fish large enough for breakfast. On such a jaunt we stopped to sit for awhile on the creek's bank in such a secluded spot that it was like being in another world. We all felt a security plus unity with nature at its best. My feeling of safety was shattered, however, as Mrs. Matney rowed us away. I looked back to see a fringe of bush parting and a large, black bear lumber out. I shrieked, That bear's just where we were! Little Olive smiled and spoke reassuringly from the knowledge of a pioneer.

"Mrs. Mandy, that bear wouldn't have hurt us none. He come out to see what we look like. Glad he ain't a mean grizzly. Mamma don't have her gun along. If she did and any old bear started something, she'd shoot. Mamma's a good shot. She never misses."

The only books in the Matney home were elementary readers, beginner's mathematics and the Bible. There were, however, religious tracts and copies of an Alaskan magazine devoted to northern adventure. Arthur and Olive had never read or heard fairy tales which were such a lovely part of my childhood. I decided to tell them some of the best loved and started with Cinderella. My telling was cut short by Harvey.

"Stop, Mrs. Mandy. Cinderella, I know, is a fairy tale. My children mustn't hear it. I hold only with the truth and that story is not true.

Fairy tales ain't at all moral."

The children were disappointed but so disciplined they yielded without a murmur to "what papa thinks best". Well, I thought, their interest indicates they are story hungry, so I must draw from memory tales papa will accept. Harvey heard me tell dramatically the touching incident of George Washington kneeling in the snow at Valley Forge to pray for his poorly clad, barefoot soldiers encamped there. It had brought tears to my eyes when I was a child and did now. Harvey was so moved that he clapped his hands in approval.

"More true stories like that is fine," he assured me. "You can tell Arthur and Olive about Abraham Lincoln, too. I want you kids to know he was president of the United States. Folks called him 'honest Abe'. Yes, a right good man he was and he was a pioneer same as you younguns, me and your mother."

Both the children on this farm had their share of daily duties, including feeding the chickens and collecting eggs. The morning I went with them to assist in these essential chores, Olive carried not only a basket for the eggs but also a pail. The bucket, she said, was for the milk she'd get from a goat tethered a considerable distance from the house. We had walked only a little way when Arthur went into a fenced pasture, collared a bull and, attaching a rope to the collar, led him to our pathway. He kept as much space as possible between himself and the bull and the gun he carried was ready for action. Arthur explained his walk with the bull casually and fearlessly.

"Papa wants him moved to another pasture."

I eyed that creature warily and whispered, Do you think it safe to walk with a bull? Arthur sounded positive in his response.

"Sure I do. I won't let him hurt you none. If he tries, I'll shoot. Don't worry."

I did worry for the safety of both the children and myself should there be a shooting. Olive tried to relieve my nervousness by asserting what she believed.

"No need to get upset. He's so gentle he wouldn't even brush a fly off his back."

I wanted to believe her but I couldn't breathe normally until the bull was herded into a meadow with a good fence around it which included a strong gate. We went on until we sighted a belligerent looking goat and Olive ran ahead to pet her. The question she asked when I came up beside her was alarming.

"Wouldn't you like to milk the goat?"

I avoided a direct answer by saying, Maybe she wouldn't want me to milk her."

"Oh yes she would," insisted Olive. "She's friendly. I'll show you how to do it."

The goat stood quietly for Olive's demonstration and then I approached her slowly and, seating myself on a low stool, stretched out my trembling hands. That old goat turned her head and while defiantly looking me in the eye kicked the partially filled bucket. This reaction surprised me and in trying to jump up I lost my balance and fell to the ground. The children helped me up anxiously asking, "Are you hurt?" I recognized a comedy scene and brushing the dirt from my face and hair laughed loudly. Only then did that brother and sister laugh and I certainly agreed with Olive's following comment. "Mrs. Mandy, you'd better stick to teaching. You do that good. Milking is not right for you."

Harvey and I continued our debates for awhile and then I finally stopped arguing. Agreement or compromise was impossible and we admired each other for having the courage to adhere to our personal convictions. Moreover, Mr. Matney commanded respect for he was a sincere and good man and wanted the best for his family, striving for it the only way he knew. I listened sympathetically to a summary of paradise on his island.

"Mrs. Mandy," he said, "me and mine lives well here. Game, fish and wild fruit is all around. We gets milk from a cow and a goat, eggs from chickens which is good to eat and has lots of vegetables that grows like weeds. My biggest crop is rutabagas and I sells them in Ketchikan to Scandinavians. They calls that squash the Swedish turnip. We're happy because we're busy as folks should be. Best of all, we're away from the wicked world so's Arthur and Olive can't learn wrong things. Don't you think my children act good?"

There was just one answer. I certainly do and I wish there were more children on the outside like them.

The Matneys decided to give me a special treat of a drive one evening. I was puzzled about this suggested kindness because there was no auto or road on the island. Imagine my surprise when I saw their unusual type of conveyance and where I would be riding! Arthur and Olive took me to a vehicle which stood on a large, fenced field. Arthur pointed to it with enthusiasm in his spoken description.

"Mrs. Mandy, that's papa's big tractor. Fine machine, don't you think? It rides good and I'm going to drive you all over this garden patch in it."

I didn't know anything about tractors but judged this one was very powerful. It was much too high for me to climb into so I asked for a boost and was pushed up to sit beside Arthur. He took me around and around the field from which rutabagas had been harvested, cutting a rut to follow in the shape of a square and then diagonally crossing and criss-crossing. The vehicle had no room for Olive but she happily waved from a fence post seat whenever we passed her. No chauffeur of a Rolls Royce could have sat more proudly at the wheel of his car than Arthur as the driver of his father's tractor. He told me about the mechanism and operation of tractors, trapping in the winter, his work on the farm and how his father developed huge rutabagas which sold for a good price. An hour passed before we stopped. After being helped to the ground, I told these delightful children, You've given me my most unforgettable ride and I really enjoyed it. That was absolutely true!

Three weeks passed before Joe returned from his expedition and he was eager to hear of my activities on the island. All were told except the hike with the bull, for that would have disturbed him. I inquired about his trip and he said the Unuk River was frightening, even to the experienced river men with him. Bears presented another danger. At one point going up river they had to portage because an enormous grizzly bear defied passage from a sandbar in midstream. His journey had been hazardous and difficult on both river and trail but worthwhile in the acquiring of important information.

Joe now had to get back to Prince Rupert to assemble his report from examinations, consultations, notes and samples. I almost wished I didn't have to return to the rush and problems of the outside. I had enjoyed unique and pleasurable days living with a pioneer family on their Alaskan island and sadly said goodby to Mrs. Matney, Olive and Arthur, knowing we might never meet again. My farewell to Harvey Matney was said at Ketchikan where he took Joe and me in his small, motor-powered boat. The craft was primarily used for transporting vegetables and furs from trapping to market in that coastal town. I was given the only shelter provided, a section covered by a canvas top. The men were protected by waterproof suits and hats and didn't seem to mind the light rain falling. I amused myself by reliving those three weeks with the Matney family and recalled with astonishment my brief career there as teacher of geography, history and typing.

I felt rewarded for my typing instruction when Olive wrote me a letter "by touch" in the fall. She enclosed a copy of a story she had written and sent to the Alaskan Sportsman Magazine. The tale had been published as submitted with composition and spelling inaccuracies due to Olive's lack of education. I thought it excellent for a little girl who had lived in the wilds and had never attended school or been taught by correspondence courses. Here it is:

### WHO'S AFRAID OF THE BIG BROWN BEAR?
#### by Olive Matney
(This story is published just as Olive wrote it)

I am a girl of 10 years, but I like good stories and that is why I like the Alaskan Sportsman. but I notice that most stories are for big people so I would like to write one for little people.

We live up here on the Unuk Valley and we see a lot of wild life up here. we have bear for neighbours, and it is a very common thing to go out in the pasture and find the fences tore down where bear have gone through and they dont shut the gates behind them. One day Mamma and I decided to go out and pick berries up above our place. there are a lot of sloughs and rivers and the banks are covered with willow and berrybushes. and all through the brush are all sorts of bear trails and bear tracks.

we tried to be very careful not to go back in the brush to far because of bear.

After we had our baskets nearley full we decided to start home and in looking where we had been picking berries there was a log partly in the water and partely on the bank and coming down the log was an ugly brown bear. befor I could think what had happened Mamma saw a fly on his neck and decided to brush it off with the only gun we had with us, 25-20.

but the hair on his neck being so short the bullet went through, and for a moment we thot he was going to fall into the water but somehow his claws sunk in the log so far he managed to keep from falling.

then he went up the log and disappeared. and down the slough a short ways a brown bear ran and jumped in the slough and went

182

Wilderness bridges came in a variety of heart-stopping designs. This one is over Raspberry Creek, south of Telegraph Creek.

across but still in sight he shook the water out of his fur and glared at us for a moment then decided to go on for a moment we thot it was the same bear but wondered how it got there without any noise going through the brush.

we finally decided to go back to the log and find out and at the top of the log there about 25 feet from where Mamma shot him, (at least Mamma said it was) was the bear. it took quite a bit of courage to go up to it because he was laying like an old house dog. his hind feet up under him and his front feet were straight out in front and his head out on his front paws. we dident know if he was playing dead or not.

Finally Mamma had thrown enough sticks at him and he dident move she was going to save only his head because his fur was not good.

She was going to mount it for a novelty every time she would start to cut his head off we would hear something in the bush. thinking it must be a bears nest we thot Daddy needed supper right QUICK so we came home with his head.

Please excuse this bedtime story for little people but someday when I grow up I will write a big bear story for big people.

Miss Olive Matney
P.O. Bell Island
(Unuk River)

Like all trail blazers, Joe and I and the prospecting men we met in the uninhabited Unuk River Region left a part of ourselves behind us for encouragement to other explorers. We shall be there when future developers and settlers come, silently supporting them from Mackay Lake, Prout Plateau, Sam Coulter Creek, Harrymel Creek, Melville Glacier, Joe Mandy Creek, Madge Lake and Mount Madge.

# ANYOX COPPER, ALICE ARM SILVER

I had always liked the brightness and colour of copper trays, plates, kitchenware and jewelry but had never given a thought to where and how copper was mined. My ignorance was corrected when Joe took me to the coastal town of Anyox, one hundred and twenty miles north of Prince Rupert. A brochure from my husband's files told me the first recorded mineral claims in the secluded wilderness of the Anyox Creek area (Anyox the Tsimpsean Indian name meaning hidden water) were in 1900. They were not considered to have potential value until ten years later. Then the Granby Company's examinations led to development of one of the largest copper mines with smelter in Canada and a thriving community called Anyox which became known as "the wonder mining town of British Columbia". I looked forward to seeing the town and its residents and the mine.

Up to this time I had only become familiar with prospecting for gold and diverse operations in the mining of that valuable mineral. Copper offered another mining interest on an extremely large scale of production at Anyox. I knew the huge mine would not be dangerous in the same way as the old workings into which I had gone with my husband. That safety factor was foremost in Joe's mind when he answered my question, Can I go into this famous mine and see how copper is converted to commercial use?

"Well," he answered, "taking a woman underground there is usually frowned on because going through is tiring and there's always the risk of possible injury. A tour of the Anyox mine is reasonably safe or I should advise against it. I'll speak to the mine's General Superintendent, Rufus Lindsay, a friend of mine since I worked briefly as a field engineer for the Granby Company. He can probably arrange for you to be conducted through a part of the operation. If you don't see it now you probably never will. The mine is scheduled for complete closure next year. This is due to a main body of ore mined out and a declining price for copper. Becoming a ghost is the distressing fate of all mines and mining communities. In this instance, I'm glad to say, the Anyox mine has contributed so much mineral wealth to the world that it will have an honoured place in the annals of history."

We travelled to Anyox by steamer through Observatory Inlet and, like all of British Columbia's evergreen coast, enjoyed its inspiring scenic beauty. There was, however, a drastic change in surroundings as we neared the mining town which was surprising and unpleasant to see. The normally lush vegetation, stretching for miles on either side of the approach, was dead. Bare trees, outlined like skeletons against the sky, with many twisted by wind and storm, completed a picture of desolation. I shivered and clutched Joe's arm asking, What happened here? Looks as if there had been a mighty forest fire. But where's the fireweed with its magenta flowers which usually springs up after burning?

Joe had a ready answer. "Fumes of sulphur gas from the furnaces of Anyox's smelter kill plant growth. Such devastation is a shock to strangers. However, Anyox residents become so accustomed to it that outsiders have to remind them of their depressing entry."

The gloomy introduction was forgotten as the ship docked. Lights from windows blazed a welcome and there was a spectacular sky of red over the plant where coke came out of the furnaces. A special round trip to Vancouver, advertised by the steamship company, had resulted in some seventy people taking advantage of a price reduction which made an excursion south affordable. About the same number, including men, women and children, had gathered on the wharf to see them off, several joining passengers in their cabins for a jolly party before the ship sailed. Joe and I collected our baggage, since there were no porters to help us, pushed our way through the crowd and started with it to the nearby hotel. We were stopped by a shout.

"Dr. Mandy! Hold on. Wait a minute."

We stopped and stood still until a smiling and alert young chap caught up with us. Joe introduced him to me with "Meet Ted Kergin, nephew of our Prince Rupert family doctor and a worker in the Anyox mine." With the characteristic kindness of northerners, Ted relieved me of the bags with which I was struggling and led us on the shortest way to the town's only hotel, talking as we walked along.

"Great to see you in Anyox again, Dr. Mandy. This is your first visit, Mrs. Mandy, so I'd better tell you something about the people here and the place itself. Look around and you'll see hills and flats. Folks live on both, hills for the high-ups in the Granby Company and flats for common miners like me. The mine is back and above the town. Our Anyox is off the beaten path and nary a road or railway to connect with the interior. That don't bother us none. We keep in touch with the outside by Union Steamship Company's Catala and Cardena, Canadian National's Prince George and Prince Rupert and a few planes. We like being away from terrible things in the south where cities are. Here there's no soup kitchens and bread lines. Why, we don't even feel the Depression! Everybody in town has a job. The company treats us white and we keep busy and healthy. This is a friendly place where we're like a happy family. There's lots of reasons why I should boost Anyox."

I was astonished to see large, beautiful blossoms trailing from the hotel's porch boxes and inquired, How do they survive when vegetation all around Anyox is dead?

"With difficulty," was Ted's candid reply, "and the care you'd give a sick baby. Say, you ought to see the rain we get. It's yellow from sulphur and gas fumes that even burn holes in leaves. Oh yes, we have some leaves. They're on two wild plants that just won't die. Can you guess what they are? No? The elderberry bush is one and it's real pretty.You'll know from the name why the other is so hardy that nothing wants to touch it — the skunk cabbage. It's got a nice yellow flower that looks like a lily but the awful smell it sends out is skunky."

Joe had to report on development of the Granby Company's mine and also examine several prospects in adjacent areas. He decided the trips in these parts were too long, exhausting and hazardous for me, so I remained at the Anyox hotel. Thoughtfully, before setting off on the trail with a prospector, he and Rufus Lindsay planned a limited mine inspection for me. On the following day Mr. Lindsay drove me to a convenient starting point where Frank Buckle, a company field engineer, was waiting to be my guide. He was a long-legged, serious man in his thirties, I judged, and I could tell one step of his would mean two for my short legs. He looked at me apprehensively, which meant he hadn't been informed of my endurance on the trail with Joe. I suspected he thought I might collapse in a short time. Certainly, I promised myself, no matter how difficult I'll show him I can stand up to whatever we encounter. His comments were brief and to the point.

"Mrs. Mandy, this tour will be tiring and not easy to take. If it gets too difficult, tell me and we won't continue. Here, put on this jacket. Without it your clothes would soon be a mess. Keep that khaki hat on, too."

The heavy jacket made for a big man became a long coat on me, cumbersome and hot. I shortly realized, though, how necessary it was to keep the outfit I was wearing respectably clean. Frank said we'd first climb a hill and look at one of the big glory holes carved out by

Exterior glory hole at Granby's Anyox Copper Mine.

blasting. The hill was very steep, forcing me to crawl in places where loosened gravel formed insecure footing. We stopped for a moment at the top, perspiration dripping from my face. I quietly laughed at the thought of my Kansas students seeing grimy me, clownishly clothed, looking fearfully at an enormous opening in the ground.

"We're going down into this open pit, a glory hole from which ore has been and is being extracted," called Frank from his lead position and I descended behind him on a narrow ladder with widely separated rungs. Deep down, I watched a diamond drill at work and wondered how the diamond market for commercial enterprises compared with that for romance. We had turned to leave the glory hole when a loud shout of, "Fire," echoed across the wide space of the pit. Frank quickly pulled me onto a ledge where a man tinkered with a battery to which a wire was connected. After accounting for all people known to be in the immediate vicinity, seven men and myself huddled together, he ignited dynamite. The resulting shower of sizeable rock and splinter particles flew over and around us. I instinctively ducked and the old chap in charge of the blasting smiled and gave matter of fact advice. "Tain't no use to dodge, sister. If you're hit, you're hit and can't do nothin' about it. Work here and you get used to what's like heavy hail. Course there's a chance of gettin' killed but — makes my job excitin', don't it?"

Leaving our sheltered ledge, I saw scattered effects of the blasting and resolved to wear tightly fitting goggles to protect my eyes if I ever permitted myself to experience a similar incident. My energetic guide, far ahead of me, tried to steady a tipsy ladder. Undaunted, he climbed up quickly on it, but I did not trust the swaying steps and scrambled up slowly on solid rock, clawing my way awkwardly. A husky miner at the top reached down a hand to help me and to speak reassuringly.

"Don't have no kid gloves, lady, just strong hands. Not to worry. Hold on while I pull. No, I won't let you down. Take it easy, girl, and up you come. Here you are, safe and sound and out of that scary glory hole."

"Coming up was something of a test," observed Frank, "and you passed it with flying colours. From now on the going will be easier. Of course you won't see the whole mine, just enough to give you some idea of what we do here."

A trail to the underground working was fairly easy to descend as a rope to cling to on one side gave physical and psychological support. This took us to an entrance opening into a high, wide and electrically lighted tunnel where cars on tracks carried ore. We viewed the electrical plant and the steel shop in which rods were tempered and sharpened. I lacked the technical background to understand much of what I saw, though Frank's scientific explanations were helpful and impressive. I was getting quite tired when he prepared me for what was a highlight of the tour.

"Mrs. Mandy," he said calmly, "we're going down into the bowels of the earth in the cage you see here. Don't be afraid. Scores of men ride in it every day."

Not being a fearless miner, I was glad that Frank held my arm tightly while the elevator dropped with sickening speed to the lowest level of the mine, 885 feet below sea level. He was sure no other mine in British Columbia, at that time, had penetrated so far underground. Down there diamond drillers were so engrossed in their work that they seemed unaware of our presence. I felt trapped and goose pimples were with me until the lift carried us back to a higher level. There we walked through a shop where tapering metal used to make drills was thrust into soaring flames. Just looking at this made my skin feel scorched. On we went, miner's lamps on our hats now essential, but their feeble light did not extend far into the black void of a huge stope ("an excavation from which the ore has been extracted, either above or below a level, in a series of steps") beside which we stopped briefly. At that moment I thought of Tom Sawyer and Becky Thatcher lost in the darkness of a vast cave and stayed very close to Frank Buckle.

Going up to the surface, we passed an extensive glory hole, partially open to the sky. It looked like an illustration for a horror story. The fog within was so thick that the depth had to be imagined. Frank described the pit as unusually beclouded and wished I had seen it in winter when sometimes the haze disappeared and the height, width and depth could be seen clearly. Loaded cars passed us and men began coming off shift. Walking into the sunshine outside, I breathed deeply of fresh air and concluded I'd rather move boulders and pan for gold in Squaw Creek than work underground seeking copper and an associated gold yield in this mine of the Granby Company. Frank stated why most men would disagree with me. They preferred molelike mining to that of placer mining in creeks because working in water and often in rain was uncomfortable and the value of nuggets collected in sluice boxes was unpredictable. He cited statistics as proof.

"There are over four hundred miners here. The entire payroll, including smelter, coke plant, concentrating plant, maintenance, etc. is eleven hundred. I judge from your expressive face, you'd not choose to be an underground employee."

We met Mr. Lindsay, who was conferring with a shift boss, and the superintendent looked me over to see if I was drooping from fatigue. His pleasing comment with the prospect of another exciting day followed.

"Mrs. Mandy, your husband said you had the stamina and interest to take a quick tour of our copper mine. He was right and since you don't have to be carried out in an ore car, I know you'd stand up to inspecting the coke plant and seeing molten copper at the smelter. I'll pick you up in the morning for this second tour at six-thirty."

I waited for Mr. Lindsay on the porch of the hotel, happy to hear early risers call out a cheery, "Good morning!" We went first to the coke plant to watch the spectacular opening of the big door fronting ovens. Their flaming contents were dumped into waiting cars. The degree of heat expelled from those ovens was almost unbearable and in minutes my hair, face, body and clothing were drenched with perspiration. It was, however, fascinating to look at filled cars driven under a spray of water that caused clouds of steam to arise. This kept the coke from burning and the resulting gas escaped into long pipes. We did not linger because my guide knew the oppressive heat was making me feel faint.

The smelter to which Mr. Lindsay presently drove me was on a hilltop where Mr. Maxwell, the concentrator superintendent, joined us. Here I saw masked men raking concentrates ("that which has been reduced to a state of purity or concentration by the removal of foreign, nonessential or diluting matter") with long, iron pokers and then loading lumps of this mass into waiting cars. Whiffs of escaping gas required masks and I would have needed one had we watched for any length of time. We now climbed a succession of stairs to look at moving plates on which hot metal glowed. The air was heavy with fumes which made me cough and this atmosphere, plus the scene through which we had just passed, made me think of Dante's "Inferno", a place where the wicked would be eternally tortured in a fiery pit. Mr. Lindsay read my mind and agreed.

"Yes, Mrs. Mandy," he said, "we've been getting a look at what the after world may be like and how it would feel to burn in Hell. I'm sure Heaven is more to our liking."

There was more to see: concentrate in huge vats burned in its own heat, a flaming liquid fire of blended and brilliant colours. It was most interesting to watch the production of immense copper blisters shaped by pouring molten metal into enormous moulds, each weighing four hundred pounds. The Granby Company kept a supply of small copper ash trays here for visitors and I was given three with the warning that they would only retain their bright colouring if covered with liquid cellophane or shellac. My second tour now ended and I said to my guides, Thank you Mr. Lindsay and Mr. Maxwell for showing me outstanding features of this fabulous British Columbia mine in operation. You've given me an appreciation of copper I could get in no other way.

The men guided me outside and we looked down on Anyox from the smelter's hilltop. Mr. Lindsay spoke with enthusiasm about the community.

"We who live and work here are proud of Anyox where, unlike many company towns, we're happy folks. The Granby Company has been cooperative with employees, developing a mutually beneficial relationship and has provided comfortable homes and recreation. You'll be surprised to hear we have a nine-hole golf course. It's not laid out on velvet grass but on slag, which is the residue skimmed off metal after smelting. Ours is the only golf course of its kind in the world, popular with all ages. Wooden tennis courts attract many players, too, and moving pictures are brought in. Yes, this is quite a desirable town. We're all saddened at the thought of leaving it."

My days in Anyox, aside from the mine inspection, were filled with the hospitality of townspeople at dinner or tea in their homes or as a guest at the movie in the community hall. I was so charmed by the local residents and impressed by the Granby Mine that tears came to my eyes when Joe and I sailed away from Anyox, knowing I should never see this thriving, twenty year old town again. The mine closed as forecast, the following year of 1935. The whole place was soon deserted and became an isolated wilderness. Happily, Anyox lives on in the minds and hearts of those who resided and worked there and in the memory of all who merely visited and passed by, a symbol of daring and productive pioneering.

Joe now chartered the luxury yacht of Anyox's postmaster, Mr. Eve, for a field trip north on Observatory Inlet to Alice Arm Inlet and then on to the settlement of Alice Arm at its head. Eve piloted the boat and, as one who had explored extensively along this part of the coast, acquainted me with a bit of history about our surroundings.

"We're passing through one of the coastal beauty spots of British Columbia," he said proudly. "I can tell you some things about it you ought to know. You've heard of the famous explorer, Captain George Vancouver. He was the first European to see these mountains around Anyox and Alice Arm. I'll betcha he saw nothing prettier anywheres. Way back in 1793 he came. Being an explorer, he took soundings of the inlets and drew charts and maps for those who'd come along after he was gone. It's said he discovered coal around here, but the seam

Typical scene in Alice Arm, Anyox and Stewart areas.

hasn't been found by anyone else.

"Now then, I guess you'll be most interested in the old mining town of Alice Arm where we're headed. It got started, like most mining towns, with a stampede. Let's see — that was in 1910 when prospectors staked the Dolly Varden. By golly, they'd found high-grade silver ore and Dolly Varden became a famous mine. That silver find brought prospectors from all over. It was a silver camp but they searched for gold, too. Molybdenum showings were looked over but not mined. They weren't worth much then. Promotion of stakings went on and a few small properties had a short life. It didn't take long for the town of Alice Arm to spring up, a rip-roaring place having everything that goes with a boom. Too bad all sorts of problems closed the Dolly Varden Mine. With its payroll gone and a World War on, almost everything folded up. You'll see few people in Alice Arm today."

The town of Alice Arm was situated on tide-water and the flats of the Kitsault River, with high, snow-capped mountains on three sides and the ocean fronting the fourth. It deserved its reputation for scenic beauty but the atmosphere of decay was evident in the many vacant houses. A local boy guided us to the Alice Arm Hotel, a large, framed structure standing starkly on the side of a steep slope and reached by a series of slippery, wooden steps. The owner and manager, Ole Evindsen, was a husky Norwegian. Mr. Eve had told me he was a good-natured, reliable man who trusted others because he was so honest himself. He, with his robust Canadian wife, welcomed us as if we were kin. Their children, seventeen year old Alma and seven year old Ronald, set about making us comfortable in every way they could. We were the only guests at the moment and this lack of business gave Ole an opportunity to talk to Joe about the very limited mining activity being carried on in the vicinity.

"Thanks for your information, Ole," said my husband. "I'll be going with the few prospectors you mentioned to advise about their holdings. First, I must call on Dooley Falconer. He has written me that he and his two sons have taken a lease on the Dolly Varden Mine. Under his direction the boys are high-grading silver there. I'll make that call now. Come with me, Madge."

Dooley lived with his family in an apartment above his general store, one half of the space upstairs a hall where badminton was played and community gatherings held. The men stayed in the shop while I climbed the stairs to meet Mrs. Falconer. She was a delight, an attractive, matronly woman with a pink-tinged, velvety skin, very blue eyes, thick, snow-white hair and bubbling with friendliness. She looked and acted motherly and her greeting was a hug to which I happily responded. Her impulsive gesture made me think of my mother far away for whom I had a deep and lasting affection.

"My, I'm glad to meet you," she exclaimed. "Dr. Mandy was here a couple of years ago and captured me, you might say, with his personality and knowledge. I thought then he'd make a wonderful husband, so I'm glad he now has a wife. News travels around the coast and what I've heard about you makes me think you're just right for him. Here comes my daughter. Juanita, can you guess who this is? We've wanted to meet her ever since we heard Dr. Mandy was married. Yes, it's Mrs. Mandy! Now then, she's a university graduate and you're second year varsity and that means you two will have a lot in common to talk about. I'll go and hustle up some tea and tarts and, Mrs. Mandy, I want you to think of the Falconer home as yours while you're in Alice Arm. You must come often to share meals and conversation. It's such a treat to have a lady visitor from the outside."

I was certainly fortunate to have such hospitality as the Falconers offered, for there was no other kind of recreation in the community where I had to remain during Joe's field trips in the area. Joe had not thought it wise for me to accompany him into the adjacent mountains and I was disappointed about this until he explained why.

"Exploration here, my dear, is as difficult and dangerous as around Anyox and Stewart. I've been in this part of my district before and know trails and camping will be really tough. I know, too, you've proved yourself hardy and adjustable enough to take such punishment, but it's not sensible for you to do so. A social time you'll have here and get to know the sturdy folks who've lived through the ups and downs of mining. Ole will tell you about his exceptional background and how he and his partner discovered the big silver deposit which became the Dolly Varden Mine and how this led to the development of Alice Arm. Such firsthand history will add to your other memorabilia of the Northwest."

The Alice Arm Hotel was a large, rambling building with a big kitchen and a lounge which also served as a living room for the Evindsen family and extended into a long dining room. Upstairs were sixteen bedrooms and an attic where guests slept on cots or in sleeping bags on the floor. This was an informal lodging house where the guests gathered with one or more of the resident family in the lounge or on the verandah in the evening. On the first night of Joe's absence, I sat on the porch with Mrs. Evindsen, a pleasant and practical woman. Looking across the valley I remarked, I've lived most of my life on flat land and now, since coming to British Columbia, I've discovered the greater beauty of mountains. They are so majestic, truly inspiring, and bring to mind a thought from the Bible's 121st Psalm — "I will lift up my eyes unto the hills from whence cometh my help." Do you feel the same about the mountains, Mrs. Evindsen?

"Yes — I think I do. Though I guess I'd just say they make me feel right good."

You couldn't find a more lovely place for a home, I went on. Have you lived here long?

"Came in 1915, a city girl. Hiked all the way up the mountain to the Dolly Varden Mine, I did, on a trail I don't think a horse could put his feet on. In them days we women wore long skirts, right down to the ground. They didn't help climbing none or the things we had to do around a camp. To keep them clean was real hard. I've heard tell you know about trails and roughing it."

Yes, I do. My husband has taken me on trails which even prospectors call tough. How different from my life in a city and in a schoolroom! Those trails have been exciting, often dangerous and yet pleasurable. They've given me memorable experiences to relive. I want you to know, too, that meeting pioneers like you and your husband has given me strength and courage to "rough it". Your years here must have been quite eventful. Would you like to tell me about them?

"I sure would. Don't have many outsiders to talk to anymore. You should know what went on in days past. Going to the Dolly Varden Mine up the mountain, after me living in the city, took some doing. What I knew about the bush you could write on a match cover. Then, finding out how to run a hotel in stampede days in northern wilds was no picnic. There wasn't much money to start the businesss and prices to keep going was mighty steep. It cost $150.00 a month for a cook and $75.00 to $100.00 a month for a waitress and they had board and room too. Them was big wages then. What we paid for food was awful high — a one hundred pound sack of potatoes cost $11.00 and a case of eggs was $30.00. The boarding miners and railway workers said, 'Spuds and eggs is a must.'

"I can honestly say 'twasn't easy to look after beds, laundry, cleaning and meals for dozens of miners, railroaders and a slew of promoters coming and going. I had to plan most careful for the meals. You see, supplies was shipped in from the south and I must make do between boats. Why, sometimes two hundred men was eating with us. Ole and me had to rush, rush and never had no chance to rest. I think of them days as happy, though, and I'm glad we was able to do what we done."

I questioned farther. What was Alice Arm like during the rush?

"Oh, wild as wild could be. Like the Klondike gold rush it was, but smaller and prospectors was looking for silver and not gold. Everything a new mining camp has, we had — promoters, gamblers, drinkers, crooks, mushroom business and fast women. But there was something very good here to remember, a community spirit of folks helping each other. Money from dances, bazaars and donations built us a church, skating rink and tennis court. Labour was free, so those things didn't cost nothing but for some materials. Someone who helped Alice Arm a lot was Canon Rushbrook. He came on the Anglican Church boat, Northern Cross, and visited settlements like ours, logging camps, canneries and lone settlers. That's one minister everyone liked. Didn't ram religion down your throat. He showed what it was by what he done, as fine a Christian gentleman as ever lived."

I asked her, How did you and your husband manage to keep the hotel operating after the closure of the Dolly Varden Mine? Her answer was informative and interesting.

"I'm telling you, Mrs. Mandy, it's been a fight. Most who stayed here was miners and men abuilding the railway to the mine. They all went away and not many people has stayed with us since. Oh, some folks come from Anyox and Stewart for vacations when they don't have enough money to go to Vancouver or Victoria. You're a nice young lady and maybe I shouldn't tell you this, but our best behaved guests has been 'ladies of the night' from the red light part of Anyox. They said they came for a rest and that's what they done, just rested. I didn't have to worry about them and shenanigans. This may be hard to believe, but I swear it's true. They sat around, talked ladylike, made their own beds and helped me get meals ready. I didn't ask, but they told me the stories of their lives, so sad I cried. Some was secretly sending money to a good family to bring up a child right. That little one would never know who or what his mother was and she'd never know her son or daughter. Well, the Bible says, 'Judge not that ye be not judged.' I didn't approve of their life style but I took them women as they was in the hotel and we had a nice time together."

Before going inside to plan the next day's menu, Mrs. Evindsen said, "Guess you'd like to hear how the town of Alice Arm began. Ole helped to start it when he and his partner discovered silver. Tomorrow night he won't be busy. I'll ask him to tell you then how he came to Canada and got to this spot and found a mine. He knew the first prospectors here and all about the things that went on. Ole's a good story teller. Me and the children never gets tired of sitting around quiet listening to what we've heard hundreds of times."

It was chilly the following evening and cozy to settle down with the Evindsen family in the lounge to play a game of dominoes with young Ronald. Alma's metal needles clicked as she knitted a skirt, Mrs. Evindsen crocheted a baby jacket and Ole eased himself into a chair and toyed with an ore sample. I was still losing after a sixth game with Ronald when his parents told him it was his bedtime and he must be off to his room. The well disciplined boy left without any argument. Ole then turned to me in reminiscent mood.

"Mrs. Mandy, nice to Alice Arm you come. 'Tween 1910 and 1920 ought you to have been."

Why the years 1910 to 1920, Mr. Evindsen? I asked.

"Ole, you call me. Everone does. I speaks to you 'bout 1910, but first before where I comes from and why so. In Norway I am born, in mountains high. Village near is Odda. On fiord is it, one of big fiords in Norway. My people is not poor. No, most poor. A cow we has, sheep an' goats. Never my father know. He die when three or four months I am. My mother again marry an' gives sisters. To our village comes tourists, lots. They looks an' they says, 'Beautiful'. Yes, 'twas so. Much look like Alice Arm.

"Somethin' happen when I am boy there, I forget not. Kaiser Wilhelm come to Odda with battleships and cruiser Hohenzollern. Off goes fancey uniform an' old clothes he walks round in. One time there, what you call catastrophe happen. Young German officer, in command highest, meets pretty Norwegian girl an' picks her to marry. Kaiser is married but picks out same girl, if you know what I means. Officer gets mad an' hits Kaiser for bad thoughts of girl he loves. Black an' blue Kaiser's face is. Villagers thinks he gets what's comin'. He don't agree. Message goes out, young officer save Kaiser's life when riggin' falls an' hits him. Poor fellow knows this is end for him. He rides horse up high cliff down over an' he is dead. In Germany they tells he is killed in accident huntin'. Farmers find body an' five hundred officers comes to take him to homeland. Military funeral he has an' big monument to say he's hero. Sad is our village an' proud of dead man 'cause he die for honour."

Ole had to pause for several minutes of emotional recollection before he could continue. We listeners waited in silence and with teary eyes.

"Fourteen I am when I goes to sea on Norwegian freighter. We docks all over Europe, sails round Africa an' South America. Gettin' near Cape Horn gives somethin' to think on. Crew is puttin' up new sails for speed an' Captain wants to him rum served. He calls up, 'How long you gonna stay up there, you sons of guns?' One man shouts, 'Down soon's we can.' That terrible Captain yells, 'I'll show you talk back.' He looses rope and that sailor fall on deck an' die right off. He is sewed in canvas to bury. Then that, that - can't say name I thinks for him. Not right for ladies to hear. He order canvas open so's he can have sailor's mackinaw. One of crew gets mad an' says, 'You'd steal coat from dead man you kill? Over dead body of me.' All sailors close in an' scared Captain runs to cabin an' gets meaner."

Ole, I interjected, life on those freighters must have been hard in every way. How was the food?

"Most awful. For breakfast we has hard tack, olive oil 'stead of butter an' watered molasses on oatmeal porridge or bran mush. Noon is main meal — salt pork an' pea soup or salt meat an' soup of vegetable dehydrate pieces, little pieces. Oncet we had not potatoes for six months. Barrels of potatoes is on ship an' they is rotten, has to be throwed in sea. I eats spuds oncet or twicet a day now. Has to make up for what I not has for six months.

"That ship brings me to Victoria in 1901, January, one hundred and eighty-two day sail from Scotland. Here is kind chap. He rouns crew up for quarantine an' is pal. I takes walk and meets Russian-Finn. He asks do I like my Captain and ship. I say no an' why so. He finds out my Captain tangles with law an' to court must go. To testify is crew. Russian-Finn know Captain try my mouth to shut. So, he hide me till time to up speak. Loses his papers, do Captain. He's bad man, but one good thing happen on freighter. Some Scot sailors learn me English.

"That Russian-Finn ask me, 'How you like to go on sealin' vessel?'

Sailin' ship I ask. 'No, sealin' ship for hunt seal.' I ask, You got good food? He say yes an' if I wants to go sealin', 'You be ready at eleven tonight. Throw rope over to come down an' waitin' I'll be to row you away.' I jumps ship, best thing I ever done. I am on sealin' ship five months an' tired I am, wantin' to be on land. I goes to Vancouver an' learns me deep sea divin'. That gets me job with Hydrographic Dominion Survey what's soundin' harbour off Kaien Island. That's where Prince Rupert was abuildin'. That be June, 1906. I clears land when not divin'."

Maybe you cut down trees and blasted out stumps and rock from the spot where my home is in Prince Rupert, I surmised.

"Mebbe so. I works there till 1914. Then me an' my friends Pearson, Eik an' Carlson goes north to gold rush at Stewart. We is late. All in good claims is staked. We thinks to go prospectin' somewheres else. Gets us a boat an' supplies an' comes to top of Alice Arm fiord. Here's nothin' but prospectors Roundy, Stark an' passin' through Indians. They tells of mountain ground, prospected before not. That's good news an' we starts climbin' up that mountain, cuttin' trail through bush. Six days an' grub is low. Eik an' Carlson starts back down to get some. Me an' Pearson goes on, gettin' hungry an' tired more.

"We stops one night an' only grub we has is tin of beans. We can't has us no supper 'cause we wants to eat next day. We puts that tin in empty lard pail over campfire. Turns we takes keepin' fire goin' so's to have hot bean breakfast. Sleepin' early on, we is woke by noise an' somethin' hittin' hard in face. We jumps out of blankets an' Pearson yell, 'What in Hell?' I yells, Beans is shootin' us. They was like bullets — pop, pop, pop. What happen? Can top gets hot, blows off an' explode beans. Me, I lays me down an' groans. No grub we now has. Soon I laff when I sees what Pearson do. He's holdin' pine torch an' crawlin' on ground pickin' up beans to push in his mouth. He's smart man, I thinks, an' I grabs beans to stuff in wide open mouth of me. Them was best beans I ever et. Seasonin' is special — ashes and dirt.

"On we climbs an' camps at Indian River an' Pearson has dream of what is to be. He shakes for make me wake up to tell what dream has he. All excite, he say in dream his Uncle in Norway is longside on bush trail by canyon deep. Sudden, Uncle stop. He point at big, white boulder an' tree an' say, 'Ore here. Stake. Call claim Dolly Varden.' I thinks a little an' then I tells Pearson why of dream. Afore he leaves Stewart, comes letter his Uncle die. In mind still has he thought of good, wise Uncle who so much help him. Name for claim? That easy for know. Dolly Varden is most pretty girl in book he's readin'. That book is — oh, what you call it? You know, Mrs. Mandy."

I was glad I could reply, Yes, I do. The book is "Barnaby Rudge", a novel written by Charles Dickens.

"Is right. I 'member now. In them days when I am young, everwhere peoples read books by that Dickens man. I think Dolly Varden in that story he write be nice name for mine if one we finds. We goes on an' not long 'fore Pearson go haywire. He call out, 'Look, canyon big, white boulder an' tree like Uncle say! There we stakes an' name of claim must be Dolly Varden.' We has us big silver find an' has to start proven it is so. Eik an' Carlson comes back an' we all works hard. When grub's low, we gets smart an' catches fish to eat an' traps porcupine for meals."

I stopped his narration with the question, Is the porcupine good eating?

"For best friend, no. When hot, taste most awful. When cold, like mutton it taste. Mebbe I talks too much an' you is tired."

Oh no, I responded, I'm not a bit tired. I like your story, Ole. Please go on.

"Field man for 'leven business men in Chicago city hears 'bout our silver. Them men sends him to see silver show an' make deal. Backers gives money for tunnel-cut an' cross-cut. They what you call incorporate an' calls theirself Dolly Varden Mining Company. Pretty soon engineerin' outfit is lined up an' starts abuildin' narrow gauge eighteen mile railroad to the mine. Cars get ore out more quick than afore when horses is used packin' ore down to tide-water for shippin'. Mine is a go an' all is rosy, with me an' partners gettin' a good share till bad things comes. To think on makes sick my stomach, so I tells more when comes next night. 'Scuse an' goodnight."

What a wonderful true tale had been told! I went to bed and lay awake far into the morning picturing Ole as a boy in his native Norway, experiencing with him those frightful days sailing to Vancouver, British Columbia, on a freighter with a sadistic Captain and then his venture in prospecting which through a partner's dream terminated in the discovery of a great silver deposit. I found it hard to wait for the continuation of Ole's story. He began the following evening exactly where he'd left off.

"News 'bout rich silver mine gets out an' there is big rush. Stakin' is all round. Good is some claims, but none good like Dolly Varden. Boom town begins. Name is Alice Arm, same as fiord. I sells my shares in mine, gets me married an' I builds hotel. I figgers roomin' and boardin' miners and railway workers is help for mine and town an' makes me money. Well now, them Chicago business men is too trustin'. Word of mouth an' shake of hand is all they has with railway company. Nothin' is in writin'. They is took over by that engineer company for bad debts of railway. Them good men is right not to pay for what they doesn't owe. Law suits they is. Government what don't know nothin' 'bout the case backs Canadian engineer and he wangles mine from honest Chicagoans. That sets back minin' for years in our province. Other Americans don't wants to come for such fleecin'.

"That engineer's a slick promoter. He raises money from Vancouver an' Victoria suckers, finishes railway an' changes name to Taylor Engineering Company. Know what he do then? Takes all ore in sight. In most two years and five months his company make more'n a million dollar from Dolly Varden silver at $1.15 a ounce. Foolish fellow have no exploration for show more silver for takin' an' nobody will give him money for carry on. He shuts down mine December, 1920, an' away walks. Watchman stay on property for little while, but no real minin' from then till now. Dooley Falconer an' his boys is high gradin' there, havin' a lease, an' I says good for them."

Have you been here since 1914, Ole? I asked.

"No. Oncet I leaves Alice Arm. Not much doin' after Dolly Varden shuts down 'cept loggin' an' that don't last. I buys me a fruit farm in Vancouver, way out by Burnaby. Pays down 'thought seein' it. I finds fruit trees is there an' no leaves is on. They is dead an' only crop is caterpillars. I has no money for pay taxes on that place, so I loses no good farm. More bad luck comes. Man what buy my hotel don't pay me none an' I takes it back an' I am in Alice Arm in business some more. Depression hits an' no business. Not for me to complain. Hotel give me an' my family a home. For this, happy I am.

"Days when I am big in money from Dolly Varden, can't go nowhere 'thout five or six reporters pesterin'. Now, no money, no reporters. One thing I wants you to know. Never do I gets into shady deals with noone in stampede times. When I goes to Vancouver them days, peoples rush me to stake claims near Dolly Varden. They would pay me apiece $1000.00 for stake. They is plumb crazy to make fast buck. Workin' folks they is. No, I tells them I sells what has silver, not moose pasture. I 'member how it is to be poor an' I not take their money."

How many were here when the rush was on? was my next question.

"Mebbe three hundred an' mebbe one thousand when loggin' is takin' over 'stead of minin'. Oncet one right good mine starts up, name of Toric, havin' some silver like Dolly Varden have. It close up when silver drop price."

Ole, I said, Alice Arm has had its ups and downs. How do people here manage through hard times?

"We fishes, hunts, grow garden an' waits for somethin' to turn up an' is neighbourly. Fires is headache. 1930 big one burns up two hotels, butcher shops, lots of houses an' stores. Dooley Falconer is only man with shop left. Most peoples you meets here today is old prospectors and them as has no money to get away. Prospectors is lucky. They get grubstake an' goes out in mountains lookin' for gold. Silver not good now. Steamers don't come anymore but Bert Kergin and Harry Fowler runs a boat, name of 'The Awake', between Alice Arm and Anyox. They carries mail, freight an' folks to Anyox. Don't know how we'd get on 'thout them men. They is life line. Many a time they've saved lives rushin' sick ones to the doctor an' hospital at Anyox.

"I'd say eighty lives in Alice Arm today. In rush days we falls over people, they is so many. We has then lots of shops, dance hall, saloon, gamblin' halls, jail an' all bad things of minin' camps, long with some good. Part of Alice Arm is what you call suburb, Silver City. It's high falutin'. Crooked promoters had maps made to show big steamers sailin' up to Alice Arm an' cattle ranches close by on Nass River, tryin' to get settlers for Silver City. 'Twarn't true. But fools falls for lies an' lots mapped out sold like prospector's flapjacks in boom time. They is one bad thing we never has — a lawyer. Soon's as one of them shows up, trouble starts. Alice Arm has no bank in money days, but in 1920 a bank sets itself up and dies in 1926. Thirty kids is in first school, seven now. We has us a cemetery. Two ladies, two men and one child sleeps there. Road's washed out an' nobody gets to it now. That's why folks here stays well. I thinks Alice Arm will boom again. Why not? I knows Dolly Varden hides more silver way up there in her mountain. Mebbe I'm gone, but my girl an' boy they sees what I say is true."

Alice Arm held a great interest for me after hearing Ole's account of her origin and brief reign of prosperity as a booming mining camp. The Falconer's stories corroborated his and their hospitality, as well as that of other residents, kept me continually entertained. On another evening, Ole recalled the tale of a prospector whose life in the Alice Arm area and subsequent tragic ending proved, like the discovery of the Dolly Varden, that truth is stranger than fiction. I settled myself in a comfortable chair and listened as he unfolded what I might not have believed had Ole not been such an honest man.

"Now, I takes you 'fore 1910 back to meet Frank Roundy. He comes north for stake timber an' for gold prospectin'. Character of Roundy is what you calls genuine. He is old Yankee, straight in dealin' an' he 'spects everone to be same. He gets mighty rich off timber an' minin'. Funny thing is he puts money in banks in places all over an' has in pocket of coat $1000.00 ever day. Roundy has first cabin in Alice Arm. It is shack too little for stand up in, eight by ten. Too bad he is miser an' don't give hisself some fun. His ways is funny, too. To him bath takin' is not to be an' his clothes is dirt stiff an' smell not so good. Knives, forks an' plates is some he uses in Civil War in U.S.A. an' washed not ever. I gets to know him an' he is smart, fifty year ahead of them days.

"Roundy has high grade ore he's minin' an' he don't let nobody know where it's at. Some of his ore run $2000.00 to a ton. Long comes two beachcombers an' makes friends of this trustin' soul. He thinks they is special nice an' shows the strangers where he hides gold and silver ore under stumps an' in bush. Them lazy good-for-nothins' waits till he goes an' puts ton of his high grade in sloop an' takes off for Seattle. They find promoter called Foxy Grandpa from feller in cartoon. They says they is trappers, runs 'cross rich ore an' wants to sell. 'How much you got?' Foxy Grandpa ask. Them no-goods shows by out-stretchin' arms. He ask, 'How far it go?' Them skunks acts green an' swears twenty mile outcrop. 'What you takes for it?' ask promoter. '$2000.00,' they says.

"Foxy Grandpa give $2000.00. He is foxy but beachcombers is more foxy. In Spring, Foxy Grandpa send men for work on claims an' finds Roundy is owner. To save face he takes option an' pay Roundy $30,000.00. His gang don't know nothin' 'bout minin'. Ore they digs up don't pay shippin' freight or wages. Miners is plenty mad an' puts lien on property. Roundy is smart. He knows not good to pay Foxy Grandpa's bills an' drops claims. Two Spanish boys stakes, takes over show an' give name Esperanza to mine an' makes money by thousands. They sells an' dumb new owners don't much do but sell shares in company it now is."

Ole leaned back in his chair, lost momentarily in silent memories of the old-timer. When he went on, there was deep emotion in his voice as he related life's final chapter of a colourful character.

"Roundy is gettin' older an' can't walk an' work like he's done. His back gets bent an' he moves slow. Never complain he don't but must've hurt from rheumatiz. He don't want people in Alice Arm feelin' sorry for him, so goes off to live in Victoria. Poor chap is still miser. Has money aplenty to have good home an' help an' do you know what does he do? Rent hisself a shack that cost $1.00 for month. Comes day when little stroke hits an' what happen is soundin' like fairy tale. Policeman, oncet foreman on Dolly Varden railway and know Roundy, find him. That constable has kind heart. He take sick, old man home an' he an' wife look after poor fellow.

"Pretty soon comes awful trouble. Roundy have sister in east of U.S.A. When she hear 'bout stroke she take trip to Victoria for to see him. He has made will an' give his all to nice policeman an' wife who save his life an' take care of him. He say to sister, 'For years you doesn't pay me no notice 'cause I don't live like you does. Now, you thinks I die an' come for my money. You not gets it.' She don't like that an' starts lawsuit to change will. Policeman get Trust Company to fight for him. When battle is over, he gets money of Roundy in Canada an' sister gets U.S.A. bonds.

"Mebbe it's good Roundy never know what happen to all that lots of money he save up. Law move like snail to settle and by then he is dead. Mean sister gets court to let her take him to her house in east of U.S.A. My eyes has tears when I tells you that good man burns to death in bed at sister's home. He's set afire by pipe he's smokin'. So sad, that way to die. Never I forgets Roundy. I tells you this 'bout him. He likes me and wants for adopt me. Then I am his son an' he leaves me his money. That I cannot let him do. I likes him but to live like he do, no. Late it is gettin' an' tired my tongue is. I asks you to 'member the Dolly Varden Mine. Tell how Ole an' his partner finds silver that starts rush and begins town of Alice Arm."

Just before leaving Alice Arm, I met John Huber who had been prospecting for years in this locale. The man was dwarfishly short, with an extremely large head set squarely on a very short neck to give him the aspect of being top heavy. His unusual appearance probably accounted for him being a loner who was considered queer. After questioning Joe about ore samples in a very dirty bag, he hurried away and my husband turned to me chuckling.

"I took a trip with old John once," he mused, "and you'll get a laugh from hearing about it. I told John I'd pack some grub and he protested. 'Don't bother none carrying food along. All kinds is up the mountain.' He hiked ahead, bending down from time to time to pick up something. At noon I suggested a stop for lunch and John said, 'I ain't hungry.' I said I was. His reply to that surprised me. 'Didn't you notice? I et all the time we was aclimbing.' I asked, What did you eat? 'Grasses and leaves side of the trail. You set while I pick some for you.' Shortly he thrust a bunch of vegetation into my hands saying, 'Mighty good and mighty good for you.' I didn't find such food satisfying, but since there was nothing else I stuffed it into my mouth and chewed away.

"We stopped for the night at John's cabin, high on the mountain. There was only a conglomeration of dried weeds and roots to eat there and they did not appease my appetite. However, the prospector did brew tea from leaves pulled out of a damp tin. This quenched my thirst and somewhat revived my tired body. With growling stomach, I asked John how he knew what wilderness offerings were edible. He answered, 'I watch bears and eat same things they do.' Have you ever suffered ill effects from a bear's diet? I asked. He admitted one

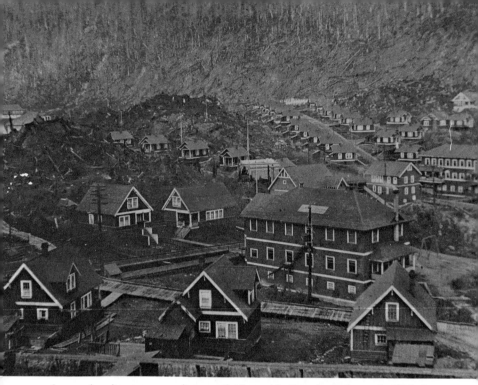

Anyox when its copper smelter was the largest in Canada. In the early 1930s it closed and the community of 3,000 disappeared.

reaction which might have been serious. 'I cut out some roots of skunk cabbage to try. They made me sweat something fierce. Then I became terrible thirsty and my throat burned. I went to sleep and slept for forty-eight hours. When I woke up I felt fine but think I took too much. I eat only a little at a meal, now, of that stinky cabbage root. Indians say one part makes you dead. Bears is knowing and don't eat any of the poison stuff in it.' John did not proffer nor did I request any of that powerful sedative which might induce longer sleep than one might want."

The quiet, sparsely populated Alice Arm I saw in the '30's was far different from the bustling mining town of yesteryear. Ole revived it for me, as did his wife and the Falconers, with memories of the silvered past. I wondered how long the mine Ole and his partner discovered would have operated had the honourable Chicago gentlemen developing the property been fairly dealt with by an associated company with mining carried on under competent, technical direction. Dolly Varden of the silver veins still sleeps in the mountain and I dream, as did Ole, of a day when she will wake to bestow upon the world her legacy of mineral wealth comparable to the richness of personality displayed by Dolly Varden, the heroine of "Barnaby Rudge".

## TERRACE, SMITHERS AND BABINE RANGE

Joe came home from his office one summer day announcing, "We're off to the Near North tomorrow. This part of my district is bordered by the Canadian National Railway and a few small towns where, for a short time, you'll stay in comfortable hotels. We'll mostly be riding packhorses and camping in the Babine mountains, a majestic range. You'll take everything in stride. After all, you're an old hand at guiding horses on very steep trails. The camp sites will be like those in the Far North — no luxury but we'll have a scenic solitude we both enjoy. What do you say to new trails to follow? Your eyes say you're eager to go."

We travelled east from Prince Rupert in a parlour car with wide windows giving us a view of the Skeena River which the railway skirted and uninhabited land with a background of the Coast Range. Joe pointed out canneries on each side of the river, some no longer active. He said there was lucrative fishing here as on the coast and the canneries employed a number of Indians, Japanese and a few whites. My husband's interest was not, however, in the wealth to be procured from the sea and river but in possible mineral riches to be found in the mountains and he talked about what had been and what might be.

"It's hard to believe that before 1913 this section of British Columbia was known to almost nobody but Indians, fur-traders and prospectors. The railway brought settlers to farm, log, build sawmills and to mine. Hardy pioneers established villages and towns in the midst of the Coast Range mountains which are not as high as those farther north but have a mineral potential of promise. In fact, these mountains have yielded productive mines, closed now because of the Depression. They could reopen one of these days and no-one knows what other ore bodies may be discovered."

A few men were lounging at the Terrace station, our first stop, to watch the train come in. For them, greeting the train's crew and speculating on a few descending passengers was entertainment. Joe hired one of the men to help carry our luggage to Mr. Willie's hotel. It was an old building heated by wood burning stoves which didn't need firing on this hot August day, but they suggested cold winters. Mr. Willie, a diminutive and genial Belgian host took time, after we signed the register, to tell us about his former vocation, so different from his present occupation.

"Confectioner was I in European hotels — in Paris, Cologne, Munich and London. Then I go to big, deluxe hotel, Dublin near. Comes there for holiday King Edward, son of long time Queen, Victoria. Mon Dieu! That old makes me, non? I go on with my story. Says manager of hotel, 'You make special, much large cake for King.' Two month works I in off time for build replica of that Irish hotel. Big is it. Inside is lights from help of electrician. Is picture here in album. See? Beautiful you thinks? It was so. King Edward likes and money piles on plates for me and helpers. We has us party and drinks champagne. Manager of hotel to me say, 'With pay, off a month.' This nice for remember, yes?"

Mr. Willie, I exclaimed, the pictured cake shows what a talent you have. I hope you still develop creations like this in Terrace. The man's eyes expressed sorrow and tears moistened them as he spread his hands in a despairing gesture to answer.

"Non, non. Today wood I chop. Garden do I. Paint put on hotel outside do I and lots more things what make hands rough. Stiff, too. Look at my hands. Condition terrible! For make confection, delicate hands must be. C'est domage!"

Mrs. Willie, a partner with her husband in operating the hotel, hurried into the lounge to be introduced. She was an amply proportioned woman with kindness stamped on her face and heard in her voice. She shook my hand and gave it a reassuring squeeze. Such a welcome made me feel I was one of her family. She brought fresh linens to our room while Joe interviewed a prospector in the lounge. With the friendly spirit of the North she talked to me while tucking sheets on the bed.

"We've been expecting you and Dr. Mandy. Prospectors hereabouts told us you'd be coming. Folks here who know your man say you're from the States. I'm from England. Been here long enough to talk like a Canadian. Of course you and I will always love the land of our birth, but isn't Canada wonderful? Where, I ask you, could you find more beautiful scenery than here in British Columbia? And I'm working at what I know best. You see, dearie, my mother was a widow. She was poor and had to support her children. A good uncle put her in charge of a public house he owned and that's where I started serving the public. Of course, running a hotel gives headaches. What does that matter when it gives us a chance to meet people from all over, generally nice. Some lemons do stop with us. Most are peaches. Anything you need, love, tell me. I want you to feel right at home."

Joe had been requested in a letter from Fred Michaud, postmarked Terrace, to meet him and his brother "for an interview on mineral matters". He knew nothing about the Michauds except from inference through reading the impressive heading of their stationery:

The Michaud Brothers, Crescent Hill Ranch; Growers and Shippers of Nursery Stock, Small fruits, vegetables, etc. Originator of the FAMOUS "SKEENA WONDER STRAWBERRY".

My husband could only presume these brothers had added prospecting to ranching and needed some geological guidance. I asked Mrs. Willie about the Michauds and she sympathetically told me their story.

"Those poor brothers! They were dears. Too sad what's happened to them."

Are they sick, Mrs. Willie? Tears were in her eyes as she answered me.

"You might rightly say both sick and dead. One did die and he's not exactly dead. The other's living and, in a way, quite dead."

Puzzled, I waited for Mrs. Willie to calm herself and clarify such ambiguous statements.

"I can tell you don't know what I'm talking about. You will when I'm finished. Don't know their background. Must have been good because they talked and acted like polished gentlemen. Fred and Bert Michaud came up here quite awhile ago from South Dakota's black hills. Seems they knew how to make things grow and did well with all kinds of fruit and vegetables that sold like hot cakes. They even produced a banana-shaped potato and the Skeena Wonder Strawberry. That berry should have made them famous and rich. Well, they weren't business men and too honest to know what tricks are played. A Michigan firm stole the secret of their strawberry when they wrote it out for them while trying to make a deal. They've dabbled in mining, too, and haven't got a cent from their claims.

"The brothers built a log house with many big rooms in it. Planned it all themselves. Nothing like it anywhere around. My, it was a beauty, a real showplace with landscaped gardens. When you walked through their rose arbour it was like being in perfume land. And the parties they had! Folks came from miles around to see their flowers, square dance and eat the best food this side of heaven. Everyone liked the Michaud brothers who treated one and all like the best friend ever. They did a lot in so many ways for Terrace and settlers in the valley."

Mrs. Willie stopped to sigh and wipe away tears with the corner of her apron. I remained silent, finding it hard to wait for her to continue the story which she resumed with a sob.

"I blubber when I think there's no more happy days for the Michauds. A fire burned their lovely house down and then they had to live in a small cabin on the ranch. They were as nice as ever but didn't have the spark they'd had before. As if that terrible fire wasn't enough trouble, Bert drowned in the Copper River not far from their place two years ago. Fred can't get over his death. No wonder. He and Bert were like the Cheeryble brothers in that novel by Charles Dickens, 'Nicholas Nickleby'. You must have read the book. Just the same as those characters, the Michauds thought alike, acted alike and were always together. Poor Fred won't believe Bert's dead. To him, Bert's still with him."

I met Fred the next morning when he came to the hotel in an old, battered Ford. He had sent a message that he'd call for the Mandys and drive us to his house. He walked slowly into the hotel's lounge and was introduced by Mrs. Willie. Fred was a very thin man of medium height with graying brown hair and his face suggested a European ancestry. His speech was soft and slow and his refined manner reflected a courtly upbringing. He bowed to me, shook hands with Joe and said, "It is a privilege to meet you, Dr. and Mrs. Mandy. It will give us pleasure to take you to our humble home."

Driving to the site of Michaud's ranch, we saw a heavy crop of weeds covering the outline of his burned house, with straggling perennials in garden borders. The once trim lawn was a mass of dandelions and other wild plants and only some blossoming roses struggling through a tilted trellis brightened the scene of ruin. Mr. Michaud kept his eyes averted from the sight of the disaster and paused for a moment after opening the door of his little cabin as if letting someone enter before us and welcomed with an apology.

"We are sorry to invite you here. This hut is where we lived when our big house was being built. It was spacious but this ·. Yes, Bert, I know we've at least a roof over our heads and must be thankful for our blessings."

The one room into which we entered had the dark walls of a log cabin and tiny windows let in little light. Fred's persistance in the pretence of his lately deceased brother's presence was so depressing and made the small hut appear to be darker than it was. When Joe and I adjusted our minds to this sad unreality and our eyes adjusted to semi-darkness, we saw a clean, orderly arrangement of everything in the room. Fred directed our attention to mineral specimens on a shelf and for better viewing tried to light a gas lamp. When unsuccessful, he seemed to confer with someone beside him, nodded in agreement and smiled as he spoke.

"We'll open the door and that will let some sunshine in so you can see our collection better. The colours in the ore mean something, don't they Dr. Mandy? We don't know exactly. Beautiful colouring, isn't it? We've prospected in several places around here and did hope one of the claims on Thornhill Mountain had gold or silver in it. Do you like the name of our claims, Mrs. Mandy? They're Sadie, St. Paul, Annie Laurie and Eureka. Maybe we won't collect any more specimens. We're getting too old to prospect. Would you look at the last samples we brought down from Thornhill, Dr. Mandy?"

Joe studied all the ore samples, placing some in sacks for assaying, and promised to send assay results as soon as possible. Michaud had been bustling about the kitchen section of the room and now came forward to say, "You must have tea with us. We've set out cups and saucers for you and a tin of biscuits. Do sit down at our table. It was hewn from a tree on our land."

The hot tea was refreshing and the imported English biscuits just right. Fred drank little and ate no sweets, choosing instead to question Joe about prospecting. He had little knowledge of geology and Joe tried to give him some practical information about minerals and how to find them, stressing the importance of gold discovery in Depression days. I remained silent, wishing I could help this lonely man face reality and live again. Three times he filled our cups and heaped more biscuits on a plate. Finally, Joe had to tell him we must get back to Terrace.

"Must you go so soon?" asked lone Fred. "We should deem it an honour to have you as guests for dinner. Please stay."

Joe was sorry to say, "We'd like to dine with you but I have scheduled interviews with several prospectors for this evening. I do regret to have to decline your invitation."

Fred replied, "We understand," and bounced us back to Terrace in his vintage car which rattled so much I thought it might start falling apart. Joe and I were properly escorted into the hotel and a smile lighted Fred's face as he bowed and said, "Goodby, and may we meet again." He watched as we started climbing the stairs to our room. Halfway up we turned to wave and received a military salute. Fred then sat down with Mrs. Willie for awhile to have a private conversation. She reported the gist of it to us the next morning.

"You know what that dear man said? 'We liked the Mandys. Dr. Mandy is a fine gentleman, well educated and knows what he's talking about and he doesn't talk down to but with prospectors.

Packer-guide Ben Nelson was one of the nicest men
Madge had ever met. As described on page 220, he
tragically died alone in the wilderness.

Hudson Bay Mountain near Smithers is a familiar
landmark to motorists on Highway 16.

We took a great fancy to Mrs. Mandy, too. She is what a wife should be — takes an interest in her husband's work, goes with him to learn about it and is the companion he needs. You know, the Mandys are like the Michaud brothers, do everything together as we do. If we go up Thornhill Mountain and get more samples to assay, do you think they'd call again? We'd like that so much.' My heart aches for Fred. Do come back and spend some time with him. I don't think he'll ever change and shouldn't be surprised if he joins his brother in the Great Beyond soon."

Joe promised, "I'll fit him into a field trip next year if possible. His devotion, though unwise, deserves the utmost kindness and compassion. Mrs. Mandy and I will be leaving around noon today, Mrs. Willie, heading through Kitsumgallum valley to Kitsumgallum Lake and on to Rosswood. Our stay there will be for a few days. Mrs. Mandy should have some memorable experiences there, don't you think?"

"Indeed I do. You'll meet characters in and around Rosswood, love, you'd not meet anywhere else. You could say they're rooted in history, likeable and honest folks you'll not forget."

Joe bought and packed food supplies and we were off in an open touring car driven by a local man. Mrs. Willie provided sandwiches, tarts and apples for a lunch along the way. Well, I remarked as we motored on a fairly good road through rolling timberland and farmed flats, This is a cushy trip. Joe sobered me with a warning.

"Partly cushy. There's a real hazard ahead which we'll laugh about when we're safe again."

I knew shortly after arrival at Kitsumgallum Lake what the hazard was. A small boat with outboard motor was waiting to carry us to the northeast end of the lake and a gloomy boatman left no doubt in my mind about possible trouble ahead.

"You're darned lucky today," drawled the pessimist. "Lake's quiet. Looks like a mirror, don't it? 'Tain't so. This here's a dangerous lake. Squalls come sudden, quick as an eye can wink. They roughs up waves that washes you out of the boat and you drowns. Seen it happen. Almost lost meself once."

We were fortunate that day, for the lake remained calm all the way to its head at Rosswood. There, a few cabins and a comparatively large log house were clustered. The latter, Joe told me, belonged to Englishman Walter Warner who had worked on the telegraph line. Here in this tiny settlement he maintained telegraph service and a post office for the isolated settlers of the valley. My husband had met him and his Indian wife on a previous trip and considered them worthy pioneers. He described Walter as an intelligent, well read and hard working man. The Warners knew we were coming and hurried to meet us, Walter speaking for himself and his shy Chrissy.

"We're glad you're with us again, Dr. Mandy. And this is the little wife? May all the best come your way, girl, and marriage the best thing that ever happened to each of you. Now there's no need to put up your tent. Our house is your headquarters. Chrissy, show Mrs. Mandy around."

The Warner's log house was adequate for them and the odd guest. It comprised a large living room, big kitchen which included dining space, an office and two medium sized bedrooms. The room for the Mandys was also used as a storeroom for sleeping bags, camping equipment, fishing tackle, guns and odds and ends. All we needed was a place to sleep and a comfortable bed crowded into a corner provided that. I said to Joe as we fitted in our dunnage, This is like quarters we had in the Unuk mining camp, only much larger and with a real bed and mattress instead of a wooden bunk. What luxury!

We were hungry and gladly accepted an invitation to have supper with the Warners, showing an appreciation of Chrissy's fresh fish and vegetables by taking seconds of everything. The evening was then devoted to a discussion of mining. Walter knew what prospecting was being carried out in the vicinity and all the prospectors who were working claims. This information helped Joe plan a series of examinations starting the following morning. He and I hiked a trail to Douglas Creek, Joe calling my attention to the boulders in this stream which flowed into Kitsumgallum Lake and was fed by small tributaries and glaciers. He also acquainted me somewhat with the placer mining partners on the creek for whom he had great respect and liking.

"Today, dearie, you'll meet a colourful couple who would have delighted Charles Dickens as suitable for a novel. Mr. and Mrs. Frank Nightwine have leases in the Douglas Creek Canyon and work together to get gold from bedrock. They have demonstrated what hard work can do. Every two days in 1931 and 1932 their clean-ups varied from $3.00 to $50.00 during the working period. That would be an average of about $14.00 for the two days of shovelling. Their needs are few so they don't require much cash and they live off game, wild fruits and a vegetable garden. Best of all, they have a peaceful existence in a lovely alpen setting. They're truly a happy couple and what the world would call characters."

We saw, when nearing a cabin settled on a knoll above Douglas Creek Canyon, a tall, broad man come outside and stand with very long arms outstretched as if to embrace the invigorating, clean air. Seeing us, he rapped out a startling whoop and loped down the trail shouting, "I'll be blowed! If it ain't Dr. Mandy! I ain't fergot your visit last year. Who's that with you? The girl from Indiana you got yourself hitched to?"

Surprised Joe answered, "Frank, how did you hear the news?"

"Up here's bush telegraph. Same's them drums in Africa you heered when a boy. Howdy, ma'am. I'm from Missouri. Ever been in that Ozark state?"

I knew it would gladden his heart that I could say, Yes, I have. Many times.

"Ain't that nice to know? Them Ozark Mountains is downright purty. Not so high as these here mountains in Canada but real purty all the same. Them was great days in Missouri, ridin' buckboards pulled by horses. And the box socials and square dances we had! We fellers kicked up our heels, the gals swung their purty skirts and we done what the caller sung out for us to do. Folks'd come for miles and miles for such doin's. What good times! My, my, them days was a long time ago. I up and left Missouri forty years back."

Have you been in Missouri since, Mr. Nightwine? I asked.

"No, I ain't. 'Tain't no use to go. Famblys all gone 'cept a sister.
She's sorta gone, too. Nun she is, shut up where she cain't see
nobody. I left home to soldier in the Spanish American War and
reckon I got used to fightin'. When comes World War, I just joins up
with Canadian Army boys and goes overseas in 1914. Was sniper in
front line trenches and comes out with nary a scratch. Know what got
me? The awful flu. I was down turrible sick with that. Mebbe flu, and
it was everwhere, killed more men than all the fightin' did. Sure was a
real bad epidemic.

"Then, war bein' over, I bummed clean across Canada and set up
with a partner to take gold outa Douglas Creek. His sister, she's a
widda woman, housekeeps. Danged if my pard didn't light dynamite
and blow hisself to Kingdom Come. Mind you, he didn't mean to.
Somethin' went wrong. Well, someone has to look after his sister and
best way I know is to marry with her. Here comes the Missus now.
Say, look who's here! Dr. Mandy and this purty, little wife of his'n.
She was American, same as me. Sorta makes us kin, don't it? My
gosh, we cain't stand here yappin'. Dr. Mandy, you gotta see what we
done in the creek. Me and you can walk the trail longside, Mrs.
Mandy. It be plenty wide but plenty rocky. I best hold your hand.
'Tain't fittin' to let you fall."

Mr. Nightwine was well over six feet tall and his long legs set a
stride that required three footsteps of mine to his one. He was an
unusual looking man with a shock of thick, frizzy, dark hair standing
high above a heavily lined face. His hands amazed me, being more
than twice the size of mine and so strong that his gentlest clasp was
painful. He never stopped talking as we were descending to the creek
and in a voice loud enough to be heard some distance away. I only
half listened because, determined to keep up with him, I had to
carefully steer my steps on the steep trail.

Mrs. Nightwine and Joe followed, my gallant husband holding her
hand, much to her delight. She walked briskly on the trail carrying a
heavy packsack, which she refused to let Joe strap on his back. When
we stopped at the placer workings she proudly declared, "I'm sixty
years old and see? I can still carry me a sixty pound pack." I admired
her strength vocally and silently deplored her permanently bent back
caused by such achievement. She had evidently cheerfully accepted
this impairment as a result of pioneering and associated mining.

Frank was a practical man, able to adapt and develop whatever was
needed for his placer mining. The sawmill where he cut poles and
lumber for sluice boxes included the power of an old Ford Engine and
a variety of junk was sheltered by him in a lean-to near Douglas Creek.
Like the Matneys on the isolated Unuk River ranch, Frank and his
missus had discovered manmade products, no matter how seemingly
useless or worn, could be utilized in wilderness living. Short lengths
of wire and string, bent nails which could be flattened and bits of
cloth could prove priceless in solving some problem. He was rich in
the possession of what outsiders would throw away.

Mrs. Nightwine waded into the cold creek beside her husband, both
shovelling gravel into sluice boxes and happily anticipating the
clean-up of gold nuggets. I watched the well coordinated couple for
awhile, studying their technique before asking, May I try shovelling?

Mrs. Nightwine shook her head negatively and Frank shouted, "No, no. Too hard for little one like you." I had to be satisfied to walk up and down and smile when the two called out such sentiments as, "Glad you come, Mrs. Mandy. Your hubby's a fine feller and we likes you too," and "This outdoors is great, ain't it?"

Mrs. Nightwine correctly reckoned time by the sun and at noon, after squinting skyward several times, laid down her shovel. She then came out of the creek, took my hand and turned me to the trail saying, "Lunch now. Frank, ask them fellers on claims longside us to eat with me, you and the Mandys. Don't have company much and oughta share when we does. Come on, Mrs. Mandy. When we gets to the cabin, I'll take off my men's

Mr. and Mrs. Frank Nightwine
placer mining at Douglas Creek.

duds and put me on a dress to look proper."

Six of us filled the one room of the Nightwine's cabin. It held a big stove in one corner, a bunk bed covered with a patchwork quilt in another, a table hewn from a log and tree stumps for chairs. Mrs. Nightwine opened a store bought tin of tongue for a special lunch and divided the meat into six equal portions. Her sandwiches, made from inch slices of buttered homemade bread enclosing a two inch slice of onion, appalled me. How would I adjust my mouth to such a size and my taste buds to so much onion? Cutlery was not on the table. Mrs. Nightwine and the men easily bit into those enormous sandwiches with gusto, eating two while I struggled with one and onion induced tears dripped down my face. Dessert, a wild blackberry pie, was delicious and seeing how much I liked it, Mrs. Nightwine gave me a jar of her canned blackberries. She advised, "Eat in pie or as is, if you wants. Good by theirselves."

Lunch was soon over and mining resumed. I took a walk above the canyon and picked a bouquet of wild flowers while Joe examined holdings beyond those of the Nightwines. The friendly Nightwines invited us to have supper with them which we happily did. The meal consisted of thick slices of buttered bread generously spread with wild strawberry jam and was accompanied by hunks of cheese and strong coffee. After supper Frank hurried away to ask the prospector lunch guests to "Come over. We'll have us a party." When the two men arrived dressed in their best clothes, Frank pulled out a long rope from under the bed.

"See this here rope, Dr. Mandy?" he asked. "It's for a trick I done back in Missouri. You ties me up with it. I tells you how and I'll get me loose quicker'n a fly can buzz."

Joe followed instructions and Frank was securely hog-tied. I was sure only a Houdini could wiggle out of the binding cord, but Nightwine freed himself in seconds. Mrs. Nightwine clapped and Joe, the prospectors and I praised his dexterity with, "Wonderful! How could you get loose so fast?"

Frank's modesty was refreshing in his reply, "Shucks, 'tain't nothin'. Jes' like stealin' from a baby. Now Dr. Mandy, you're on. Let's see iff'n you can get out of that there rope fast as me."

Joe fought the tightly bound rope with pretensions of much exertion. Ordinarily he would have persisted but, realizing Frank wanted to win the competition, gave up the struggle in a few minutes. His voice was purposely faint in admitting, "You're a stronger and smarter man then I, Frank. I can't free myself."

Frank shouted, "A hillbilly beats! You look mighty funny trussed up, Dr. Mandy. Awful funny. Jes' like them hogs on my pappy's farm."

The man from Missouri began to laugh so loudly and hysterically his whole body shook. He laughed so long and so hard he could neither sit nor stand and had to drop to the floor where he rolled over and over still laughing. Never had I seen anyone anywhere so thoroughly enjoy himself and in such a way. His laughter was infectious and caused the rest of us to become so hilarious we almost fell off our stump chairs. Frank's explosive merriment continued for some time before he gained enough control to get up and untie Joe. He was only smiling when starting another round of entertainment.

"'Scuse me for laffin', Dr. Mandy. So funny I jes' couldn't help myself. Good fun we is havin', ain't we? I got me another game to play, me and you. Ever hear of hot hands? I puts out my hands, you puts yours on top. You tries to pull one hand away 'fore I hits it. Like this, see? I gets to go on hittin' till I misses. Then you tries hittin' my hand. This goes on till me or you says to stop. The feller that hits the most wins. Ready? Here my hand comes."

My husband was not as large as Frank and his hands looked small beside Frank's huge paws. Joe was quick but Frank was quicker. He was unaware of the power in his hands and didn't know he struck with crippling force. Joe described the blows to me later as being like those of a heavy hammer. When the game concluded, winner Frank was again convulsed with laughter and had to lie down on the floor for more rolling. Finally he quieted and turned to me for conversation.

"Mrs. Mandy, did you ever see Grand Opry?"

Opry? Grand Opry? Oh, — yes I have and liked it very much.

"Did you ever see that Opry called 'Uncle Tom's Cabin'?"

Frank's Grand Opera differed from mine and a quick recollection told me why. The theatres across the United States in his youth and my early childhood were called Opera Houses. He heard literate people refer to Grand Opera and assumed all productions shown in those theatres fitted into that category. It would have been impossible to explain this so I accepted his belief in what he had seen and answered, I remember "Uncle Tom's Cabin" very well. It played every year in my home town and my brother and I liked seeing that Opry every year.

"Warn't it sad? I jes' cried and cried when they cut off little Eva's curls. Cried lots more when they lays poor Uncle Tom on that there blue grass of Kentucky."

People won't be seeing "Uncle Tom's Cabin" any more, I was sorry to tell him. Just last week a newspaper reported that, for the first time since it played in Opry Houses, no company will tour the U.S. with that Opry.

"Is that so? Too bad. Reckon I can tell you why. It's jes' too sad. Folks cain't stand up to cryin' over it no more."

Joe and I were ready to say goodnight when Frank stopped us by exclaiming, "No, you cain't go yet! Hold on till we gives Mrs. Mandy a present. You never let us give you none, Dr. Mandy. Said it warn't fittin' for a man in your job. No law agin' a weddin' present for the wife, is there? This is for her."

Mrs. Nightwine held out a gold pan in which were a number of nuggets and said, "We wants you should have one."

I knew how hard they worked to get gold from the creek for only a modest income and replied, Thank you. You're very kind but I can't take one of your precious nuggets. You need it.

Frank spoke up. "We aims to keep you here till you picks one."

He was determined to have me select a gift, so I chose a tiny nugget. There was an immediate, disapproving, "No, no. Put that back." The Nightwines then held the pan between them and rummaged until they found the perfect wedding gift, a dainty nugget shaped like a heart. Frank laid it in my hand and spoke with satisfaction.

"There, jes' right for a bride. Makes you think sweetheartin', don't it? We wants you to have the nugget made into a ring like they done in '98. Mebbe it'll make you think of your everlastin' friends on Douglas Creek."

Hiking back to Rosswood hand in hand with Joe, I felt inspired by our time with Frank and his Missus. We agreed that they were among the most sincere, unsophisticated and contented couples we'd ever met. Oh Joe, I said, I'll always treasure the Nightwine's nugget because in addition to being shaped like a heart it's a gift from their hearts.

"I'll have that nugget fashioned into a '98 style ring as soon as I can," promised Joe, "a symbol of 'everlastin' friends'. I wish there were more people with their strength of character in what Frank calls the wild outside."

Joe and I were sitting with Walter and Chrissy in their kitchen the next evening talking mining when we heard a commotion. Their husky was barking furiously and we heard additional canine yelping mingled with that of voices. We all rushed outside and saw a small procession coming into Rosswood. It was led by a slowly moving little dog, followed by a heavily bearded man bent from carrying a huge pack. A woman, obviously several months pregnant and bearing a baby strapped on top of her packsack, trailed with six children and two goats. The man dropped his heavy load and stammered a request.

"Me --- my family --- dead tired. We - we're hungry. Grub's gone. Been hiking --- seventy mile trail. Can - anyone give us - a bite to eat - and a dry -- warm place to sleep?"

Walter unlocked a one-room log cabin opposite his house, opened its door and led the weary family inside with words of welcome.

"Folks, this cabin belongs to a woman in California who comes here for vacations. I look after it while she's gone. She'd want me to put you in here. Make yourselves comfortable and food will be coming."

The little group soon settled in a shelter which was warm and cozy after the cold, damp nights on the trail. Prospectors heard through "bush grapevine" of the trek and came with bacon, crackers, cheese and jam for "the little tykes and their mamma and papa." Joe and I brought oranges from our grub sack and how the children smiled when each received the fruit. Mrs. Warner contributed loaves of bread, butter, eggs, cold meat, tea and cake. The pioneer family was left to eat by themselves and Joe and I returned later to see how they fared. We found the bed ready for the parents, the baby sleeping soundly in a big armchair with boards across the front to keep her from falling out and the six children laid on the floor tucked into a long blanket. The faithful dog dozed beside the stove in which a fire smouldered. Early in the morning the father, with his fully rested children grouped about him, told his trail story.

"My name's Sydney Fraser. Been ranching in the Nass River valley and caretaking a shut down mining operation. Grew fine vegetables with no way to get them to market. Gets a man down that does and my boy has got to an age for school. Decided suddenlike I'd best take my family to Terrace, a town where I'd likely find me a job. Started out with thirteen of us — me, the wife, a baby, six kids, a horse, two goats and a dog. Pete, the horse, was to carry our heavy loads. He didn't go far. Too old, I guess. First day out he laid down and died. Then me and the wife had to carry packs in relay — me one hundred pounds and her forty pounds with the baby atop. We'd leave the younguns on the trail with the rest of the dunnage, foot it several miles, cache what we carried and go back for the rest of the load and the kids. Our two oldest backpacked sisters when the going was tough.

"We crossed lava beds and Lava Lake in a dugout canoe we found. Made it over Cedar River on a log jam. Nine days it took. We slept good knowing our dog's bark would scare animals away. Got a mite cold when the campfire went out but we huddled together and kept tolerably warm. It was scary when grub run out and goat's milk was all we had to go on. Here comes the wife with baby Muriel. That baby's darn spunky, never cried once. Come close, kids, and be introduced proper. Sydney Earl is nine, Pearl Viola's next at seven. Verna's six, Gwendolyn five, Beryl four and Marjory two. Only one bad thing happened after Pete died. Our middle youngster fell into campfire ashes and burned a spot on her head. I can tell it still hurts but she's game, not one to make a fuss."

Chrissy and Joe took the injured girl into the Warner house and Joe held the child while Chrissy applied a native remedy with almost instant relief. The Frasers were then ready to leave and wanted to hire a boat to take them down Kitsumgallum Lake as quickly as possible en route to Terrace. Weather did not permit this as the wind-whipped waves on the water made navigation impossible. Undaunted, the family started on a hike around the lake, cheered by a whistling father. The little dog, invigorated after a night's rest, was the tireless leader and the two goats brought up the rear. I watched the marching family for some time as they touched my emotions more than any parade I had ever seen. They all exhibited the fortitude and optimism of the true pioneer.

Walter waved them off observing, "Come to think about it, there's no boat around here that'll hold all that family and the goats would be bound to kick up trouble."

Joe and I were soon bound eastward by rail to Smithers, a town on the Bulkley River in the midst of the alluring Babine Mountains. We registered at the old Bulkley Hotel presided over by owners, Mr. and Mrs. Harvey Davies, a most unlikely couple to be in such a business. Mr. Davies, a Welshman of military bearing, had fought in the Boer War, worked on a banana plantation in Costa Rica, managed tea estates in India and raised cavalry and show horses in Alberta. He had served Smithers as Magistrate, Juvenile Court Judge, Mayor and Coroner. Pleasingly plump, the white-haired Mrs. Davies was of English ancestry, born in India, educated in England and had led a lady's social life as an adult in India. She had married Harvey Davies before emigrating and coming to Canada. They kindly invited me to share their sitting room upstairs when my husband was on the trail without me.

Joe left with a group of men early the following morning and I went alone to the dining room for breakfast. The only other diner was a man on the far side of the room with a newspaper propped up in front of him. He looked up when I entered, rose and called out, "Come over here." I obeyed this characteristic, informal, northern friendliness and went to his table. He seated me and sitting down opposite began talking.

"I'm Mr. Calder, the crusty, bachelor bank manager here. You're Mrs. Mandy, aren't you? I inquired when I saw you and your husband come to the hotel yesterday. In my position it's essential to check on strangers in our town. Your hubby's gone to Hudson Bay Mountain today. I talked to him before he left. There's no reason for you to breakfast alone because he isn't here, and I'll enjoy your company. Try some of my guava jelly. I always bring a special treat for myself to go with hotel meals. I guess you don't know anything about Smithers. I'll fill in a bit for you.

"Pioneers built this town and ranching, logging, mining and the railway have kept it going. Not much mining now with the Depression on. Hope your husband can give an encouraging report on the old Duthie Mine he's examining right this minute. It was discovered in the early 1920's and bought by an American shipbuilder. My, it was rich in silver! With some intermissions the Duthie Mine carried on until tight money closed it in 1930. There's a newcomer in town, J. J. Herman, who's planning to lease the property and reopen if there's a chance for profit. That's good news for our Smithers. Great Scot! Look at the time. I've got to open the bank. If you're here when I am for lunch, I'll share local raspberries with you. Must hurry or I'll be fired."

Mrs. Davies prepared me to meet Peavine Harvey, a well known prospector and colourful character. He has an odd nickname, I said. How did he get it? She not only told me how the name originated but also about his handicap.

"Charles Gordon Harvey is really his name. He must have been past middle age when he came to Smithers in 1914 with a young wife and baby son. Trying to promote the community he always told new settlers, 'Everything in our soil grows as high as the peavine.' That's three to five feet tall. Someone started calling him Peavine and the name stuck. I'm sure youngsters here, and many adults, don't know he's Charles Gordon. Everyone likes the old chap but you can't hold a conversation with him. He's deaf to sound. The man talks a lot and in a voice so loud it can be heard the full length of our main street. Dr. Mandy tells me he's taking you up Harvey Mountain tomorrow to Peavine's mine. Remember, he won't hear a word you say."

The drive to Peavine's home along Driftwood Road was pleasant on a sunny August day and our talkative taxi driver enlightened us about Peavine, his wife and twenty-four year old son Gordon. The information he poured out was a story which could easily become a dramatic play.

"Gee, folks, I think I should tell you something about the Harveys. They're not ordinary, to say the least. Peavine's honest, hard working and a likeable cuss. He's highly respected, you know, and getting on in years. Too bad he can't hear. Spends most of his time at the mine since he and the missus don't see eye to eye. Different as day and night and that makes for a stormy marriage. In all fairness to Mrs. Harvey, she was brought up to be a lady in England. She plays the piano real well. Pioneer like Peavine, she ain't. The boy is tied to his mother's apron strings and shy as a deer. Why not? He don't get out with people. Round town Mrs. Harvey's called the goat woman. That's because she's got forty goats. Has a name for each one. That woman does something she shouldn't do. Peavine don't report it but some of us knows. She goes to Peavine's cabin on the mountain and takes away blankets and grub when he's in the mine. That's a terrible thing to do. Why, the poor fellow could die of starvation and exposure when there's a blizzard and he's trapped up there. We're near the Harvey ranch now. Get ready to meet the missus and the boy."

Mrs. Harvey, a slight woman in a chore-soiled cotton dress, a man's broad brimmed, felt hat on her head, came around the house. Her son walked behind her and some goats followed. The taxi driver got out of his car and strode toward them speaking cheerily.

"Good morning! How are you today? I've got a couple who want to meet you, Dr. and Mrs. Mandy. They're going up to the mine."

The goats crowded noisily about us and I warily edged away from them, fearing they might become belligerent. Mrs. Harvey sensed my fear and spoke defensively of her pets.

"Don't be afraid, Mrs. Mandy. My dears won't hurt you. Ben Nelson brought horses for you Mandys to ride up the mountain. Before you go, I must offer hospitality of the Harvey home. Gordon, bring glasses of milk for the Mandys. Did you know goat's milk is nutritious and should be in everyone's diet?"

The horse's were gentle and so familiar with Peavine's steep trail they automatically stopped at his one-room log cabin. Peavine was bending over a washtub in front of his little house finishing laundry, a big, powerful looking man with unruly gray hair above a heavily furrowed face. He saw us when straightening to wring water from a shirt. Wiping sudsy hands on his trousers, he walked toward us speaking in a voice louder than any I had ever heard.

"Ben told me you'd be here today. Stay where you're at. After I put on some other duds you can come into my place."

Soon, dressed in clean shirt and pants, Peavine appeared in his doorway to loudly shout, "Well, don't stand there and waste time. Come in and set down. It's time to eat. I'll give you lunch. Oh, you brung your grub and extra for me? Thank you kindly. I'll heat up the breakfast coffee to wash it down. See the pad and pencil on the table? Write there what you say. My eyes are good but my ears don't hear."

Conversation consisted of Peavine's monologue on mining

Prospector and miner Peavine Harvey.

and Joe's paper recorded advice. Interspersed to amuse me, Peavine told tall tales of wild times in the Klondike gold rush of '98. He ended the meal abruptly with, "We must go into the mine right now, Dr. Mandy."

Joe wrote on the pad, "Don't you want Mrs. Mandy to go with us?"

There was a violent shake of his head as Peavine answered, "No, too dangerous. Might have a slide or cave-in. She's too little anyway. I could fall over her. Mine's dark you know. Why I might not see the girl and knock her down, break her leg or squash her. Take a walk, Mrs. Mandy, and look at wild flowers. Help yourself to coffee and biscuits in the cabin. Let's go, Dr. Mandy."

I cleared the table of dishes and washed and dried them before starting out on Peavine's suggested walk. It wasn't possible to walk very far on this slope of Harvey Mountain without the physical and psychological support of a companion. I lingered quite awhile on a floral carpeted incline and picked a bouquet of wild flowers which I arranged in an empty coffee can on Peavine's table. I had felt invigorated by crisp mountain air and inspired by the loveliness of the Babine Range stretching high and far in the distance. Consequently, the small cabin seemed stuffy and restraining when I returned to it. I really had to find something to occupy my mind. A pile of western magazines offered a solution and I curled up in a worn armchair to read a few.

The men came back in the late afternoon and Joe spent an exhausting hour conferring with Peavine by writing his part of discussion. Peavine asked us to stay for supper with the assurance, "I got plenty to eat." Joe answered on a writing pad, "Thanks, but we haven't time. I must get ready for a trip in other parts of the Babine Mountains."

Joe was on the trail for three days with a prospector after we visited Peavine and I remained in the hotel to type some notes and business letters for him and to attend to personal correspondence. On the third day I decided to have a little rest away from the typewriter and walked a short distance to the local drug store. On the way, I heard an extremely loud voice coming from an open window of the barber shop. I asked the druggist, Why is a radio allowed to disturb the peace of the town? There was a chuckle with his answer.

"That was not a radio you heard, just Peavine Harvey."

I was the only customer in the shop and had selected a dozen post cards and a leather bookmark to buy when I heard someone come in. I did not look up until a thunderous, "Hello!" sounded beside me. It was Peavine Harvey, freshly barbered and dressed in his best clothes, complete with a tightly knotted necktie. He snatched the bookmark from my hand and put it on the counter. Then, he told me what to do.

"You don't want that bookmark. It's not genuine leather. I know what is. Give me those cards you picked out. I'll choose better. You shouldn't have any more than six. Don't waste your money. Here you are, a better selection. Now then, let's go back to where there's a table. I'll set you up to a dish of plain ice cream. You don't need anything fancy on it. I always have ice cream when I come to town."

I followed the friendly man, thinking he recognized me. As he talked I knew he didn't and that was understandable. A dress, stockings and slippers and a bare head had changed my appearance from the trail rider in breeks, boy's shirt and jacket, high leather boots and a broad brimmed hat concealing my hair and shadowing my face. Peavine talked and I listened, unable to respond since I had no pad and pencil to show him what I was thinking. I laughed silently while hearing Pevine's appraisal of me, enjoying the incident thoroughly.

"'Tain't often I come to town," he drawled. "Have me a mine to work with drill, shovel and wheelbarrow. A government man was up there day before yesterday. He brung his wife along, a little lady about your size. She picked a bokay for my table. That was real nice, wasn't it? Right smart girl and might have been purty if she'd dressed proper. I don't hold with women in pants. Her husband calls hisself a doctor, not medicine mind you. Might say a rock doctor, name of Mandy. Fine man. He looks everywhere in my mine, crawls and gets dirty same as me. Him and his wife can come up the mountain to my mine any day. I want you to know I'm a strong man and I'll be working my mine for years to come. Why am I healthy? I drink milk and eat half a pound of sugar every day. Yes, I buy fifteen pounds a month of the sweet stuff. Sugar keeps a man going. Got to get back to the mine, sister. Thanks for eating ice cream with me."

Peavine must have been puzzled about my identity and on his way out of the shop stopped beside the druggist who knew me by sight and also knew of the Mandy's visit to the old mine on Harvey Mountain. I had heard him laughing during Peavine's chat with me. He had become serious when Peavine approached him to ask, "The girl I had ice cream with, I don't know her do I?"

The considerate druggist spared him embarrassment. "How could you? She's someone passing through Smithers," he wrote in answer.

Peavine read, smiled and walked out vigorously shouting, "Hello," to everyone he met. His dream of great riches never materialized but his legacy of land along the Driftwood Creek, given to the Park Branch of the government by his son Gordon, is a lasting source of wealth for British Columbia. It is now called Driftwood Provincial Park and is a tourist attraction. Tom Schroeter, the District Geologist stationed at Smithers, described the contribution to me in the following statement:

"Driftwood Provincial Park covers a major tourist attraction — fossil beds. The age of the rocks is fifty million years and fossils such as fish and bugs are found here. Gordon had some spectacular samples of fossil fish. The area is very unique for western Canada and thus geologically very important."

There were several potentially valuable prospects in the Babine Mountains and Joe and I were guided to them by Ben Nelson on pack horses. We were accompanied at the outset by Arch Harer, an old prospector from Smithers. He walked the trail convinced that, "My two feet are as good as a horse's four." We made camp at the Lorraine and La Marr claims in which Arch had an interest. At the latter Arch stretched out under a tree and slept while Joe, assisted by Ben, examined his property. Another tree near an old cabin shaded me from the sun as I recorded notes about this trip. On waking, Arch rushed over to me to impart some astonishing information.

"Mrs. Mandy, I'll be confidential with you. First a bit about my background. I was a school teacher in Pennsylvania when a young man and teaching didn't satisfy me. Too tame. I wanted adventure and Canada promised that, especially in prospecting for gold. And I'm lucky. I'll be very rich in a year or so and have a summer home here and a winter home in Vancouver. See that rusty looking mountain off to your right? I'm going to stake on it and I'll whisper to you why. Don't tell anybody my secret. If word got around, there'd be a rush and I don't want that. What you're looking at is a mountain of solid gold."

How do you know it is solid gold? I asked.

"I went to the top with an engineer. He said it was solid gold and that there's enough gold in it to operate a thousand ton mill for one hundred years and maybe as much in other mountains around here. Let me show you his report. Nobody's seen it but me and I keep the report hidden in this old cabin beside you. I'll fetch it."

By now I was familiar with mining reports and this one written for Arch was the most amazing promotional nonsense I had ever read. The document verified Arch's contention of the enormous amount of gold in the rusty mountain. Appended to the signature of the writer's prediction and conclusion was, "Practical Mining Engineer". I analyzed the contents for Arch and emphasized the fact that universities and colleges do not grant the degree of Practical Mining Engineer. The optimistic man held fast to his anticipation of mining a solid gold mountain. I made no further attempt to discourage his belief thinking, at his advanced age, why not indulge in fantasy? After all, who has not been cheered by an impossible dream?

Our party soon numbered three people as Arch was so tired he had to return home for a rest. During the remainder of explorations my interest centred on Ben, leader of the packtrain, rather than on mineral outcrops. He was a small, softly spoken man, picturesque in traditional cowboy garb, the outfit's high hat making him appear taller than he was. His manner was so gentle that his horses responded to him like loving companions. He provided as much comfort for us as possible on a wilderness trail. Ben got up very early each morning to build a roaring fire in front of our tent to warm us as Joe and I

A Mandy campsite in the Babine Range

rolled out of sleeping bags in the chilly mountain air. I was thankful he had a pot of water heating over the campfire to facilitate Joe's daily shave and the washing of my face and hands. It was a pleasure to take the trail with Ben for he was a competent wrangler, an excellent camp cook and always cheerful. Conversation flowed as we sat around a glowing campfire in the evenings where Ben's reserve as a "loner" faded and he talked about his ancestry, days of wandering and mining history in the Babine Range.

"You might say I've been around and most times more or less alone. I like it that way. My mother's parents were Spanish musicians who moved to Denmark where I was born. Their daughter married a Danish gentleman, my father, who liked reading good books. Guess I get my liking for music and reading from my people. Books help a man get a decent vocabulary and learn about the world. Travel was in my blood and I went to the eastern part of the United States to farm with an uncle. Too young to settle down, I was soon off to Arizona and Texas. When the American army started chasing Pancho Villa and his men onto the Mexican side of the Rio Grande, I joined up for the fight. That over, I worked on ranches all the way to Canada and found British Columbia a good place to live. I have a ranch on Driftwood Creek next to Peavine Harvey's farm. It's not very big but I've built a house on it and raise vegetables and fruit. I trap, run a packtrain and prospect. Some day I'll stumble onto a big deposit of gold or silver and maybe get to be a millionaire. Then I'll be able to help a lot of people who've been unlucky.

"Only once did I tangle with the law. Trapping one winter, I stopped in a cabin to warm up. The man who owned it was away on his trapline. My gosh, that cabin was an awful mess. I cleaned it up, burnt old papers and junk and dried out some mouldy clothes. Next time I was in Smithers the constable showed me a warrant for my arrest. Couldn't think what I'd done wrong. That constable had common sense. He laughed and tore up the warrant for vandalism. You see, he'd stayed in that cabin. He said a complaint that I stole woolen underwear knitted by the trapper's mother was downright silly because not even a skunk could have stood the smelly clothes there. And, you know, the trapper reported months later he was wearing the longjohns he'd accused me of stealing. You've not been in the Babines before, so another time I'll tell you about what's gone on in mining in these mountains."

As promised, Ben gave us historical data on our last camp night. "There's been prospecting in the Babine Range for a long time. Good luck and bad luck has gone along with the prospectors. Of course you know, Dr. Mandy, mining is gambling and you lose more times than you win. There's that James Cronin. From 1907 to 1923, that's a long time, he was getting his mine in shape to cash in. Yes sir, everything was ready to go. Cronin had put in about $200,000 of his own money in it and the government had put in a road to the property. I heard there were 50,000 tons of ore blocked out at $30.00 a ton, a good price then. Let's see, that was in 1923. Then you know what happens? Cronin was riding down the mountain and his horse stumbled. That threw him off and he was hurt bad. His mine didn't open and he died in 1926. It did start up in 1928 called the Cronin Mine but nobody's working there now. Too bad. It'll open one of these days I think. Good values there. You've been to the Victory I hear, Dr. Mandy. Donald Simpson put in a lot of tunnels there in twenty years. He had good ore and not enough for a big mine.

"There's the Duthie Mine on Hudson Bay Mountain, a big help to Smithers. The man behind it was Duthie, a shipbuilder from Seattle. He bought a group of claims in 1919. By 1923 he discovered a rich silver vein that paid back what the claims had cost him. Then he needed money to develop and sold a controlling interest to the Federal Mining and Smelting Company which was part of the Guggenheim outfit. Those big shots closed down the workings in 1924. Duthie wasn't a man to give in. He reopened the mine in 1925. Everything went smooth after that. Duthie had his own mill by 1927 and a little village grew up there on the mountain with enough men and their families to start a school. Reports were so good that shares offered to the public in 1928 were oversubscribed. Yes, the Duthie Mine was a big payroll for Smithers till the stock crash of '29 shut it down in 1930. No mining there since. Dr. Mandy, I'm told you've been up there with J. J. Herman. He wants to lease the old mine. Well, he's a go-getter and should have the Duthie a producer again.

"I must say, a prospector is an optimist and never gives up. That describes me. My living is made by trapping and packing and I ought to be satisfied. I'm not. I still prospect and keep looking for a mine. Who knows? Maybe I'll find it. Say, it's past time to get into a sleeping bag. Sure do enjoy the trail with you two. Hope my horses and me can take you out in these mountains again. Good night."

Ben Nelson was a guide and packer to be remembered and Joe and I were saddened to read in the press a year later that he had been lost on a prospecting trip. How could a good guide like Ben be lost? I asked Joe. His answer was logical.

"It's hard to understand why he started prospecting at the wrong time of year in the Cassiar. That part of the province was unknown to him. Circumstances must have occurred there with which he could not cope. Lost alone in winter wilderness is dangerous. Let's hope he'll be rescued."

We did not know the facts concerning Ben's disappearance and subsequent finding. I was informed of them after Joe had been called to the Great Beyond. In 1980 the Historical Society of Smithers sent me that year's February 6th issue of the Smithers News which featured articles about yesterday's local pioneers. Ben Nelson was one of those so honoured. The story of his ill fated prospecting trip was related, the substance of which I have condensed as follows:

"Ben Nelson set out with another man in the fall of 1940 to prospect. His partner, fearing winter hardships, soon left him and Ben spent the winter in the Groundhog country of the Cassiar. In April of 1941, P. M. Moncton who was in charge of snow measurement in mountain passes along the proposed route of the Alaskan Highway, met Ben on the trail. Since he knew the territory into which Ben was going, Moncton drew him a map with useful guiding instructions. At that time, Ben had packhorses and about two hundred and fifty pounds of mostly mining steel on a sleigh and three guns. Moncton traded him some provisions and noted that except for sugar he was well stocked with food. About May first, Caribou Hide Indians found a note attached to the door of an abandoned trading post saying Ben had lost his horses and all his belongings when a raft collapsed in an attempt to cross a river. Police from Smithers started a search for the missing man. Ben's remains were discovered in late summer in the Chuckachida Lake area. Evidently unable to withstand the severity of winter months and loss of provisions and horses, Ben had died of starvation and weakness."

Thinking of the tragic way Ben Nelson died made me cry. Finally I said to myself, Ben would want you to think of him as he was, guiding the Mandys on Babine Mountain trails. Those were days to fondly recall and relive. I remembered Ben had wanted to become rich from finding gold or silver. He had not achieved his goal and yet for many years enjoyed the pursuit of it. That probably gave him more happiness than becoming a millionaire.

My husband's last examination in the Babine Range was of an old mine first staked in 1914 which had been worked by several companies. Owners Alex Chisholm and Arthur Cope, in that year of 1938, wanted a report which they hoped would be favourable enough to attract a purchaser. The mine was located on Dome Mountain, twenty-six miles east of Telkwa. To get to it, Joe and I motored twelve miles from Smithers to Telkwa and seven miles beyond to the Latchford ranch. Horses were available from Latchford and with Cope we rode them on an easy trail to Paradise Lake and then on a steep, narrow cliffside trail. The mine site looked like a tiny village with five sleeping cabins, cookhouse, barn, hayshed and two small stilt caches. Cope had said we needn't bring any grub because he had plenty at the camp for our two days there, but Joe supplemented his provisions with head lettuce, oranges and bananas.

I appointed myself cook and Cope and Joe were soon underground for examinations. The afternoon hours were pleasant, as the surrounding beauty was inspiration to compose the poem for an annual Mandy Christmas card. Supper required a minimum of work with tinned meat, canned corn and peas quickly heated on a wood burning stove and served with wedges of head lettuce. A dessert of oranges and bananas was accompanied by coffee. After the meal we sat outside the cookhouse and Cope told of his successes and failures in prospecting. Joe and I talked of experiences before marriage and together in the north. What a contented evening it was in a tranquil setting Joe said. As we slipped into our sleeping bags he added:

"On Dome Mountain we are close to God, where the materialism of the world does not touch us. In such serenity we can see fully the wonderful work of the Creator and feel the hand of the Divine. My dear, little wife, we could be happy here forever."

Mr. Cope was the breakfast cook, stuffing the three of us with big, thick sourdough flapjacks smothered in syrup or spread with strawberry jam and, of course, brewing strong coffee to drink. After this meal the men were off to the mine, back for lunch at noon and then away for further examination. Shortly after lunch I began to feel ill and quite miserable and the men looked sick when they joined me. None of us could eat supper and each suffered during the night with stomach pain and vomiting. In the morning Joe investigated and concluded the source of our collective illness was mixed vegetables I had served as part of our lunch. Evidently the can of vegetables had frozen during winter storage with resulting almost invisible perforations. Those tiny holes allowed summer heat to enter and develop harmful bacteria in the contents. Calmly and cheerily he predicted quick recovery.

"We merely have a light case of ptomaine poisoning. That's nothing to worry about. We'll be back to normal in a couple of days thinking only of the peace and sublimity of Dome Mountain. Riding down the mountain on sure footed horses in fresh, clear air will be an antidote."

Joe was transferred by the Department Of Mines from Prince Rupert to a Vancouver office in 1943. He and I were sorry to leave the north but the compensation was more educational opportunities for our young son. We established a home in Burnaby, a city of 35,000 then, adjoining Vancouver. Here we had a ranch style house of our design built on a corner facing a major thoroughfare and overlooking the side street of Alberta Avenue. We were happily surprised one day when the municipality changed the name of Alberta to Mandy Avenue. This, we inferred, was a token of appreciation for improvements in our section of Burnaby made possible through our organizing a neighbourhood Ratepayers' Association of which Joe was elected president with me as secretary. Among constructive achievements of the Association were mail delivery, which had not existed in this Burnaby division previously, and the widening of Alberta Avenue by forcing encroachers to restore the portion of road allowance wrongfully acquired.

Joe's years of mineral exploration in the harshness of wilderness trails took their toll. After his retirement, crippling arthritis and a heart condition caused him to remain at home, seldom able to greet visitors. It was my privilege to be his nurse, but eventually surgery for both my eyes necessitated a housekeeper assistant. I found her in a remarkable little lady, Gina Russoski, who was kind, sympathetic, understanding and efficient. She fitted into our household so well that in a short time she was like a daughter to Joe and a sister to me. Gina thought it sad that Joe's illness allowed few callers until Joe told her what was constantly in his mind.

"Mrs. Mandy and I don't really need them. Our love makes us sufficient to each other."

During this period of isolation, Joe insisted I continue activities which involved meetings one afternoon and one evening monthly. His health had not permitted him to participate in the problems of the British Columbia Retired Government Employees Association of which he was a member and where he was wanted as an executive of the Vancouver Branch. He declined the honour and was delighted that I was asked to serve in his place. This position I accepted and regret he did not live long enough to know I was an executive of the Branch and a member of the Provincial Executive for fifteen years before resigning when my eyesight made attendance difficult. Projects for the Association and the presentation of a book review at the West Burnaby United Church's Agenda Unit, combined with fellowship in these groups, helped to relieve the stress of watching my dear partner fading away.

Joe's prophetic words concerning the peaceful and spiritual atmosphere of Dome Mountain came back to him as his life's trail neared the end. With those words in mind he dictated his final request:

"My ashes are to be scattered over the last campsite together of the Mandys in 1938 having been owned by J. J. Cope and partner Alex Chisholm of Smithers, British Columbia; Dome Mountain prominently lying 5700 feet elevation on the east flank of the southerly end of the Babine Range; at about latitude 54° 44' 22" North, longitude 126° 38' 17" West. The easterly slopes drain into Fulton River, Fulton Lake and Babine Lake (elevation 2,200 feet). Babine Lake is about 27 miles east of Dome Mountain and Babine Gold Mine's camp on Dome Mountain is 26 miles easterly of Telkwa, British Columbia."

Joe then asked me to make arrangements for the fulfillment of his last wish, to temper the sadness of our parting, months before the actuality. This was very difficult for me to do for our trail, both in days of wilderness exploration and residence in the city, had been that of constant, compatible togetherness bonded by true love. How, I asked tearfully, could I go on without my loving and beloved partner? Joe eased my despair by reminding, "Love is eternal and will live on to comfort and inspirit." Fortified by this assurance I wrote to Bill Harrison, son of long time prospector friend Cliff Harrison, who lived at Burns Lake. Bill was a pilot with his own airline company which serviced an area including Dome Mountain. I asked if his company could carry out Joe's wish to go back to the north of our memorable adventure-filled years. A typical northern response came immediately from Bill and his wife Rosemary, both fondly known to us for several years. They wrote:

"We're sorry to hear Dr. Mandy is so ill. We want you to know we'll do whatever Dr. Mandy wishes without charge, since we've always thought so much of both of you."

My husband was called away on October 15th, 1968, and after a Memorial Service the Harrisons were informed of the train transporting his ashes and the time of arrival in Burns Lake. A letter from them shortly afterward contained a comforting report. Rosemary had met the train to reverently receive an urn bearing the last vestige of the virile and romantic man who had given me undying affection and unusual adventure. Bill had carried out Joe's wish to rest on Dome Mountain as soon as weather permitted a flight to it. The two brought tears of gratitude to my eyes in a concluding sentence:

"We'd be honoured to carry out your desire to return to Dome Mountain, as Dr. Mandy has done, when you are called away."

Of course I have missed the physical presence of my trail partner but I have not been alone. Dear Joe's love continues to encircle me and he is with me in spirit to encourage and cheer as foretold in what he so sincerely said two months before leaving for an unknown realm.

"You look as young and beautiful to me as when I met you over tough chicken on the Princess Louise. No matter what happens, remember I love you every minute of the day and night. I always shall and I'll always be with you."

My heart yet clings to beautiful northern British Columbia where memories linger to happily sustain me in sunset years. The Mandy's trail led northwest and it still does, for one glad day I shall join my husband there. Yes, I must have subconsciously foreseen our final resting place when composing the poem on Dome Mountain for our 1938 Christmas card:

Fragrant pines amid peaks of the Babine Range
Stand guard in Nature's vast realm of love,
Where all is kindred, nothing is strange
From fundament rock to blue heaven above;
Where a chorus of joy is the song of the streams
And Peace and Goodwill follow the trail we roam.
To you this is wafted with all that it means
From God's own temple and our wilderness home.

# EPILOGUE

Many years have passed since I started life's journey and I am still an optimist. Contentment is mine living in the house my Joe and I designed together, for I have cheering memories, the supportive love of grandchildren Adrian and Carla whose father, my son, died some time ago, and good friends to extend a helping hand when needed. Here, pictures and artifacts constantly remind me of golden days on the wilderness trail and of an extremely happy marriage. These and the guidance of a Divine Power who answers prayer sustain me as well as Joe's challenging commendation the day before he suffered a fatal heart attack. He called me to his room to say, "You are the strongest person I have ever known." I thanked him for such a heart-warming appraisal of my character. His praise was a parting gift to help me maintain fortitude in the future.

Recently, I have realized that Joe and I played a part in provincial history which, with our blissful love story, should be shared. Consequently, my glaucoma-dimmed eyes and arthritic fingers cooperated with memory and trail notes to enable me to write the book, OUR TRAIL LED NORTHWEST. The project completed, I can take time in sunset days to relax in home and garden. Floral beauty surrounding my home encourages recollection where among flowers I smile thinking of the name given the Mandy home — a combination of Joe's birthplace, Africa, and mine, Indiana. AFRIANA sounds as harmonious as the lives of Joe and Madge Mandy together have been. Obviously, I can joyously dedicate our story to my beloved husband who made the northwestern trail possible and our united years a glorious adventure and a gladsome romance.

Madge in the garden of her Burnaby home.